DAN EGONSSON
Lund University,
Sweden

DIMENSIONS OF DIGNITY

The Moral Importance of Being Human

KLUWER ACADEMIC PUBLISHERS
DORDRECHT / BOSTON / LONDON

A C.I.P. Catalogue record for this book is available from the Library of Congress.

ISBN 0-7923-5068-5

Published by Kluwer Academic Publishers,
P.O. Box 17, 3300 AA Dordrecht, The Netherlands.

Sold and distributed in North, Central and South America
by Kluwer Academic Publishers,
101 Philip Drive, Norwell, MA 02061, U.S.A.

In all other countries, sold and distributed
by Kluwer Academic Publishers,
P.O. Box 322, 3300 AH Dordrecht, The Netherlands.

Printed on acid-free paper

Printed in the Netherlands

To my son Harry
with much love

Contents

x

Acknowledgements

It took four years to write this book. During these eventful years I have discussed my ethical ideas with many people. Here, unfortunately, I can only mention those who have affected the content and shape of my book in a direct fashion. But my gratitude includes also those persons who have contributed to the prehistory of the book.

Two friends have never failed to show interest in my at one stage fairly thick manuscript. Toni Rønnow-Rasmussen has encouraged me a great deal during the different phases of the work. He has also closely scrutinized several parts of it and inspired me to make substantial cuts in the original manuscript. Ed Damron has read the whole manuscript, mostly during intervals behind the scenes of Malmö Municipal Theatre, and then made constructive suggestions.

Special thanks are due to Ingmar Persson, who has meant a lot for both my philosophical and my working life and with whom I have had conversations about the book and its topics. Thanks also to Wlodek Rabinowicz, who read parts of the manuscript and made comments and suggestions.

Tom Regan suggested that a chapter on Kant should be published separately. I have followed his advice, which I think was good.

The following, randomly listed, persons have influenced and helped me in various ways: Birgitta Forsman, Jonas Josefsson, Björn Petersson, Alan Crozier, Johan Laserna, Shelly Kagan and, especially helpful, Lena Halldenius. Lena read the whole manuscript and corrected many errors that would have disturbed me. Moreover, I thank the participants at the philosophical seminars in Lund and at philosophical conferences in Umeå, Odense, Leeds and Lund.

The publication of this book was supported by a generous grant from Erik and Gurli Hultengren's Foundation for Philosophy. I am grateful for this financial help.

Lilla Ry, November 1997
D. E.

PART I
PROBLEM AND METHOD

CHAPTER 1

INTRODUCTION

One idea has been almost universally embraced among people in the West, namely that there is something special about being human. This idea is rather vague and that is partly due, I believe, to the fact that it has been taken for granted for a very long time and not been much reflected upon until rather recently. For example, it is not clear whether the thought is (1) that being a human being is important in itself, or (2) it is important to be like a human being, that is, to have the capacities which a normal grown-up human being has. It is also possible to claim that both things are important; if two beings have exactly the same mental and physical capacities, it will make a difference to hear that one of the beings is a human one and the other not, and analogously if we have two human beings it may in some situations make a difference to hear that one is a normal adult and the other chronically unconscious. However, making distinctions within the class of human beings in this way is not normally considered morally correct.

Let us compare with Aristotle. First of all, he believes it is the capacity to reason that gives someone her superiority. This superiority can make it right for her to use an inferior being as an instrument for the accomplishment of various kinds of work, for example in the household. Thus we may have masters and slaves and slaves can be the master's possession, that is, the master's instrument of action.

This means first that Aristotle definitely believes there are important differences among human beings. For instance, slavery is defended in the following way:

For he who can foresee with his mind is by nature intended to be lord and master, and he who can work with his body is a subject, and by nature a slave (1943: 250).

Aristotle would, of course, also say that there is a difference between human beings and animals. Therefore, if the master is better than his slave, the slave may be better than an animal:

For he who can be and therefore is another's, and who participates in reason enough to understand but not to have reason, is a slave by nature. Whereas the lower animals cannot even understand reason; they obey their instincts (1943: 256).

However, even if Aristotle thinks that the possession of reason is distinctive of the human species and human function, he also believes that the value of a single human being may be lower than that of an animal:

For man, when perfected, is the best of animals, but, when separated from law and justice, he is worst of all; [...] if he have not virtue, he is the most unholy and the most savage of animals (1943: 253).

So in two fundamental respects Aristotle's view on this topic will differ from our traditional view. First, he does not believe that all human beings are equally valuable. Second, it seems that he does not believe that a human being automatically is more valuable than an animal.

The Western tradition is derived from Christianity, and that will explain these differences. In the Bible we read that God has created man in his own image and, according to Christian tradition, since every human being is made in this way, even the slave and the poor, it is wrong to regard some human beings as being more valuable than others. But it is not wrong in Christian thought to think that human beings are more valuable than animals. On the contrary, just because we are created in the image of God we are unique, and this is a uniqueness which all of us have in relation to the rest of creation, and it consists of our having an immortal soul.

The Western tradition stands in sharp contrast to the Eastern tradition. Both traditions believe in the doctrine of the sanctity of life, but the Eastern tradition seems to give a more literal and consistent interpretation of it. When talking about life, what is meant is *all* kinds of life. It is a well-known fact that the most devoted practitioners of the Indian religion Jainism desire to avoid *any* injury to life. The Jain monk wears a gauze mask to prevent the inhalation of insects, he goes naked to avoid crushing insects in the pleats of his clothes, he always sweeps the ground before him so as not to kill any living beings with his footsteps. And, of course, he does not eat animals.[1]

If the doctrine of sanctity of life is about life generally we also have to say something about plants. To my knowledge very few Christians have claimed that also plants, and not only humans and animals, ought to be protected and showed concern (Albert Schweitzer is the great exception). But this thought is part of the Eastern tradition. For example, many Buddhists believe that it is wrong to eat seeds, the reason being that eating these seeds will prevent them from growing. For some believers this rule applies not only to seeds but also to the growing plant. Therefore, the later in the plant's vegetation period one eats it the better. So whenever it is possible to avoid taking and destroying life, whether it is an animal's or a plant's, one should do one's best to realize this possibility.[2]

---

[1] See Ninian Smart (1984: 93).
[2] However, the latter extension is probably not representative of the Eastern tradition, meaning by this a tradition where the thought of reincarnation plays a fundamental role. To my knowledge, one seldom believes that a plant is an incarnation of a human soul. But an animal might be. Therefore, an important distinction between different forms of life, between a plant's and an animal's life, can also be discerned in the Eastern tradition.

Recently the Western tradition has been charged with having two conspicuous shortcomings: (a) that it pays too little respect to non-humans, and (b) that it pays too much respect to humans. Let us look at these objections in turn.

(a) I believe that most of the major thinkers in the West in one way or another have depreciated the non-human experiences in comparison to the human ones. David DeGrazia claims that "there can be no denying that Western civilization reveals a history of substantial bias against animals" (1996: 52). Some influential thinkers have totally denied the existence of such experiences in animals, although I think that this category after all is rather small. A well-known example is Descartes, who denied that animals were conscious and then drew the practical conclusion that any treatment of animals was permitted. (However, to judge from the eye-witnesses and others, the Cartesians and mechanists who applied these ideas to animals dissected alive in their laboratories were extraordinary in their view of animal pain and were regarded as such by many of their contemporaries.)

Descartes was criticized for his assertion that animals were incapable of feeling any pain. But it is worth noting that one possible view is to say that whatever the truth of it, we should show concern for animals. Aquinas and Kant said there could be *indirect* reasons not to maltreat animals, that is, reasons which are not primarily about animals but about human beings themselves. For instance, Kant says that:

so far as animals are concerned, we have no direct duties. Animals are not self-conscious and are there merely as a means to an end. That end is man. [...] we have duties towards the animals because thus we cultivate the corresponding duties towards human beings. [...] for he who is cruel to animals becomes hard also in his dealing with men (1976: 122).

The idea is that there are many similarities between animals and human beings and this means first that it may be psychologically hard not to treat them as being roughly in the same moral category, the possible difference being a matter of degree rather than kind. Second, notwithstanding this psychological question, it would not be advisable to fail to care for animals, since it could have negative effects on our attitudes to other human beings, once again because of the analogies between human and animal nature. It becomes easier to be cruel to other human beings if we are used to acting cruelly to animals.[3]

But then, would Kant say that animals are conscious of this cruel treatment—can they be harmed? Much of what he has written indicates that he believes that animals *can* be harmed. There are several passages which suggest that animals are endowed with fairly sophisticated capacities. For instance, here is a passage in the same work.

---

[3] Elsewhere (1997) I have tried to argue that this is a position with fairly far-reaching consequences.

The more we come in contact with animals and observe their behaviour, the more we love them, for we see how great is their care for their young. It is then difficult for us to be cruel in our thought even to a wolf (1976: 123).

Kant's position seems to be radically different from Descartes'. There is a profound difference between humans and animals, according to Kant, but not in the sense that animals lack all human feelings. It is doubtful whether or not Descartes believes that animals are completely void of sensations, but evidently he is prepared to acknowledge less in them than is Kant.

(b) James Rachels claims that "the Western tradition places too much value on human life" (1986: 24). Here we are back where we started when we pointed out the influence of Christianity on our moral attitudes—there is something (very) special of each member of humankind. We have seen what consequences this attitude might have, as when it legitimates treating animals as mere means to our human ends. Here we have an attitude which we as human beings seem to gain from.

But this is not the whole story. Rachels does not object solely to an "egoistic" and "chauvinistic" attitude, but also to a view that harms many people. The book from where the quotation is taken is about euthanasia and the traditional attitude is negative towards this practice. In most Western countries it may be accepted under certain circumstances—for instance, as a method of letting people die by abstaining from giving them life-sustaining treatment, but not as a method of actively killing them. The thought is that there is value in the existence of a human being whether or not she wants to go on existing. So here we have a case where it seems that human beings might lose on their high respect of humankind.

Other areas where we have the same situation are for instance abortion and especially selective abortion, i.e. where the abortion is done because one knows or expects that the foetus has certain properties. Let us first talk of abortion generally. Many pro-life advocates think that all innocent human lives command absolute protection. This may be good for the foetus, which may then develop into a fully fledged person in due time, but it is not good for the woman, who would have her autonomy curtailed by being forced to carry the child to term. Here the attitude in question will befall very many women in a negative way. Exactly how negative is hard to say and varies from case to case, though many would say that the physical and psychological consequences imposed by pregnancy are profound. There are also fanatical pro-life advocates who refuse to countenance any exceptions to the proscription of abortion, no matter if the pregnancy is a result of incest or rape. The negative effect of this will be extremely large, but nevertheless it is an attitude that is very natural to take for the one who believes in the importance of innocent human lives, since one cannot reasonably think that it matters "how or why the sex occurred or the sex began" (Tribe, 1990: 132).[4] The value of the human life to be protected would be the same.

[4] Observe that Tribe is a critic of this extreme position.

As far as the selective abortion is concerned one might claim that the pro-life attitudes may also have negative effects on the foetus. If it is meaningful to talk of a life not worth living (which the advocates of euthanasia and suicide have to do) this will be directly applicable to the question of abortion as well.

There certainly is a difference between abortion and euthanasia in that we may let the person herself *judge* whether it is better for her to die. But most people who accept euthanasia also think that in certain cases, for instance if we talk of a human being in irreversible coma who cannot request death, it would be right for another person to make the judgement whether or not this life is worth living (and should be ended). And we can claim that we have a morally analogous case when we talk of a foetus which, if allowed to develop into a child, will live a life which we judge will not be worth living. Letting these children be born with reference to their value as human beings as such would of course be worse for them.

So far I have tried to be rather neutral in the questions considered. The objective for the remaining chapters will be to look into these problems in more detail, considering both the arguments of the advocates and critics of the Western tradition. In principle I agree with many of the critics, but I also think it possible to compromise on these questions. In other words, I believe there is such a thing as a special human value or worth. What this value is and whether there are acceptable arguments for it will be considered in due time.

Earlier I pointed out that the Western tradition concerning the value of being human contains two ideas. First, that human beings are more valuable than animals. Second, that all human beings are equally valuable. This study will be particularly about the first of these ideas. The second one will only receive a very brief treatment.

Furthermore, the major part of the study will concentrate on the importance of being (a living) human *per se*, although towards the end I will also discuss and criticize two attempts to show that being (a living) human is a morally significant property only because of what normally is connected with this property. So whereas Part II discusses question (1)—see the opening of this chapter—Part III deals with question (2).

CHAPTER 2

METHODOLOGICAL BACKGROUND

> Philosophers these days frequently elicit "our intuitions" about
> this or that and appeal, implicitly or explicitly, to our feelings
> and sentiments, and to moral consensus. They invent imaginary
> cases and tell us bizarre stories which are intended to illuminate
> these intuitions. Pick up any recent journal or Moral Problems
> anthology, and it seems as if everyone is going about ethics in
> a similar way.
>
> William Shaw "Intuition and Moral Philosophy"

> Whatever the *avowed* methodological stance, it's a radically
> rare ethicist who'll actually advocate, and continue to maintain,
> a morally substantive proposition that's strongly at odds with
> his reactions to more than a few cases he considers.
>
> Peter Unger *Living High and Letting Die*

There are many ways of criticizing a moral theory or principle, and it is not
my intention to propose a formal procedure to accomplish this task. I will
mention some features upon which I think it might be useful to reflect. Some
of them will have direct relevance for the discussion of human dignity; others
only indirect relevance.

2.1 Simplicity

Many of the rules in connection with fundamental theoretical proposals
in ethics ought to be the same as the rules in e.g. the physical sciences—
a theory should be simple, for instance, although I believe that the rationale for this may be slightly different in the physical sciences compared to
ethics.

A scientist usually believes that a simple theory is better than a more
complicated one, even if both theories provide equally good explanations.
The reason might simply be that a simple theory is more handy than a more
complicated one. But the reason why she wants a simple theory might also
be that she believes it probably will prove to be the true one in the long
run. So a scientist, for instance a physicist, might want her theories to be
simple, since she believes that this is how nature works—nature chooses
economy.

Scientists also have aesthetic preferences. They may think that a simple
theory or principle is more beautiful than a complicated one. But a scientist

who has to choose between a very simple but slightly incorrect theory or explanation and a more complicated but more correct theory would probably choose the latter one, assuming that her ambition was to know what is true or false about nature. So the aesthetic considerations would in this case be secondary to these other considerations.

If we look at the person who constructs ethical theories we will probably find certain differences here. First, we may question whether there is a procedure available for the moral philosopher which is analogous to the empirical testing of physical theories. We can try to compare observations in empirical sciences with intuitions in ethics—to be in accordance with certain kinds of intuitions is a demand to be put on an ethical theory, just as a physical theory has to harmonize with certain observations (this can be put in the negative form as well: we may demand that an ethical theory should be able to be falsified by intuitions just as a physical theory should by observations).[1] Then, whatever the demands to be put on a theory in the empirical sciences as far as observations are concerned, there is an analogous demand to be put on the ethical theory as far as intuitions are concerned.[2]

I will soon consider whether there is a place for intuitions in the justification of an ethical theory. I believe there is, but I am not sure that we can let the intuitions play the same leading role in ethics as observations in the physical sciences.

If there is no perfect analogy in ethics to questions of truth and falsehood, there should also naturally be more room for such ideals as simplicity, and it becomes easier to see this primarily as an aesthetic ideal. In that case, I believe it easier to make compromises between simplicity and intuitions than between simplicity and observations, at least if we are sure that the observations are correct; many people stick to utilitarianism also when they know that this theory is counter-intuitive in certain fundamental respects and believe it is important for a moral theory *not* to be so.

There is another difference as far as simplicity is concerned. In a moral theory there may be an extra dimension associated with simplicity over and above the aesthetic one, a dimension probably not important to a theory of physical reality. A scientist's ambition is normally not to teach lay people how to view reality but instead to describe and explain it accurately. She is more concerned about this than about giving her ideas a form which has an appeal to other people, whether or not they are scientists. The ambition of a moral philosopher is normally different, since her objective may well concern

---

[1] Cf. M. White (1981) and also W. D. Ross who has claimed that "the moral convictions of thoughtful and well-educated people are the data of ethics just as sense-perceptions are the data of natural science" (1930: 41).

[2] If this is what we think, we will use a sense of intuition which in D. D. Raphael's terms leads more to probability than to necessity, i.e. if having an intuition is analogous to making an observation, then it must be something weaker than "an intellectual grasp of a necessary truth" (1994: 63).

how to change the world in accordance with what she thinks is right.[3] We may want the world to fit our moral theories but e.g. physical theories to fit reality. As Roy A. Sorensen puts it: "science tries to make words fit the world, ethics tries to make the world fit the words" (1992: 13). If there is a discrepancy between the world and our theories, we can strive to change the world if we are moral philosophers, but if we are scientists we instead change our theories.

If we accept this as a rough description of what the ambitions of the two subject matters normally look like and how they are pursued, then we may also realize what the moral philosopher needs but not the scientist—she needs to shape her theories in a form which is *possible* to use as an instrument to change the world. This is why she may want her theories to be simple in the sense that they have an appeal to people and can be practised. And it explains why so many ethical debates tend to circle around whether a Kantian or a utilitarian moral outlook is correct. Kant is by no means a philosopher with simple ideas, but his theory is built upon the categorical imperative, the main thought of which can be explained in a fairly simple way and with references to the Golden Rule. Pretty much the same is true of utilitarianism— when carefully analysed it proves to be anything but simple—but the main thought of the theory has a kind of pedagogical simplicity; the idea is clear and easily understood. So there is a kind of social dimension of moral philosophy which may explain why simplicity is an attractive feature of an ethical theory. Of course, the same reasoning can apply also to science. A scientist might well have an instrumental view of constructing scientific theories. But the difference I want to point to is that the scientist has a freedom of choice here that the moral philosopher has not. A non-applicable scientific theory is in itself less queer than a non-applicable moral theory.

The relevance of this for our subject will become quite obvious as we continue this study, since one of its central ideas is fairly simple, namely that there is a special value in being human in so far as people actually believe or feel that such a value exists.

2.2 Consistency

Consistency is often expressed as a theoretical *demand*, that is, it is always correct to criticize a theory, whether it be a moral or scientific one, if it either contains explicitly contradictory statements or statements from which other explicitly contradictory statements can be derived. Simplicity, on the other hand, is more like an *ideal*—objections to simplicity are not fatal.

---

[3] The ambition may concern both direct and indirect changes, i.e. either changing the world oneself or changing the people (by putting moral pressure on them, for instance) so that they change the world.

It is commonly held that it is a consistency demand which makes it impossible for the same action to be right in one situation and wrong in another, if the only difference between the situations is that they occur at different places or at different times or with different individuals figuring in them.

One of the earlier formulations of a universalizability requirement is Henry Sidgwick's:

whatever action any of us judges to be right for himself, he implicitly judges to be right for all similar persons in similar circumstances. Or, as we may otherwise put it, "if a kind of conduct that is right (or wrong) for me is not right (or wrong) for some one else, it must be on the ground of some difference between the two cases, other than the fact that I and he are different persons." (1907: 379)

The most well-known modern proponent of the principle is R. M. Hare, who says:

if we make different moral judgements about situations which we admit to be identical in their universal descriptive properties, we contradict ourselves (1981: 21).[4]

This means that I am not allowed to say that it is wrong for a person to inflict suffering on me in situation S, but not wrong for this person to inflict suffering on another person in S, although he and I are exactly similar as far as the universal properties are concerned. But what is a universal property? To be *me* is not, that is, to be the particular person who is writing this sentence right now. So the fact that I am *I* cannot be used as a reason why it is morally wrong to inflict suffering on me. And as I understand the requirement of universalizability, it applies to moral judgements, principles and reasons.

In the quotation Hare seems to regard the principle of universalizability as a demand for consistency. However, Toni Rønnow-Rasmussen has argued that it is not merely a consistency requirement (1993: esp. Ch. III).[5] We will soon return to this question, but in the meantime I want to point out that my treatment of universalizability will not presuppose that it is in all parts a consistency requirement. Neither will I presuppose that it is a requirement that follows logically from the moral language (I believe that these two questions are connected).

What about a claim regarding the importance of species membership? Can it be wrong to hit someone with reference to the fact that she belongs to a certain species? In one sense "yes", since there are many universal properties accompanying species membership—for instance the capacity to experience pain and suffering.

---

[4] In his first articles on the subject Hare thought that the universalizability requirement is conceptually tied to the word "moral". Later his thesis seems instead to be that it is tied to the word "ought". See Hare (1963: 37).
[5] Cf. John Deigh (1995: 751) who seems to claim that it is not at all a consistency requirement in the sense of a demand not to contradict oneself.

But what about someone claiming that species membership *in itself* is a morally relevant factor for this question? Compare two situations. One where I claim that the reason why suffering ought not to be inflicted is that it is inflicted on *me*. Another where I claim that the reason is that it is inflicted on a member of the species *Homo sapiens*. These situations seem to be similar since the reason in both situations focuses on my own identity—in the first situation on my own identity as an individual and in the second situation on my identity as belonging to a group. If it cannot in itself matter morally upon *whom* the suffering is inflicted, how can it matter upon *which body of individuals* the suffering is inflicted?

This question hides an important distinction. If the reason why the suffering ought not be inflicted on us simply is that we are we, then something is wrong. This is exactly the same kind of reason as when I say that this should not be done to me simply because I am I. But if by saying this I intend to say that it should not be done because I am the *kind* of person that I am, then what I say may make sense. And the same is true if I say that something is wrong because it is done to a member of the species *Homo sapiens*. To be such a member is, I will assume, to be a certain *kind* of being and if this is what my reason concerns then it may be all right.

But observe, it may also be correct to say that species membership is important *in itself* and not primarily that certain important properties accompany the species membership. To belong to a certain species is a universal property.

To say that suffering should not be inflicted on a certain individual because she is a human being is to commit oneself, other things being equal, to the same judgement of any human individual—if an individual is a human individual suffering should not be inflicted on her either, other things being equal. This makes sense in a way in which it does not, in my view, make sense to universalize a judgement that this should not be done to me simply because *I am I*—what does it mean to subscribe to a judgement to the effect that of any other individual who proved herself to be me, I have to say that this should not be done to her either?

On the other hand, it *does* seem to make sense to imagine what it would be like to be placed *in another person's shoes*, that is to say, what it would be like to have (all or only some of) her descriptive properties just as it does make sense to imagine what to say about a situation where another person is placed in my shoes.[6] I may imagine what it would be like to be the *kind* of

---

[6] Here, just as Hare seems to do (1988: 284), I have to assume that Leibniz's so-called principle of indiscernibles which in Rønnow-Rasmussen's formulation states that "exact similarity amounts to identity" (1993: 111) might be false. Otherwise being in another's exact shoes would be the same as being identical with her. This principle can of course be called into question. See for instance Zeno Vendler, who claims that "there are bodies, and there are persons, but there are no 'I's'. If I imagine being you, I do not fancy 'transporting' something into your body, or 'mixing' two entities. What I do is assume, as far as it is in the power of my imagination, the

person that another person is—i.e. having her personal characteristics, psychological set up, and so on—or to have a universal descriptive property of hers just as I may imagine what it would be for another person to be the kind of person that I am or to have a universal and descriptive property of mine. That is one way of explaining why I may refer to these properties when I give the reasons why she or I ought to be treated in a certain way.

This is a result of the fact that I prefer to interpret the principle of universalizability in the following way.[7] I am not allowed to give moral reasons which are built on the fact that I am I, i.e. that *I* am D.E., since it is impossible to imagine what it would be like for someone else to be D.E. The universalizability in my interpretation requires that I accept the following conditionals: (a) if the property P is morally relevant when I have it, then it will also have to be relevant when another individual in my position has got it; (b) if P is relevant when another individual has got it, then it will also have to be relevant when I have it when placed in her position. That I am I (D.E.) or that you are you (N.N.) can for obvious reasons not meet this requirement (one cannot change particulars). On the contrary, the fact that I have the universal property UP can meet the requirement, since whatever the property is, it will be possible that another individual than the one who actually has got it might have it instead.

One problem with this explication of the principle of universalizability is that (a)–(b) seem to be neither sufficient nor necessary for universalizability.[8] For the following reason it is not sufficient. I may apply the reasoning described in (a)–(b) to non-universal properties as well. For instance, suppose I claim that A ought to be discriminated against because B dislikes her, where B of course refers to a particular person. It might well be the case that I accept that I also ought to be discriminated against when placed in A's position; that is to say, I accept that if I was disliked by B, then I ought to be discriminated against. Nevertheless, being disliked by B is not a universal property. Therefore, I suggest we use (a)–(b) merely as a criterion, or test. A

coherent set of experiences corresponding to your present situation (your 'Humean self' as it were). But, as Hume pointed out, there is no specific experience of an 'I' in that totality. Nor is there one in mine. The 'I' as such has no content: it is the empty frame of consciousness indifferent to content. Consequently, by constructing in my fancy the image of what I would experience in your situation, I *ipso facto* represent your experiences" (1988: 176). Thus, imagining being another person I just imagine what it would be like to see a situation from his perspective. I believe, however, that there is a distinction here between imagining being like another and imagining being another, since the last expression is equivalent to saying that one imagines that one particular thing is not that particular thing but instead another particular thing, and that does not sound intelligible in my ears. I am not claiming that this will refute Vendler's view; what I am doing is more like *describing* an alternative view. But, once again, one reason why I feel free to reject the principle of indiscernibles without any strong argument is that also Hare seems to reject it, at least the strong version described above.

[7] What I say of universalizability should not be seen as a faithful interpretation of Hare.
[8] I owe this reflection to Wlodek Rabinowicz.

reason, principle, or property might satisfy the principle of universalizability, given that I accept the conditionals (a)–(b) concerning the property, but it does not have to. So, it is merely a first test.

But is it even a criterion? One might claim that some universal properties are essential for me as a person and that I cannot, consequently, imagine what it would be like to lack them while still remaining a person (and the same holds of course for the condition under which I remain *the same* person). Take for instance sentiency. I might claim that a certain treatment of A is morally right or acceptable in virtue of the fact that A lacks sentiency. But in view of what we have said above and what it means to be a person, it seems that it makes no sense imagining what it would be like to be myself as a person placed in a non-sentient being's position. I cannot imagine being the same person under conditions where I lack properties that are essential for personhood. However, this problem is partly a result of a misunderstanding of (a)–(b), since what I am to imagine is not in my view that I *as a person* am placed in another's shoes but rather that I *as an individual* am thus placed. And sentiency is not an essential property for me as an individual, nor is, as far as I can see, any other universal property essential for me as an individual, not even the property of being an animal—human or non-human. Therefore, I think we *can* use the conditionals (a)–(b) as a first test of universalizability.

So when you discriminate against some individuals (e.g. by denying them protection from what causes suffering to them), the reason for doing this must not refer to the identity of these individuals, but only to their universal properties or to the lack of some universal properties of these individuals. Therefore, if you think you have moral reason to discriminate against an individual merely because this individual is an animal, the principle of universalizability will also mean a commitment to the following statements. If the individual was *not* an animal you would not have this reason to discriminate against it. Moreover, if *you* were an animal others would have reason to discriminate against you. The test concerns whether or not the reason I cite for making a moral judgement is such that it involves a preparedness to make the same moral judgement concerning any individual who has the property that I hold to be decisive for making the judgement in question. This I take to be different aspects of the test of universalizability.

However, in this test we have assumed that it is possible to make certain kinds of thought experiments, for example, one in which we imagine what it would be like to belong to a another species. Is this kind of thought experiment possible?[9]

---

[9] Bernard Williams, for instance, does not think so: "We just don't know what we are talking about if we suppose that that very person hadn't been a human being" (1990: 178). See also Saul Kripke who expresses this idea somewhat more guardedly: "supposing Nixon is in fact a human being, it would seem that we cannot think of a possible counterfactual situation in which he was, say, an inanimate object; perhaps it is not even possible for him not to have been a human being" (1980: 46).

2.3 The Species Concept

The answer to this question depends on how we define the notion of species. I will discuss two main alternatives[10] but then, in the end, suggest that we make some kind of compromise.

The first alternative is a species concept which relies on the notion of essential properties as defining properties of each species.[11] Elliot Sober remarks that *essentialism*

is a standard philosophical view about natural kinds. It holds that each natural kind can be defined in terms of properties that are possessed by all and only the members of that kind. [...] A natural kind is to be characterized by a property that is both necessary *and* sufficient for membership (1993: 145).

Now, since it might be convenient to describe an organism's morphological properties, morphology is traditionally used for species descriptions. Therefore, I will call this a "morphological species concept".

An alternative is to use what has been called a "biological species concept". Ernst Mayr is commonly regarded as being a proponent of this concept. He holds that "*Species are groups of interbreeding natural populations that are reproductively isolated from other such groups*" (1976: 270).[12]

According to Sober this is to be interpreted as a kind of non-essentialism. A species is here not a *kind* but instead an *individual*. Similarity is neither necessary nor sufficient for two parts to belong to the same individual. Sober writes:

I'll use the term "breeding population" to denote a set of local demes linked to each other by reproductive ties but not so linked to demes outside the set. For example, the herd of deer living in a particular valley constitutes a single deme. Within the herd, there is reproduction. Moreover, this herd is reproductively linked to other such herds because of the entry and exit of individual organisms. A breeding population thus constitutes a *gene pool* whose parts are integrated by reproductive interactions (1993: 153–4).

As a third alternative I suggest a compromise between these views, namely that we regard species as a natural kind, defined in terms of the genetic structure that is possessed by all and only the members of that kind. We thus take the essentialism from the first alternative and the reference to genes from the second. Let us call this the "genetic species concept".[13]

---

[10] Cf. Slobodchikoff (1976: 1).

[11] Observe that *essentialism* in this context is fairly innocent and concerns merely properties essential for membership in a species. Certain properties are thus defining properties of a species or a natural kind. There is also a non-trivial form of essentialism, according to which these properties defining a natural kind are essential for the *individual* that possesses them. Sober interprets essentialism in the innocent way.

[12] See also Mayr (1963: 19 ff.).

[13] These are not the only alternatives. For instance, there are variants of the second alternative not discussed here. D. L. Hull (1976) wants to define species merely in terms of its continuity in space and time. See also Elliot Sober (1993), who holds that species are historical entities. The

The advantage of the third view compared to the first one is that I believe there is a tendency in biology to regard the genetic concept as primary in relation to the morphological one. This is, I think, what Roger Trigg catches when he writes:

> Someone who looked and behaved like a human, but whose genetic composition was utterly different from the human, and who could not interbreed with members of the species *Homo sapiens*, could not from the biological point of view be classified as a member of that species (1982: 101).

Then what is the advantage of the third concept over the second one? I am not claiming that we should replace the second one with the third one, but merely that from the perspective of this study, it seems that the third one is the simpler alternative. So when nothing else is said, the concept of a human being is taken in its genetic sense. This is commonly the sense which those philosophers and writers who believe that being human may be important *per se* at least *say* they have in mind.[14]

So far our discussion of the species concept has circled around two questions. First of all, whether species membership is of any fundamental importance to the question of personal identity, that is, for example, whether it is impossible to imagine being the same person or being while changing species membership. The other question concerned whether the genes are of any fundamental importance to the concept of species membership. If the answer to this last question is "yes", we could safely conclude that the answer to the first one is "no"—with a genetic concept species membership does not make any fundamental difference to personal identity. However, it is possible to claim that we can answer "no" to the first question even with a morphological species criterion, although the answer perhaps will not be *that* obvious. So the answer to the first question is not quite determined by the answer to the second one.

Suppose you wake up one morning, just like the hero in Kafka's short story, and realize you have been transformed into a big beetle. It is a purely bodily change—you think and react as you did before. This is probably the reason why the story seems so dreadful.

Now suppose you adhere to a purely morphological species criterion (which will not allow for the possibility of looking exactly like a big beetle but at the same time being human). This means that you have literally turned into another species; it is literally true that you as a human mammal have been transformed into an insect.

Is it in some way odd that Gregor Samsa still thinks he is Gregor Samsa? No, it is not and you too, if you were in Samsa's "shoes", would probably

---

main problem with this suggestion is, in my view, that it yields an unnecessary indeterminacy of classification. Who could tell whether we humans consist of one or two species?

[14] See also Roger Trigg (1982: 95).

think you were (numerically) the same individual after the transformation. You would think of yourself as the same person having changed species membership, which means that in the common-sense perspective species membership is not of any fundamental importance to the question of individual identity.

There is reason to believe, therefore, that an individual can change species membership while retaining her identity as a particular individual.[15] This means in turn that we may, as far as the demand of universalizability is concerned, have a moral principle to the effect that suffering should not be inflicted upon human beings, because it is in itself morally important to be a human.

2.4 Universalizability and Utilitarianism

Peter Singer, among others, has tried to draw more far-reaching conclusions from the principle of universalizability. He says:

The universal aspect of ethics, I suggest, does provide a persuasive, although not conclusive, reason for taking a broadly utilitarian position (1993: 12).

He reasons in the following way. The first step is to reject the bias to oneself and this follows directly from the principle of universalizability. When I accept this requirement of ethical judgement, then I am also "accepting that my own interests cannot, simply because they are my interests, count more than the interests of anyone else" (1993: 12). This excludes ethical egoism, Singer says, since "my very natural concern that my own interests be looked after must, when I think ethically, be extended to the interests of others" (1993: 12–3).

The second step is reached by imagining what to do in a situation where we think ethically and have to decide between two possible courses of action. Since ethics takes a universal point of view...

I now have to take into account the interests of all those affected by my decision. This requires me to weigh up all these interests and adopt the course of action most likely to maximise the interests of those affected (1993: 13).

I will soon comment on Singer's argument.

---

[15] Being a human being is therefore a non-essential property for me as an individual. But it is also what P. F. Snowdon calls a *non-abiding* sort, which is a sort "to which a thing can belong at a given time and then cease to belong, despite remaining in existence" (1990: 87). Observe, however, that Snowdon thinks that "being an animal" is an *abiding* sort, meaning that if an animal belongs to it "at a given time, then that entity must belong to it as long as that entity remains in being" (1990: 87). For a discussion of this distinction, see also Stefan Berglund (1995: 28–9, 48–9). Observe that the question of essentialism concerns what property one has to have in every possible world, whereas the question of abidingness concerns what property one can have in this world *and then lose.*

Let us ask whether or not Hare believes that ethical judgements require that we abandon an egoistic concern for ourselves. He says of universality that it "means merely the logical property of being governed by a universal quantifier and not containing individual constants" (1981: 41). As Rønnow-Rasmussen makes clear, the last part of the sentence is about *ineliminable* individual constants (1993: 110). I tried to make the same point when I claimed that a moral principle may refer to an individual in so far as what is important in the principle is the universal properties of the individual.

It is clear that we actually have two parts of the universalizability requirement here, which seem to have different standing and different functions. Partly the idea is that an ought judgement requires universalizability in the sense of being governed by a universal quantifier and partly that reference to individual constants is not allowed in such judgements. Hare describes these parts as a weaker and a stronger sense of universalizability with the demand on universal quantification being a result of a supervenience relation whereas the exclusion of individual references is a further requirement (1989: 74). I am not going to analyse the relationship between these parts.[16] However, it seems clear that it is easier to regard the first part of the requirement as a consistency demand than the second one; furthermore, it is easier to regard the first part as a conceptual demand than the second one. In the following I assume that we are talking of a principle containing both these parts when we consider Hare's universalizability requirement.

Does this exclude egoism? Hare's thesis is that it is not the case that all kinds of egoism are excluded by the principle of universalizability. For instance, "if we say 'Everyone ought to look out only for himself', that is logically (formally) speaking universal" (1988: 249). This means that the principle does not prohibit one from being partial to oneself, as long as one admits that this partiality commits one to say that it is also all right for another person to be partial to herself. If I say that everyone ought to look out only for herself, this implies that I also say that I ought to look out only for myself and that she ought to look out only for herself.

What I want to show is that even *universal* egoism has a special standing if we accept the principle of universalizability, in the sense that there seems to be a very small room for applying the principle particularly to those judgements that can be derived from universal egoism and that universal egoism in this sense differs from other kinds of partiality. If this is right, then Singer might use at least some version of a universalizability requirement to take the first step (concerning rejection of the bias to oneself) in his argument. However, I do not believe the requirement will help him to take the second step as well.

---

[16] This as well as other aspects of the universalizability thesis has been treated in depth by other philosophers. See, for instance, Rønnow-Rasmussen (1993), Wlodek Rabinowicz (1979) and Torbjörn Tännsjö (1974).

If I accept the principle of universal egoism, then it trivially follows that I accept a principle of egoism applied to my own case, since if it is true that everyone ought to be self-interested then I ought to be self-interested as well. This was described above. But then it seems that I may derive from a principle which Hare claims satisfies the universalizability requirement another principle which does not satisfy it, if by the requirement we mean a ban on reasons for my actions which, as Sidgwick says, are built on the fact that I and someone else are different persons. If the principle exhorts me to be self-interested, then it exhorts me to follow a principle that makes essential reference to me as an individual—and what the universalizability requirement says is, in Wlodek Rabinowicz's formulation, that "purely 'individual' or [...] 'numerical' aspects" (1979: 11) are not morally essential. But if I am to practise self-interested principles, then the fact that I am I *will* have a fundamental moral importance for me.

And observe that this is not an example of the trivial fact that we may derive a singular moral judgement from any moral judgement. From the moral principle "One ought to carry old ladies' bags (if the ladies so wish)!" it naturally follows that I too ought to do so. But when I try to live in accordance with such a principle—"I ought to carry old ladies' bags (if...)!", I will apply a principle in which the reference to myself in no way is essential for me—that I ought to carry these bags has nothing to do with the fact that I am I, or generally with a fact about personal or individual identity.

On the other hand, if we look at the self-interest principle we see that it *does* contain an essential reference to an indexical term. In fact it contains one inessential and one essential reference of this kind. If I state the principle "I ought to satisfy my own interests first of all!", we see that the first "I" is an eliminable individual constant whereas "my own" does not seem to be so. The reason is that since I am a universal egoist I will subscribe to the principle that it is also true of any person similar or exactly similar to me that she ought to satisfy her own interest first of all. However, what this principle says is that *any* person in my position should lay stress on the fact that she is she and *not* that any person in my position should satisfy the interests of any person in my position first of all. If I follow a principle which does not make essential reference to individual aspects, then I will not at all be following an egoistic principle.

Consider the following objection.[17] It is not necessary to interpret being egoistic or self-interested the way I have. Being self-interested does not necessarily entail that the property of being me makes a difference for me, but can also mean that I lay stress on being the agent of the action. So being self-interested might be interpreted as *acting in the interest of the agent*, and here we have no essential reference to me as an individual. So actually we seem to have two kinds of universal egoism: universal *non-universalizable*

---

[17] Which I owe to Wlodek Rabinowicz.

egoism and universal *universalizable* egoism. The point about universal egoism that I make above concerns only the former kind of universal non-universalizable egoism.

I believe that universal universalizable egoism is a theoretically possible but psychologically implausible position. When a universal egoist proclaims that "Everyone ought to look out only for herself!" she is not expecting everyone to be self-interested in the sense of giving priorities to the agent of the action. This is not how egoism works, and it is not the way a universal egoist thinks. One may even wonder if it should be designated "egoism" at all. Therefore, I believe we may side-step this problem with reference to common-sense knowledge of psychology. And the following point still remains: from a principle which satisfies the test of universalizability, namely the principle of universal egoism, we can derive another principle which does *not* satisfy the universalizability test.

But what will this mean? In one sense I find this a bit puzzling, since how, from the point of view of universalizability, can it be that a principle that exhorts *everyone* to lay stress on her personal identity is better than a principle which only exhorts *one* person to do that? If the universalizability requirement claims that morality is essentially independent of individual aspects (see Rabinowicz above), then how can it be better if many people refer to these aspects than if few people—perhaps only one—do so? Another way of formulating this question is to wonder whether the requirement should not only sort out such principles of mine which make essential reference to the fact that I am I but also principles from which such principles can be derived. It seems that universal egoism contains the essential individual reference which will make such derivations possible.

Where exactly lies the problem—if it is a problem? Does it lie in the fact that the universalizability requirement does allow principles in which there is an essential individual reference? No, I do not think so, since that would not only affect universal egoism but any other kind of universal partiality as well (and this would easily take us to Singer's conclusion). Instead the point is that universal egoism seems to have a special standing compared to other kinds of universal partialities, since it does not make *any* room, or only a small room, for the various aspects of what we have called the test of universalizability.

For a contrast, consider partiality to one's own children. It is clear that in one sense this will contain an ineliminable reference to myself, since when I claim that someone should not inflict suffering on my children, then I am not claiming that any person in his exact position should not inflict suffering on the children of any other person exactly similar to me. Instead I prohibit the infliction of suffering on these children just because they are mine (since just as above and for the same reason as above, I consider the most plausible form of universal partiality to one's own children to be the non-universalizable one). Therefore, the fact that my children are *mine* is of fundamental importance to me.

I may apply the universalizability test to a case like this one nevertheless. Recall that one aspect of this requirement was a demand that the reason cited for why someone is treated in a certain way involves a preparedness to treat any individual, *ceteris paribus*, who has the property that I hold to be morally decisive in the same way. Now, if I claim that someone ought to be treated favourably just because he is my child, then I am committed to the view that, other things being equal, any individual who is my child should be treated this favourably. There is a room for testing whether or not I am prepared to stick to my judgement also under conditions where the identity of those individuals that my judgement is about would be different. And it is not only possible to *apply* this test, it is also possible to pass it—if I treat someone favourably and as a moral defence state that this individual is my (biological) child, then it is very plausible to assume that I *would* accept a judgement to the effect that I ought to treat any individual who turns out to be my (biological) child this way.

And I have already explained that I do not believe that this kind of test is applicable in a case where I propose that someone ought to be treated favourably because this someone is me—it does not, in my view, make sense to ask myself whether I would be prepared to treat any individual who turned out to be me in the same way, if by "any individual" we mean any individual whatever her numerical identity.

This has to be qualified. One might object that there is room for applying the universalizability test also to egoism, namely to non-universal egoism. Suppose that I believe that everyone acts morally correctly if they act in *my* interest. Then it follows that I would say that A's action is morally right if it promotes my interest. But I may also ask myself—and answer in the affirmative—whether or not I would be prepared to give the same judgement in a situation where it was instead *B's* action that promoted my interest. So there is room for the test here.

However, there is *more* room for the test if we compare with non-universal partiality towards one's own children, where the important thing is that everyone promotes the interests of my children. Here I can apply the test in two ways when I say that A ought to be treated favourably by B because A is my child, since I am committed to the view that, other things being equal, *any* individual who is my child should be treated favourably by *anyone* who is in B's position.

So the asymmetry seems to remain. In both universal and non-universal egoism there seems to be less room for the universalizability test compared to other kinds of partiality. At least this is true as long as we talk of partiality where there is an essential reference to myself as an individual.

I am not in any way claiming that this is a startling difference between universal egoism and other kinds of partiality, since I believe it follows rather trivially from what it means to have oneself as the primary object of one's egoistic concerns and to have someone else—for instance one's child—

as such an object. What I wanted to do was merely to point to this fact: that universal egoism is further from the spirit of the universalizability require-ment—since it leaves no room for any aspect of the test—than other kinds of partiality, and that this means that the step from this requirement to the ban on egoism, even universal egoism, indeed is fairly small.

Therefore, there is a grain of truth when Singer claims that the universal aspect of ethics provides a persuasive reason for not accepting even universal egoism and thus for taking the first step on the road to utilitarianism.

But Singer cannot justify the second step by the requirement. The universal aspect of ethics does not force us to take into consideration the interests of *all* others. So the difficulties of ethical egoism do not automatically yield universal altruism. Also a more confined form of altruism, e.g. kin altruism, will do, since it does not seem to carry with it the problems that pertain to egoism, to the effect that there is no room at all for applying the univer-salizability test. And neither does the requirement force us (not even mildly) to adopt utilitarianism in which we *maximize* the satisfaction of interests of all those affected by our action.

And the second step is unjustified even if we choose an interpretation of the universalizability requirement in which *all* references to individual terms are forbidden, which would be a ban on all kinds of agent-relativity. It is true that we in that case cannot defend partiality to our own children any more, but we can still be partial to our own species if we merely formulate this partiality without any references to ourselves. And I repeat that this can be done. Then it will not be true that "an ethical principle cannot be justified in relation to any partial or sectional group" (1993: 11). Therefore not even a literal interpretation will take us to utilitarianism.

It is true that Singer very carefully claims that the universal aspect of ethics provides "a *persuasive*, although *not conclusive*, reason for taking a broadly utilitarian position" (1993: 12, my emphasis). However, given tradi-tional formulations of the universalizability thesis, it is not strong enough to sort out various kinds of partiality.[18]

I conclude that in so far as we subscribe to the principle of universalizability, it seems all right to be partial towards one's own species. So our methodological remarks on consistency interpreted as a demand for universalizability are not directly able to sort out the kind of attitude which this study particularly is about. Neither do they bring us to utilitarianism, which indeed would sort out this attitude.

---

[18] Which is an effect of the fact that universalizability discussed here is not an impartiality thesis, but instead a thesis about what Richard Norman has called *consistency and impersonality* (1983: 117).

2.5 Intuitions

In the following sections I will only consider some facets of the academic debate on intuitionism in a fairly unsystematic and random way. I do not strive for systematic completeness even on an elementary level.

The question of intuitions is a hard problem in ethics, in the sense that it is difficult to have a consistent attitude towards it. The reason for this in turn is that we strongly feel that there are both great advantages and disadvantages in letting our intuitions or feelings determine what moral principles to accept and what to think morally of different examples from life and thought experiments.

One of the advantages is that it seems like a handy procedure to solve a problem just by asking oneself what one feels about it. If the problem is whether or not a certain principle is morally acceptable, a simple form of reliance on intuition will say that the principle is morally acceptable if you have no negative moral feelings against it.[19]

Perhaps someone thinks that one problem here is how to determine when a feeling is a *moral* one and when it is something else, that is, how does one determine the moral quality of the feelings which are roused by considering the principle? One simple answer would be to say that *all* feelings excited by a moral principle and which are relevant to the decision whether or not to accept the principle are moral feelings. Then what you need when deciding whether or not a feeling is a moral one is merely an independent method of telling when a *principle* is a moral one.

This answer is not fully satisfactory. If one believes that feelings have something to tell us in moral matters, then it is also reasonable to discriminate between different kinds of feelings concerning their moral relevance. For instance, if considering whether it is equally wrong to kill a boar and a deer one would like to think that the kind of tender feelings one has towards deer and which are caused by their pretty faces, ought to have no (or less) voice in the matter. Furthermore, if one really does think that it is possible to tell when a principle is a moral one, then it must also be possible to decide whether or not a certain feeling is a moral one. Some of the criteria may apply both to the principle and the feeling, some may not, perhaps because although both a principle and a feeling have a propositional content, the exact content of a feeling may be harder to formulate.

If this is true, the handiness of the intuitionism considered here is already a little bit decreased. We cannot listen only to our feelings when determining the moral status of a principle, an action or state of affairs—we have to make sure that we listen to the right kind of feelings.

---

[19] My account of moral intuitions will be meta-ethically neutral in so far as the nature of these intuitions is concerned. Therefore I will speak interchangeably of moral intuitions, moral beliefs, moral feelings and moral preferences. Nevertheless, I believe that a meta-ethical analysis has to do justice to the fact that all these aspects of a moral attitude somehow coexist.

This can be expanded further. One can say that not only should one discriminate between kinds of feelings as an intuitionist, but one should also say something about whether or not one has considered and reflected upon the feelings in question. In other words, an intuitionist may say that we have to listen to our feelings with a critical attitude and investigate them in a special way before letting them decide whether, for instance, a moral principle is acceptable or not.

This means that also the conditions under which a feeling is aroused can be relevant—the feeling is more reliable when it is a result of careful reflection of the principle or action to be judged, when the subject has tried to get all the information relevant for making a judgement and when the feeling tends to be stable even when this cognitive process is repeated.

Here we can also see an analogy to natural science. At the beginning of this chapter we asked if there was any procedure available for the moral philosopher which was roughly analogous to the empirical testing of e.g. a physical theory. If intuitionism is true, then we have reason to believe there exists such a procedure—intuitions play roughly the same role for some moral philosophers as observations do for (some) physicists. And this analogy[20] also supports the point made above—natural scientists also put certain demands on the kinds of observations with which to support their theories and the conditions under which the observations are made. Science work with experiments, that is, with observations made under controlled conditions. The analogous demand to be put on a moral philosopher is that she listens to her moral feelings under controlled conditions, in the way described above, and that she also tries to repeat this procedure just as a natural scientist will repeat her experiments to make sure that she can rely on them.

This means that the advantage of intuitionism mentioned above probably is undermined. This way of getting knowledge in ethical matters turned out not to be so handy after all. We may still think it advantageous to have a view in which there at least exists a possibility to *get* moral knowledge and to confirm or disconfirm moral principles. But this is not what was initially claimed, and it may support the suspicion that also intuitionists will claim that only the experts can tell whether or not a moral theory is acceptable, just as in physics only an expert can tell whether or not a physical theory is acceptable. Much of the spontaneous support of intuitionism will be lost if this is true.

We may still believe that intuitionism has advantages. To my mind, intuitionism is attractive mainly because we all have strong feelings in connection with moral principles and situations which we believe are morally interesting and it seems so natural to let these feelings (spontaneously or after they have been considered) determine what to think about the principle or situation.[21] So intuitionism is a very natural standpoint, since I believe it

---

[20] Some of the problems with such an alleged analogy are discussed by James Griffin (1996: 12 ff.).
[21] The distinction between principles and situations seems to provide room for a choice between generalism and particularism, for instance the kind of particularism defended by Jonathan Dancy

is true of most people that they actually let their moral feelings solve their moral problems—most of us, whether philosophers or non-philosophers, treat our moral feelings or intuitions as authorities. Furthermore, one might claim that there is no *better* ethical method than the intuitionistic one,[22] but I am not able to show this here.

2.6 Problems of Intuitionism

This will tell both for and against intuitionism. It tells for it in so far as most of us seem in reality to believe in some kind of intuitionism—it is not a far-fetched choice. But it also tells against the theory, since we may claim that since most of us function as intuitionists of a kind, we lack an effective instrument for solving our moral disagreements. The well-known problem with intuitions is that they diverge, and if we believe it comfortable to rely on intuitions in moral matters for our own part, we mostly think it uncomfortable when our moral antagonists rely on *their* intuitions and therefore cannot be reached by our arguments (if we have any).

There is also a problem of conservatism in connection with intuitionism. We often have feelings which stand in sharp contrast to our intellectual convictions, feelings which may harmonize more with our *previous* convictions, and to which we therefore do not want to attach importance. It is a grave problem with intuitions, I believe, that they demand from us that we listen to them although we also feel that they will not always accord with our present moral thinking.

One example from my own experience is the distinction often made between killing and letting die. My intellectual conviction in this matter is rather firm—if we have two cases which are completely similar as far as the motivation of the involved persons is concerned, the result of their actions (and inactions), and so on, I am intellectually convinced that if the *only* difference between them is that one case can be described as killing a person while another case can be described as letting a person die, then there is no moral difference between them.[23] So out of these convictions I cannot attach

---

(1993a) and (1981). But observe that Dancy rejects the universalizability thesis that we took for granted in the previous chapter. Compare also John McDowell (1985).

[22] Compare William Shaw: "The basic justification for intuitionistic procedures is simply that, despite difficulties, there is no other way to proceed, no alternative to pulling ourselves up by our own bootstraps" (1980: 130). Compare also Samuel Scheffler: "it is difficult for me to see how there could be any plausible conception of ethical justification that did not assign a substantial role of some kind of ethical beliefs and intuitions" (1992: 144). See also Walter Sinnott-Armstrong who writes that the "most common way to argue for intuitionism is to rule out its alternatives one by one" (1992: 629).

[23] Jonathan Bennett calls this "the neutrality thesis", which is equivalent to a negative answer to the following question: "If someone's behavior has a bad state of affairs as a consequence, is the morality of his conduct affected by whether he *made* the consequence obtain or only *allowed* it to do so?" (1993: 76).

any weight to the distinction and therefore I am not prepared to subscribe to moral principles supporting such a difference.

Nevertheless, my feelings keep on trying to convince me that there *is* a difference between killing and letting die, even in these arranged thought experiments where every factor is held constant except for the fact that one case means to kill a person and the other to let a person die. In a well-known article Philippa Foot expresses this (intuitive) conviction in the following way:

> Most of us allow people to die of starvation in India and Africa, and there is surely something wrong with us that we do; it would be nonsense, however, to pretend that it is only in law that we make a distinction between allowing people in the undeveloped countries to die of starvation and sending them poisoned food. There is worked into our moral system a distinction between what we owe people in the form of aid and what we owe them in the way of non-interference (1967: 11).

The problem with this deep intuitive conviction which is worked into our moral system is that it is both so hard to dismiss and, as it seems, so easy to explain away. The explanation is that in our actual world there probably *is* a difference between allowing people to die in India and sending poisoned food to them—the difference is that only evil people do the latter while the former can happen for various reasons. In this world people who kill are more dangerous than people who allow people to die; if you knowingly send poisoned food you are *interested in* the death of these people. Most of us who allow people to die are *not* interested in knowing that people die as a result of our inactions; we do not refrain from giving food *in order to* let these people die. On the contrary, most of us regret the fact that our inactions have these effects. But if you send poisoned food it has to be because you have morbid attitudes—you are not the kind of person who feels bad about other people dying as a result of your actions or inactions. And the point is that there are many ways in which we can show that the former attitude is morally preferable to the latter—and that it is this fact which is reflected in our intuitions.

So we tend to apply intuitions which presuppose conditions in the actual world also to cases in which these conditions do not hold. This is certainly a kind of conservatism in so far as if the conditions change in the world we will still tend to judge it from the perspective of the old world and the moral thinking we made in that world and which perhaps did fit that world.

Hare claims that this is also the reason why we cannot use unrealistic thought experiments in moral debates and thinking to test whether or not a principle is morally acceptable. Referring to an opponent of utilitarianism who uses fantastic examples to show that utilitarianism is implausible, he says:

> his audience's intuitions are the product of their moral upbringings [...], and, however good these may have been, they were designed to prepare them to deal with moral situations which are likely to be encountered [...]; there is no guarantee at all that they will be appropriate to unusual cases (1981: 132).

I interpret this as a dismissal of any test of intuitions on unrealistic examples and therefore in practice a dismissal of the traditional moral thought experiments.[24] I will soon consider whether this is the conclusion to draw from the fact that it is problematic to rely on intuitions in situations for which these intuitions are unprepared.

Another difficulty with intuitionism is that, in spite of what was said above, it seems to suggest the existence of objective values which are detected by our intuitions. There are many kinds of intuitionism and we have not in this discussion defined exactly what kind of moral theory or feature of a moral theory we consider when we talk of "intuitionism". But intuitionists are traditionally attributed two theses. First, that moral judgements or moral principles can be true and false and that we can know whether they are true or false. Second, that they are, as Dancy says, "known in a special and unfamiliar way, perhaps even by a special faculty called intuition" (1993: 411). So the thesis is that *we* do not create the values, they do not come from us and do not directly depend on our attitudes, which means that they have an objective existence—they are there for us to detect and they will exist independently of whether we succeed in detecting them or not. There are many familiar arguments against such a theory. J. L. Mackie's criticism is well-known (1977, Ch. 1), and I will not repeat it here.[25]

2.7 Basic and Derived Moral Principles

There is an important distinction to be made between moral principles which are basic for a person and principles which are derived. The main difference is that derived principles rest upon one or several factual premises. For instance, from the basic moral principle to create as much happiness as possible you may derive another principle exhorting you to have as many children as possible. This second principle is derived since it is a result of an adherence to the basic principle together with a factual belief that having as many children as possible will be a means towards the observance of the basic principle.

One suggestion is that we preferably should listen to intuitions concerning basic moral principles.[26] But this suggestion is problematic. As far as I can see, the problem is that intuitions concerning basic principles are often more

[24] One point which Hare makes here, but which I have not tried to make, is about the genesis of intuitions. Hare believes that they are shaped by ourselves or alternatively by our moral upbringing, which may be a result of our own or someone else's efforts. Moral intuitions are in his view chosen and implanted in order to reach a moral result determined independently of any moral intuitions.

[25] Mackie's arguments are by no means fatal to every version of objectivism. One way to escape his argument is simply to challenge the Humean account of motivation on which the criticism is built. Cf. also Thomas Nagel (1986) and John McDowell (1985).

[26] See Michael Tooley (1983: 29).

hesitant or at least more vulnerable than those intuitions that concern derived principles—we seem to attach more importance to intuitions concerning derived principles than to intuitions concerning basic ones. At least, this is so if by talking of a basic principle we mean a principle that tends to be general and if by talking of a derived principle we mean a principle that tends to be specific.

A common belief in these matters is that pre-reflective intuitions are less important than reflected ones and that there is a direct correlation between the importance and the degree of reflection of a moral intuition, feeling or belief. It seems reasonable to trust a conviction which you have considered in detail more than a spontaneous conviction which you have not considered in detail.

One natural way of accomplishing this consideration of a principle or an intuition concerning a principle is to try to draw the consequences of the principle and then assess them. The easiest way is to see how the principle works in a concrete situation, that is, to see how it works in different factual situations. A derived principle is by nature more considered in this respect, since by definition the facts are an important part of the principle.

I believe this is the same idea as the one Rachels in a recent article describes in the following way:

Moral principles tend to be vague and abstract; we hardly know what they mean until we see exactly what particular judgments follow from them. Suppose, for example, we start with an "axiom" that seems self-evident, but then, upon investigating its consequences, we discover that it leads to the conclusion that murder is permissible (1993: 117).

Just like Rachels, my claim is only about a *tendency* of the basic principles. We may have concrete basic principles but as a rule they are abstract and general in character.[27] Therefore, if we accept that some degree of reflection is important in these matters, that will also explain why we preferably should listen to our intuitions concerning derived principles instead of those concerning basic ones, at least when the latter concern abstract and general principles.

I am not claiming that an intuition or feeling *has* to be considered in order to be relevant in our moral reasoning. We may also lay stress on an untutored intuition, for instance, if there is no conflict between it and a more considered one. Even if we have an ideal prescribing that *all* intuitions, feelings and

---

[27] We may also have derived moral principles that are not very specific. For instance, consider Mill's *On Liberty*, where he states a very general principle, namely the well-known principle saying that "the only purpose for which power can be rightfully exercised over any member of a civilized community, against his will, is to prevent harm to others" (1978: 9), and from which he derives fundamental human liberties, such as freedom of pursuing our own good in our own way. Observe that this principle is *not* a basic one, but instead derived in turn from the principle of utility. Given some important facts of human life, for instance that a society in order to prosper has to promote and encourage personality and individuality, the principle of utility will yield something like Mill's liberty principle.

beliefs of ours should be as carefully considered as possible, I think this kind of rationality ideal preferably is important when we have a *conflict* between beliefs or intuitions and where some of these are less rational than others. Where there is no such conflict, the fact that some of our beliefs and attitudes are irrational, i.e. not considered, will not be a problem for us.

On the other hand, it is also problematic to say that we should preferably listen to our intuitions concerning derived principles, since these principles depend on facts that might well be different. Therefore, what would better express my position is that intuitions concerning particular cases are more reliable than intuitions concerning general principles and that the distinction between intuitions concerning basic and derived principles is relevant only in so far as it matches the distinction between general principles and particular cases.[28]

Where does all this leave us? Part of the reason for discussing the problems with intuitionism has been to hint at the kind of intuitionism that I myself would like to defend, which indeed is not a theory but more an establishment of the fact that most of us, whether we want to or not, *do* rely on intuitions at some stage of our moral reasoning. And it is not so much a justification for doing so.

I will assume that we are allowed to do what most of us cannot actually refrain from doing—namely, taking moral intuitions seriously.

But actually I make two different assumptions in my study. One stronger assumption that moral intuitions in themselves have a value as evidence and one weaker assumption that it is important to take into account the fact that we have certain intuitions, whatever their intrinsic value as evidence.

---

[28] Again, I am not here defending pure particularism against generalism, at least not if particularism involves denial of the universalizability thesis. But I think there is a case for giving priority to the reactions to the particular case before the reactions to general principles without claiming that the second kind of reaction is without *any* value. So in the end the reasonable position might be some kind of coherentism which weighs intuitions concerning particular situations against intuitions concerning general principles but which, in view of these arguments, places the former kind of intuition slightly before the latter. Cf. also Tom L. Beauchamp's and James F. Childress' discussion of deductivism, inductivism and coherentism (1994: 14 ff.). See also Peter Unger, who would describe the conflict discussed here as a conflict between "our *moral intuitions on particular cases*" on the one hand and "our *general moral common sense*" on the other (1996: 28).

PART II
DIRECT IMPORTANCE

CHAPTER 3

A "STANDARD ATTITUDE" (SA)

Philosophers are ordinary folk.

Michael Smith *The Moral Problem*

I am strongly inclined to believe that whatever attitude we have towards
intuitions, that is, whether we want to take them seriously in our moral
reasoning or not, most of us share the intuition which tells us that what we
do to a human being compared to a non-human one has a special moral
relevance, at least in certain situations. This is an intuition which in one way
or another is important to most of us—as a putative source of moral
knowledge or as something we believe we have to fight against.

3.1 The Standard Attitude

Roger Wertheimer describes this attitude or belief in the following way:

Let us call the kind of moral status most people ascribe to human beings *human (moral) status*.
The term refers to a kind of independent and superior consideration to be accorded an entity,
not to the kind of entity to be accorded the consideration, so it is not a definitional truth that
human beings have human status. But most people believe that being human has *moral cachet*:
viz., a human being has human status in virtue of being a human being (and thus each human
being has human status). Call this the *Standard Belief*. That most people accept it is an empirical
fact (1974: 107-8).

(Let us in the following call this intuition "the Standard Attitude" or just
SA. The reason for this will be considered in due time.) The intuition, as I
understand it, is one you may have whether or not you are prepared to lay
stress on it; it is more like an instinctive—but not necessarily irrational—
reaction which you have independently of the kind of moral principles you
accept and defend.

The exact content of the intuition is difficult to determine. I do not *want*
to make any precise definition of the Standard Attitude. The reason is that
I can make my points without taking any definitive standpoint as to what is
the exact content of the Standard Attitude. In Chapter 6 I will just note
some possible elements in the phenomenology of the Standard Attitude.
What is more, I believe also that I can make my points even if people have
slightly different opinions as to what the Standard Attitude says.

One thing might be cleared out right from the beginning. I say that the
Standard Attitude is about the importance of being human. This is only part

of the truth and should be understood henceforth rather as saying that the Standard Attitude is particularly about the importance of human *life*. It is the fact that a *life* is human that the Standard Attitude values, not the fact that anything—for instance a dead organism—is human. So the Standard Attitude does not ascribe value to dead human bodies. It is true that in some cases this might be called into question (see Chapter 8), but this is at most an untypical understanding of the Standard Attitude and I would prefer to define it as being about the value of human *life* nevertheless. And when I henceforth talk of the "value of being human", this should be understood as a shortened form of the more ungainly "value of being a human life".

There is an important question to be put about the content of such intuitions. They tell us, for instance, that the death of a human being is worse than the death of a non-human one. But the question now is whether the intuition in question can tell us *why* humans appear to be more important than non-humans in this regard. Is it because they are humans *per se* or is it because they have certain properties (typical of humans) which make them special in comparison to non-humans?

This is the very distinction with which this study started. My suspicion is that often our intuitions are too vague to determine this straight away. No doubt, just as we noticed in connection with the distinction between killing and letting die, the Standard Attitude is coloured by the conditions in the actual world. In our world humans typically *do* have certain properties (over and above the fact that they are humans) and the intuitions we have are of course adjusted to the conditions in the actual world, since that is the place where they should work.

This will give us two problems. Firstly, that it can be hard to determine whether our intuitions are about the property of being a human being *per se* or about something else. Secondly, that *if*, in spite of this difficulty, we have intuitive support for the thought that it is the property of being human *in itself* which is important, then it seems that this is something easily explainable given facts about us and the world. If certain properties always (or nearly always) have followed the property of being a human being, then how do we make sure that our belief in the intrinsic importance of being human is not ultimately explained by the fact that humans (nearly always) have these properties? Similar phenomena occur in other areas. For instance, there is a tendency for people to look upon money as something of intrinsic value (the miser saves his money not to spend it but to watch it grow). Obviously, we have here a case of a value transferring from being indirect to becoming direct. And generally, it seems to be a fact that we tend to look upon things with an indirect value as if their value in fact were direct.

In some cases the origin of an intuition will affect our attitude towards it. For instance, suppose that one very important intuition or belief of ours prescribes that our intuitions as far as possible should be rational and considered. Perhaps we accept a kind of intuitionism saying that we may give an intuitive foundation for our morality, but should listen preferably to those intuitions which will not be eliminated by a rational process in which they are scrutinized in various ways (exactly what kind of process we are talking of here will of course be determined by what exactly we want the concept of a rational intuition to mean). That would at least be the kind of intuitionism I would ascribe to myself—a kind of morality founded on those of our intuitions which we cannot get rid of anyway, i.e. that are rational enough to survive rational criticism.

The next question is psychological: what reason do we have to believe the Standard Attitude would disappear after we have realized its origin? We have to guess here and again look for similar experiences in other domains.

Will the Standard Attitude be affected by the kind of knowledge of which we are talking here? I do not think it will disappear altogether, just as I find it hard to believe that the miser can get rid of his attitude to money simply by considering the fact that its value can ultimately be explained as stemming from the fact that one can do things with it (apart from just saving it).[1]

This is not to say that such knowledge will not in any way *affect* his (the miser's) attitude. It seems reasonable to suppose it will, or at least it seems reasonable, assuming folk psychology, to think that if *anything* will affect this kind of attitude, it has to be considering this and similar truths. This can be done in various ways—by meditations, reading novels (for instance Dickens), simply repeating facts to oneself, and so on. And if there is some truth in this, it seems reasonable also to suppose that our attitude to the property of being human will be affected by a similar process—so our liability to regard being human as something intrinsically important will perhaps be somewhat reduced once we realize from where it comes.

On the other hand, if part of the attitude in question really remains after this procedure, then we may find it hard to say with absolute confidence that the attitude *is* a result exclusively of a psychological mistake. We may admit that part of the reason why we think it directly important to be a human being is that we take what was originally indirectly important to be something else, but claim that this need not be the whole truth. Our attitude may also have other sources. Therefore, the result of the mistake in question is rather a reinforcement of an attitude which might have existed even without the mistake in question being made—*it is the strength of the attitude rather than its existence which we should ascribe to the mistake.*

One question which I believe I will leave fairly open in this discussion is the nature of these other sources. Why do most of us endorse a Standard Attitude (or something similar to it) which cannot be explained as a result of the mistake discussed? I do not think we have to answer this question, at least not for the moment.

[1] Cf. R. B. Brandt (1979: 122). Furthermore, there do indeed exist arguments to the effect not that money has intrinsic value (for instance in a utilitarian perspective), but instead that money in a sense has an *independent* value. See for instance Ian Carter (1995: 835).

3.2 Is it Important *per se* to Belong to a Certain Biological Species?

Wertheimer, as we have seen, formulates what he calls a Standard Belief, which says that "a human being has human status [i.e. a special moral status] in virtue of being a human being (and thus each human being has human status)" (1974: 109). A simple reading of this is that any member of the species *Homo sapiens* has human status, and this is also what Wertheimer seems to be saying: "The term 'human being' is correctly applied to all and only the members of our biological species" (1974: 114).

However, when Wertheimer discusses ethical problems of abortion one may doubt if this is what he means:[2]

People disagree over whether and when abortions are morally objectionable primarily, if not solely, because they disagree over whether and when a fetus is a human being. [...] While people may disagree about what overriding considerations may legitimize killing a human being, most people believe that killing a human being is in principle wrong and that, if a fetus is a full-fledged human being, it may be destroyed only for those reasons that justify destroying any other human being (1974: 108).

Here it seems that Wertheimer means something more with "human being" than merely a member of a particular species, since I doubt that this is what the abortion debate is about; I doubt that the person who believes that we may be morally justified in aborting a 16-week-old foetus will support her belief primarily by pointing to the fact that the foetus is not a human being in the biological sense.

Of course, there will always be some people who try to support their opinion with arguments which are out of touch with reality, but Wertheimer is not talking here of unusual ways of arguing against abortion but instead of the usual ones, and no doubt the denial of membership of our species is *not* a customary argument against abortion. And you may wonder: *if* a foetus of this age is not a member of *Homo sapiens*, what is it then? It would be absurd to claim that it is a member of another species, but it also seems bizarre to say it is a member of no species whatsoever. That is to say, if we admit that the foetus is a being it is implausible not to say it is a *human* being.

This is something which could be questioned, that is, whether we have a being or something else in front of us. We may ask whether a one-week-old embryo really is a human being or merely a piece of human life. Many would like to think that human life begins at the moment of conception, but it does seem a bit more problematic to claim that the life of a *being* or an *individual* begins at that time.[3] For instance, it is well-known that the fertilized

---

[2] Tooley also has this kind of problem when interpreting Wertheimer's Standard Belief (1983: 80–1).

[3] John Harris thinks that the claim that human *life* begins at the moment of conception is problematic also: "of course the egg is alive well before conception and indeed it undergoes a process of development and maturation without which conception is impossible. The sperm, too, is alive and wriggling" (1985: 10).

egg may split and form twins and we may have our doubts as to whether we are prepared to say that it is possible for one individual or being to become two (the reason for these doubts can be logical or just semantic).[4]

Here is a situation in which it seems biologically realistic to ask whether we have in front of us a human being or something else. Furthermore, if this is the situation we have in mind it would also be reasonable to think of the property of being a human being as a gradual process, which Wertheimer seems to do. As John Harris says: "Life, then, is a continuum and the emergence of the individual occurs gradually" (1985: 11). But this process will of course come to an end one day (even if we cannot specify exactly which day) in the sense that there is a stage in the development of a foetus where we can say for sure that this being is a human being. I assume that most people believe that this is something which occurs before the foetus is 16 weeks old (this was the example chosen above). Therefore, we will reduce the abortion debate to be about very early abortions if we claim that the debate concerns whether or not the embryo or foetus is a human being.

So there is after all (or at least there could be) a place for disagreement in the abortion debate as to whether a prenatal human organism is a human being or not, but this is a fairly small place, and it does not seem to be what Wertheimer has in mind, since he obviously believes that this question is one of the most important touchstones (or even the most important one) in the abortion debate (at least among non-philosophers).

Wertheimer, therefore, has to have something else in mind when he uses the expression "human being" than merely a being's membership of a biological species. What then does he have in mind?

Tooley says: "It seems to me more likely that he uses it, instead, to mean something like: *mature*, or *fully developed* member of the species *Homo sapiens*" (1983: 81). There is no way of determining the exact content of the expression, but I believe that Tooley suggests too strong a reading of Wertheimer, since there is an obvious sense in which a foetus at no stage of development can be considered a *fully developed* member of the human species. Who wants to deny that a foetus is an organism in development? You may say that there

---

[4] Of course, things can be said also *for* the moment of conception as the start of individual human life. For instance, Vinit Haksar writes: "A powerful case can be made for the view that an individual human being begins to exist at conception. Any other criteria, such as the moment the foetus becomes viable, or the moment the human individual infant is born, seem arbitrary. The moment of conception, unlike other moments in the history of the foetus, seems radically discontinuous with what preceded it. If you believe in the simple view of personal identity, then it would be natural to assume that a person begins to exist all of a sudden, rather than gradually, and the moment of conception seems the least non-arbitrary moment for the beginning of human life. Moreover, at conception the individual acquires the genetic code that will remain with the human being throughout its adult life. And it is at conception that we seem to find the beginning of the spatio-temporal chain that links the foetus to the adult human being" (1979: 86–7).

are alternative interpretations of what it means to be fully developed, but then the rhetorical question has to be: is there *any* sense of this expression in which a foetus at some stage of its development becomes fully developed or could be considered as a candidate for being fully developed? The only sense concerns the genetic constitution of the organism, but if that is what we refer to when using the expression we are back to the question of species membership. And we did agree that Wertheimer had something more in mind.

I am not sure about how to interpret the Standard Attitude in the light of these difficulties, but I would like to think that Wertheimer, when he talks of full-fledged human beings, has in mind human beings in which certain characteristics can be found. We can only speculate as to what these characteristics are. One property of a foetus, often suggested to be morally important, is sentiency, and more exactly the capacity to experience pleasure and pain. But it is a bit problematic to lay stress on this particular property in the abortion issue, since you may wonder whether this capacity is relevant to the *killing* of a being. Observe that this is what Wertheimer is talking of in the first place—it is the *killing* of a foetus that some people obviously would justify by claiming that the foetus is not a full-fledged human being. Sentience will enter into the question of killing only in an indirect way—it may be an empirical fact that we cannot carry out an abortion without causing some pain to the foetus. It appears therefore that although sentiency may be important for the abortion issue, you may claim it is not directly relevant to the question of killing as such.

In spite of this I think Wertheimer really does have a property like sentiency in mind when he is talking of a full-fledged human being, but I do not think this is the only property he has in mind. I believe he refers to a collection of certain properties which is commonly associated with being a human being, with emphasis both on *human* and *being*. At least a primitive form of sentiency would have to be included in this collection, but also, I think, certain physical traits. We are not willing to call something a full-fledged human being unless it looks like one and works (biologically) like one. That is one of the reasons why I suspect that we are reluctant to call a newly fertilized egg (whatever we want to call it—a "zygote" or an "embryo")[5] a complete human being—it seems much too different in physical terms.

The chief aim of this discussion has been to point out the problems that remain even after it is decided that the Standard Attitude concerns the direct importance of being human. In Wertheimer's case the problem, as I see it, is that he slips back to a version of the Standard Attitude according to which the property of being human acquires a more indirect importance—as a kind of guarantee of the presence of those properties which are associated with human beings.

[5] Mary Warnock has suggested that we call it a "pre-embryo" until the Primitive Streak appears on the fourteenth or fifteenth day after fertilization (1987: 11–12).

To me the natural interpretation of Wertheimer is that he falters between different interpretations of the Standard Attitude—as being about mere biological membership on one hand and about something more than that on the other. If this is true and if we interpret his claim (1974: 113) that the Standard Attitude is rejected by virtually all philosophers as something which is preferably true of the first biological reading of the Standard Attitude, then we are free to say that the other reading of it—which evidently is not rejected by virtually all philosophers—concerns the indirect importance of being human: the morally important properties may be all those properties (or only some of them) which come with being a human being.

3.3 William E. May's Position

Let us leave Wertheimer and look instead at an example which at least in certain respects is more typical. It is also an example of the difficulty of knowing exactly what content to give the belief in the importance of being human and also of knowing whether it is about direct or indirect importance. William E. May has tried to argue for the belief in question in the following way:

My position is that our belief that a human being is a moral being and thus subject of moral rights is based on a belief that human beings differ radically in kind from other animals: men are moral beings not because of something that they achieve or do but because of what they are. [...] I am—and you are—a being of moral worth not because of anything that I have done or actually can do but simply because I am. On this latter view each of us holds our humanity as a gift, a gift (for those who are religiously motivated) from God, a gift (for those motivated by a humanistic spirit) from our fellow men (1974: 23–4).

I believe we have reason to ask the same question to May as we did to Wertheimer: what do we mean when we are talking of a human being here? Is it simply a member of the species *Homo sapiens* or is it something else? Both interpretations can be supported.

One reason to believe that May is talking of biological species membership is that he presents his view as a denial of certain philosophers' views—Fletcher's, Tooley's, and others—which hold that "membership in a species is of no moral significance" (1974: 23). What May says is that this is true only if one can also show that the moral importance of man originates in a difference of degree between man and other animals and not in a difference in kind. What May believes is of course that there exists a difference in kind between man and other animals, and this could easily be interpreted as a claim that membership of the human species has moral significance after all.

A second reason for this interpretation is that it seems that May wants to claim that all members of the human species are morally important, and that is why what he says has relevance for the abortion debate. A being is a human one "simply because he is and is present (even if hidden in the womb) to his fellow men" (1974: 24).

On the other hand we may also find reason to doubt whether this is really what May is after. For instance, he is talking of humanity "in the sense of being an entity that is the subject of rights" (1974: 23) as an endowment or gift and not an achievement. Here he explicitly states what should be understood by "humanity" and it seems clear that it is something other than or at least not equivalent to mere membership of a certain species.

A second reason for doubting that what May has in mind is simply membership of a species is his claim that being human is a gift—from God or (if we prefer) from other human beings. And obviously, we are used to thinking of membership of a biological species as something that could not be assigned to others as a gift. But thinking of humanity as a gift will open up the possibility of being a member of the biological species *Homo sapiens* without having the gift of humanity. Therefore, being a human being does not seem to be equivalent to being a member of a species in this interpretation.

There is also a related tension between May's claim that humans are morally important "because of what they are" (see the first quotation) and his claim that they have their significance because of something given to them by other humans. These seem to be two different ideas even if we do not interpret the idea of what we are in terms of species membership. It is one thing to be something, or, as he says in the last quotation, to simply be, and quite another thing to have something given to one from others.

3.4 Humanity as a Gift

Let us look at the idea that what is special about human beings is that other human beings have a certain attitude to such a being; May is taking humanity as a kind of gift from our fellow men. This is a rather problematic idea, in several respects.

First of all, the status of the idea is unclear. Should this be taken as a justification of the special worth of human beings? If that is the case, there is a risk of circularity: our attitudes to other human beings should be governed by considerations about what human beings are (and not what they can do or have achieved). What human beings are, on the other hand, is determined by the attitudes of other human beings.

Leaving the issue of justification aside for a moment, May's ideas are problematic also if we take them to be about a criterion of a special moral worth, for instance, that a being has this worth if and only if she is an object of certain attitudes of other human beings (where an important element of these attitudes is to regard the being in question as having a special moral worth). The trouble is that he in that case gets a problem which seems to be inherent in most criteria of human dignity, namely that they appear to be both too narrow and too wide if we want to claim that every human being (biologically determined) has human dignity and that this is a trait which is unique to human beings. And a natural interpretation of May is that this is what he wants to say.

These are the problems:

(1) One obvious reason why it is true that not every member of the human species has an appropriate attitude directed towards her, is that very many such members are not objects of such attitudes at all. There are members of the human species that are totally unrecognized and if what May says is true, i.e. that the worth of another human being is a function of the attitude directed at it, it seems that these members will lack this special moral worth. One clear case is when a women is unaware of the fact that she is pregnant, which normally is the case up until several weeks after the moment of conception. It seems that this is a period of time in which a human individual lives in a kind of mental no man's land. And how could we give gifts to individuals the existence of which we do not know anything about?

Under what condition is an individual the object of an attitude? The typical case is of course when someone has direct knowledge of an individual and therefore has certain attitudes to her. If we talk about the abortion issue this will be the case after the 16th week (if not before) when at least in Sweden most couples—or mothers—come into direct contact with their children for the first time through a diagnostic test with ultrasound. But there are also many unclear cases. For instance, suppose a couple is not yet aware of the fact that the woman is pregnant. Nevertheless the couple has many plans in which their future children are included, for instance they want to take care of their future children in the best possible way and that is part of the reason why they want to be vegetarians and live in the country, have a compost heap and grow their own vegetables. Does the existence of these plans imply that the couple have attitudes toward the growing foetus in the mother's stomach? Is it an example of having an attitude to a being to have attitudes towards the kind of being which the being in question will become in the future? Is May talking of attitudes to the concrete individual or the more abstract individuals, i.e. attitudes to the kind of individual which one happens to be or the group of beings to which one belongs?

If May does not demand more than the kind of impersonal attitudinal relationship manifested by the last alternative, then I will have to admit that all members of the human species can be covered by attitudes which confer humanity on them.

(2) But if so he will have the problem of showing that his ideas will not in the end result in a too *inclusive* view of humanity. The simple question is: will it be possible to put any restrictions on *which beings* may come into question for the gift of humanity? What if someone wants to confer this special moral worth on a being which does not belong to our species? And of course, this is not just a far-fetched possibility, it is a reality: people actually treat members of other biological species as if they had a worth comparable to the worth that according to the Standard Attitude human beings have.

We all know that people may treat their pets as if they were real persons, and that is precisely the kind of situation I have in mind.

3.5 A Religious Foundation of Human Dignity

I believe that May's theory of human dignity presupposes the kind of religious motivation according to which our humanity is a gift from God, since this alternative will not yield the same problems as the other alternative does.[6] You could say that God is directly aware of all human beings, even those who just have started their existence, and therefore he may have an attitude towards all such beings, no one excluded. This is possible, and without stretching the concept of having an attitude to someone. The other problem could also be solved on theological grounds, since you may say that God has not endowed any of the non-human animals with this gift—not even our dearest pets.

This way of interpreting May is also supported by a statement he makes in a note, where he says:

My basic point is that *being* a human being *does* make a significant moral difference because the difference between man and other animals demands, for its sufficient explanation, the presence within man's makeup, that is, within his being, of an element not found at all in other animals, namely spirit (1974: 34).

I assume, with some hesitation, that "spirit" could be interpreted as "soul" and therefore that May is giving a religious argument for the existence of a special moral status of humans.

However, if this is May's basic point new problems will emerge instead. For instance, as he describes the matter in the quotation above it is not sure that being a man (human) really is something morally important *in itself*, i.e. the basic point does not seem to be to protect someone because he is a human being but instead because he is a being endowed with a spirit or soul. But then we should not view May's position as necessarily opposing the position "of Fletcher, Tooley and those who would agree with them [...] that 'membership in a species is of no moral significance'" (1974: 23), since what they mean is that such membership is of no moral importance *in itself*.[7]

As far as I can see, none of these philosophers would deny that if you could establish a difference between humans and non-humans which *goes*

---

[6] Usually this kind of foundation of human dignity utilizes the concept of sanctity. John Kleinig says: "The language of 'sanctity' is often used to invest life with a certain kind of religious significance—a sacredness" (1991: 18). But he also notes that "religious" can be understood in many different way. Thus he says: "for others, it is not its devotion to God that constitutes or underlies its sanctity, but its own character as life. [...] We may stand before life as we stand before God" (1991: 18).

[7] This is a qualification which May forgets or simply leaves out, with the result that the position becomes highly distorted (cf. Tooley, 1983: 76).

with the fact that all humans belong to a certain species or which *coincides* with this fact, then you may be justified in giving special treatment to humans. Surely they would deny that there exists such a difference, one that places all human beings in a distinct category compared to all non-human ones, but that is another question and not the same kind of controversy. Whether or not all humans have a spirit which all non-humans lack is a theological question which is irrelevant to the question whether species membership is morally important in itself.

It can be noted that there remain problems with this idea even when you assume as a theological fact that all humans have a soul. For instance, one of the thoughts behind the Standard Attitude is that human beings are special in the sense that it is morally more serious to kill them than killing non-humans. But why is this so? Why is it more serious to kill a being with a soul than a being without one?

Once possibility is to say that if you kill such a being you destroy not only a biological organism but the soul which it lodges as well.[8] One might claim that the fact that *more* entities are destroyed when a human being is killed explains its seriousness—more of God's creation disappears when a soul is destroyed together with a biological organism. According to this idea the Standard Attitude would be about a mathematical relationship.

This is problematic, since I assume that the killing of one human being is held to be morally more serious even compared to the killing of *two* non-human ones, and therefore the principle cannot simply be to refrain from destroying as many created things as possible, but also to distinguish between different kinds of created entities. The destruction of a biological organism is not equivalent to the destruction of a human soul. So the idea has to be that there is something special about the human soul precisely because it is a *soul*, for instance, that a soul is more like its creator than the rest of the creation.

This idea assumes that it is *possible* to destroy a human soul, although the religious tradition often takes it for granted that the human soul is *immortal*, and that this is precisely what makes it a human soul and something different from whatever is the governing principle of a non-human life. The reluctance to speak of non-humans having souls should be understood, I imagine, as a reluctance to ascribe this kind of immortality to them. But if the human soul is immortal, it is hard to see what sense is to be made of the prohibition against destroying it, since, as it seems, we would *not* destroy the soul by killing the biological organism.[9] And if "ought" implies "can" there is no

---

[8] Some of the arguments which follow can be found also in Christian Munthe's comprehensive book on abortion (1992: 87 ff.).

[9] It may be (theologically) uncertain whether there is any possibility for a human soul to perish—maybe it can if God wishes or if the person herself behaves very badly and consequently comes to Hell, which according to some people should be understood not as a positive (in the non-evaluative sense) state but as a negative one, i.e. not as a state in which human souls

point in morally requiring people to abstain from doing what they in fact cannot do.[10]

Suppose that the Standard Attitude does not only say that the *killing* of a human being has a special weight but also that the *causing of suffering* has. This is something which could possibly be explained by pointing to the immortality of the human soul. The suffering of a human being means in that case the suffering of an entity which exists much longer in time (and perhaps eternally) than the non-human one does, with all the possibilities this will give—of indelible impressions and memories, and so on. It seems that the effects of harming an entity will or might be more far-reaching, other things being equal, the longer the entity in question exists.

---

continue to exist in negative (evaluatively speaking) conditions but as a state of non-existence or death. This would also take care of the argument that B. E. Rollin describes in the following way: "As Cardinal Bellarmine pointed out, in fact, the absence of a soul can well be used as an argument *in favor* of moral consideration of animals, indeed in favor of *better* treatment of animals than of people, since people would be rewarded in the afterlife, whereas animals had only one crack at existence" (1983: 107). If we understand Hell as a negative state, in the non-evaluative sense, that will deprive Cardinal Bellarmine's point of general validity.

[10] I have interpreted May's talk of a human spirit as a quasi-religious argument, since if by "spirit" we refer instead to some kind of an intellectual capacity it will obviously not work to explain the Standard Attitude, since what it says is that a human being *independently of her intellectual capacities* has a special status compared to a non-human one; this is at least the interpretation May would probably choose. But then, how should a religiously inspired argument about the wrongness of killing humans be interpreted if we stick to the fact that part of the explanation will be that humans have souls. Tooley has suggested (1983: 325–32) that we interpret it as saying that killing a human being is wrong because it deprives her of the "opportunity of enjoying a more extended earthly existence". Therefore in a case of abortion, if we suppose there exists an immaterial soul that will survive the destruction of the body, "killing a human nonperson makes it the case that there *will be* a person later on who will have been deprived of the opportunity of enjoying any earthly existence at all" (1983: 327). However, this reasoning rests on a very important factual assumption, namely that earthly existence is better than the existence the person gets if killed (as a foetus or later on), i.e. that earthly existence really is in the interest of the person. For instance, if the soul when the biological organism is destroyed comes to Paradise it seems that the killing would lie in its interests instead. As Helga Kuhse claims: "[...] it seems quite plausible to hold, for example, that the body is a tomb or prison from which the immortal soul seeks to be set free [...]" (1987: 19). There are different theories about what happens to the human soul after death and especially interesting are the theories about what happens to the foetus or young child which is not yet baptized when killed. Christian Munthe (1992: 87 ff.) discusses—from a philosophical perspective—some possibilities here. Due to original sin it may come either to Hell or to a kind of world which is neutral in value, called "Limbo". Munthe claims that if the former is the case we have an argument against killing these non-humans, but no argument against killing them after they have been baptized. If the latter is the case the status of the killing will depend on what kind of existence they will have if not killed. The conclusion to draw is that much (metaphysical) work has to be done before it can be shown that it is wrong to kill humans because they have immortal souls, and that is no doubt a drawback of the argument. This is also a good illustration of the general problem of relying on theological or semi-theological arguments in ethical discussions, namely that *if* ethical problems are solved with theological tools, they are so at the price of being saddled with problems in the philosophy of religion instead. And many people would regard that as a Pyrrhic victory.

3.6 When Does a Human Being Get a Soul?

It is true that we live in a secular time. Nevertheless, I believe that this idea of a unique human soul underlying the unique moral standing of humans is fairly widespread. I would therefore like to take this opportunity to discuss the idea in some detail.

There is one important question to be put, according to this hypothesis, namely when do we humans get our soul? If you want to say that every human organism from conception should be given a special kind of moral protection (and once again, I believe that this is what e.g. May wants to say), then you have to assume also that the fertilized egg gets its soul the moment it is fertilized. This gives rise to two problems, one which is primarily logical and which questions whether it is logically possible to combine the theological assumptions with certain physiological facts, and one which is more downright theological.

One theological assumption seems to be that a human soul is not only immaterial and immortal but also indivisible, something which can be hard to reconcile with the fact that it is possible for a fertilized egg to split and form twins as late as two weeks after fertilization if you also claim that every human life, i.e. every member of the biological species *Homo sapiens*, is morally valuable. If a human organism has its value due to the fact that she has a soul, it seems that the zygote will get its value after the point of time when it can no longer divide, unless we also believe it possible for a soul to divide.

Therefore, one of these assumptions—either that a human organism gets its moral significance from conception or that the soul is indivisible—has to be dropped if you want to stick to the explanation according to which the value of a human is founded on the fact that she has a soul. If our presentation of May above is adequate, it seems that, on pain of inconsistency, he would have to drop the latter assumption.

Other writers have chosen the other alternative; Joseph Donceel is one of them (1984). According to him the splitting of one soul into two is metaphysically impossible and therefore the foetus gets its soul about ten days after the conception at the earliest, i.e. when the implantation is completed. Donceel describes the division of a human soul as a metaphysical impossibility, which could be interpreted simply as saying that this is how a human soul works, whatever the reason we give for this belief, theological or other.

But the same, or at least almost the same, point could be described in logical terms. If a fertilized egg is an individual and splits into two, we have one individual who becomes two individuals. But this way of describing the matter is odd, since it seems to imply that if both the split individuals are identical with the original one then they also are identical with each other,[11]

---

[11] The reason is that I have assumed that the individual identity relation (i.e. a relation between individuals which are not yet persons) is transitive just as it has been assumed that personal identity is a transitive relation: "A relation *F* is *transitive* if it is true that, if *X* is F-related to *Y*, and *Y* is F-related to *Z*, *X* and *Z* *must* be F-related" (Parfit, 1984: 206).

which is absurd for many reasons. This problem could be avoided in the same way that Donceel avoids the metaphysical problem, by saying that there exists no human individual the first two weeks after conception, even if this sounds queerer than the denial of a soul in the foetus before that point.[12]

Returning now to the problems with the human soul, we have made an important assumption, namely, that there may exist only one soul in a zygote and that this soul then has to divide when the human organism does. This assumption can be questioned. For instance, Munthe plays with the idea that in a case when the fertilized egg splits we may assume that there have been right from the beginning two coexisting souls in the egg, and that this is the explanation why the egg splits and forms twins (1992: 86). A fertilized egg which in the future will split may be regarded as a kind of Siamese twins right from the conception, with the difference that their physical parts not only are closely related but actually identical. The point is that if we believe that there may be more than one soul in a fertilized egg we can regard the egg as valuable right from the conception without committing the metaphysical mistakes Donceel talks of, since if the egg splits this can be seen as a result of the fact that the fertilized egg actually lodged two souls.

This may solve the metaphysical part of the problem, i.e. the problem about souls. But it seems more problematic to translate this solution to the problem of individual identity, since a similar kind of solution to this problem would have to suppose that when an egg splits this is the result of the fact that the egg right from fertilization actually was two individuals melted together in one body or organism.

If our criterion of identity of a human individual is physical this amounts to saying that an organism which is two individuals has to be physically different from an organism which is one. The organism has to have a physical property in virtue of which we can claim that it is two individuals. But does there exist such a property? Is a fertilized egg which in the future will split in any way physically different from one which in the future will not split? Indeed, there has to be an *explanation* why one egg splits and another does not, and one natural explanation seems to be that the splitting is caused by some physical property of the fertilized egg.

But with modern technology it is possible to *induce* the splitting of an *in vitro* fertilized egg, which means that the splitting of these eggs will not be a result of—which here means "not be intitiated by"—some physical or other property of the egg, but instead of actions performed by us. That would also

---

[12] There is another phenomenon, to which Munthe (1992: 86) draws our attention and which causes the same kind of both metaphysical and logical problems, namely the possibility of two fertilized eggs melting together and forming one individual. If we do not think that one soul possibly could split into two we probably would not believe it possible for two souls to merge together into one either. The problem of the transitivity of the individual identity is equally salient here—the fused individual cannot be identical with both the fertilized eggs, since they cannot be identical with each other.

mean that the eggs which actually will split are not necessarily physically different before they split compared to the eggs that will not split—they are not in any way "marked out" physically.[13]

I conclude this discussion by saying that we have found several reasons, of which some are logical, for claiming that a human individual begins its existence only after the possibility of twin formation has ceased to exist. Whether or not we want to tie the identity relation to the existence of a soul does not seem to affect this conclusion. However, the problem was primarily addressed to those who believe that a human being gets her uniqueness by virtue of her soul.

3.7 Concluding Remarks

Let us try to sum up the main points of the discussion in this chapter. The discussion has circled around a thesis or belief or intuition which we have called "the Standard Attitude". The term is inspired by Roger Wertheimer. This attitude is roughly a belief in the direct moral importance of being human. What this means more exactly was not settled, since I believe that so long as we talk about intuitive reactions, it may be difficult to state the exact content of the Standard Attitude. It is part of the nature of our intuitions that they are often vague. In order to make them precise we have to reflect on them and test them against different kinds of examples. The risk we take when doing so is that during this process our original convictions will cool down or alternatively will not allow for precision, i.e. they will be present only as fairly general beliefs or patterns of reactions. If this is the result of our looking more carefully to our intuitions, then I would like to think that their credibility is negatively affected. The reason for this ultimately has to do with the ideal of rationality—it will be difficult to build a coherent moral attitude on intuition with this kind of compliance, or whatever term one prefers.

We have tried to penetrate two ethical works which are built on the Standard Attitude—Wertheimer's and May's. And we put two main questions. First, do these writers really believe that being a human is important *in itself* or do they mean something else? Second, when talking of human beings do they refer to a biological species or do they refer to something else? We noted that

---

[13] Munthe points to the relevance of this possibility for the soul problem (1992: 86). How do we reconcile the possibility of induced splitting with the claim that twin formation is explained by the fact that there were right from the beginning—conception—two souls lodging in the same fertilized egg? We need an explanation of what seems to be a coincidence, namely that we choose to induce the splitting on those eggs which from the start contained two souls. What makes us choose these very eggs, which as far as I can see before the splitting are not in any detectable way different from the eggs which will not split (now I am talking of a detectable difference which is not necessarily physical)?

neither Wertheimer nor May gave a decisive answer to these questions. And that was also the reason why they were chosen, since I believe that the vagueness displayed in their interpretation of the Standard Attitude is representative of the majority of the adherents of the belief.

Before we try to criticize this belief I would like to scrutinize in more detail what the importance of *Homo sapiens* amounts to. Above we considered the difficulties of determining whether a property which we value really is valuable *per se*. Now I want to consider what it means when a property is really valued in that way, and particularly when the property of belonging to the human species is valued in that way. In what follows I will understand the Standard Attitude as an attitude to the importance of *Homo sapiens*.

CHAPTER 4

THE DIRECT VALUE OF BEING HUMAN

> Should people agree on treating human beings as having dignity
> because it is good, or is it good because people agree on it?
>
> Bertram Morris "The Dignity of Man"

To claim that some property is of direct moral importance may be ambiguous. It can mean that the property in question is important in itself and not because of the fact that the property is typically found together with some other property; it can also mean that the property is important in itself and not only as an instrument or necessary condition for the actualization of other properties.

Above we have discussed primarily the first distinction in connection with the property of being human (even if the second distinction is mentioned in some of the examples). For instance, we have asked whether it is the fact that a human being belongs to the species *Homo sapiens* that makes her morally special or whether it is the fact that members of this species typically have certain properties that make them special, e.g. a high degree of consciousness.

It is easy to *combine* these distinctions when talking of those properties with which the property of being a *Homo sapiens* is typically associated, for instance consciousness and especially self-consciousness. If you believe that a human being is morally important since she typically displays self-consciousness, this is not the same as believing that the property of being self-conscious is important *per se*. You may very well think that this property is valuable in virtue of what it makes possible.

For instance, many philosophers think that in order to be able to want something you have to have a concept of the object of your want.[1] If the attitude of desiring is a propositional attitude, or involves such an attitude, a necessary condition of having such an attitude seems to be understanding the proposition one desires to be true. A necessary condition of this understanding in turn seems to be having the concepts figuring in it.[2]

---

[1] If you believe there is an analytical connection between wants and happiness, the same will be true of the attitude of being happy about an object. Lennart Nordenfelt suggests that such a connection exists and says: "In order for a person to be happy about something (including life itself) it is required that he or she at least believes that this object constitutes the realisation of a want that he or she has" (1993: 49). Ignoring whether or not there exists such a connection, to me it seems intuitively easier to agree with Nordenfelt that the attitude of being happy about something requires a concept of the object of this attitude, rather than the attitude of wanting something. However, in the end we may nevertheless decide to put a conceptual requirement on a wanter. For a general account of the role of cognitions in emotions, see John Deigh (1994).

[2] Cf. Tooley (1983: 104).

If this reasoning is correct, you cannot desire to continue life unless you have a concept of your future life, and in order to have such a concept you have to be self-conscious, at least to a certain degree. Thus, if you believe it morally important not to thwart a desire to go on living, you will also think that the capacity for self-consciousness is a morally significant property. But this will not be an intrinsic significance, since an individual may have this capacity without caring whether or not she will exist in the future; that is, self-consciousness according to this reasoning is relevant only as a prerequisite of a desire to go on living (or of a desire not to go on living).[3]

In short, we have considered two distinctions which can be hidden in talking of the direct importance of a property: first, properties which have an *intrinsic* importance in contrast to being *associated* with other properties (which can be directly or indirectly important) and, second, properties which are *intrinsically* important in contrast to being *instrumentally* important.[4] I believe that being a human may be indirectly important in both these senses, though commonly it is the first sense we have in mind when endowing the property in question with indirect importance. On the other hand we may well regard the properties which are associated with being a human as being indirectly important in the second sense, that is, valuable as instruments for other things.

---

[3] This is an example of one possible way in which self-consciousness can have importance as a necessary condition of something else. It is not the only one. You can claim that many important wants of a person presuppose the capacity in question, for instance, the want to not be an object of foul slander, the want to be respected as an artist, scientist, teacher... In fact, every want concerning oneself as a conscious being will, according to this reasoning, presuppose self-consciousness.

[4] As I interpret Moore in *Principia Ethica*, he is discussing the second alternative in terms of intrinsicality and instrumentality. However, there is reason to believe that Moore also means something else by "intrinsic value". To call something "intrinsically good" is also to say that this something does not get its value from the fact that it stands in relation to something else. To be intrinsically valuable is, according to this interpretation, to be *independently* valuable. See Moore (1922: 253–75). Christine M. Korsgaard wants us to distinguish between, on one hand, "the distinction between things valued for their own sakes and things valued for the sake of something else—between ends and means, or final and instrumental goods" (1983: 170) and, on the other hand, between "things which have their value in themselves and things which derive their value from some other source: intrinsically good things versus extrinsically good things" (1983: 170). (Elizabeth Anderson (1993: 38) regards instrumental value as one kind of extrinsic value.) Although I believe that Korsgaard correctly makes a distinction between the two distinctions, I will here use the expression "intrinsic value" as referring both to "final value" and "value independently of its relation to other things" or "value in virtue of its internal characteristics". But I hope the context will indicate in what sense I use the expression. I will also employ the distinction between objective and subjective value in order to separate some of these ideas. Furthermore, notice that many philosophers ignore the distinction in question. Cf. also Wlodek Rabinowicz & Jan Österberg (1996: n. 1).

4.1 Objectivism and Subjectivism

One important meta-ethical problem concerns whether something can be valuable only in relation to a valuing subject or if something can be valuable— given that there exists something valuable—independently of whether or not a subject has any attitude towards it, whether it be a cognitive or conative attitude.[5] This is the classical problem of subjectivism *versus* objectivism, and it is a problem which was touched upon before.[6] One problem which the subjectivists have to solve is how to account for the fact that we normally seem to have moral attitudes towards objects because we think these objects valuable (positively or negatively) in some way or another, whereas the truth according to subjectivism has to be described the other way round: objects are valuable in virtue of subjects having attitudes towards them.[7] One problem with objectivism, on the other hand, has to do with explaining what kind of fact it is that something is valuable, if it is not ultimately a fact about our own or another's attitudes. Furthermore, how do you as an objectivist explain the fact that a value judgement is intrinsically motivating in a way that a factual judgement is not?

The point here is not to show that the problems with objectivism are more difficult to solve than the problems with subjectivism but rather to show that you may believe that being human is in itself morally important whether you are an objectivist or subjectivist about values. If you believe that being human is intrinsically important you can, if you are a subjectivist, by this mean that the property is intrinsically important *for humans*, i.e. human beings place a special value on being human in itself, a value which is not dependent upon what is associated with belonging to that species, and that is what makes being human morally important. Or, you may, if you are an objectivist, intend to say that being human has an intrinsic value which is independent of the fact that this is valued by us humans.

---

[5] This has to be qualified. You may be an objectivist even if you think that values are tied to attitudes. The important thing, I would say, is that objectivism denies that all positive values do result from pro-attitudes and all negative values do result from con-attitudes. Therefore, it would be objectivism to claim also that human knowledge is valuable and that the existence of this value does not depend on the fact that humans positively value knowledge either for what it is in itself or for what it leads to.

[6] I use the term "subjectivism" in roughly the same way as Connie S. Rosati: "By 'subjectivist theories', I mean theories according to which a person's good either consists in or crucially depends upon certain positive psychological states or proattitudes, such as pleasure or (actual or counterfactual) desires" (1996: 299, n. 5). See also R. B. Perry (1954: 125) and Peter Railton (1986: 9).

[7] Steve F. Sapontzis calls this "an affective value theory" which "holds that values originate with feelings, such as pleasure and pain, fulfilment and frustration, joy and sorrow, excitement and depression, and so forth" (1993: 271).

4.2 "Valued by" as an Active Process and "Valuable for"

What does it mean to say that something is valued by someone? We may distinguish between two cases: one in which a certain property is *valued by* someone and one in which a property is *valuable for* someone. These cases are distinct since a property may be valuable for someone without being valued by this someone. It is easy to find examples: a carrot's properties may be valuable for my ten-year-old boy without necessarily being valued by him. Furthermore, to say that something is valuable for someone, it is enough that this someone has a good, and to have a good, I believe, does not require being a valuing subject. Thus if plants have a good (and obviously they have—their good consists of growing and multiplying) certain things will also be valuable for them. I assume that this is in line with normal language.[8]

Obviously, when talking of a property like the property of being human having intrinsic value for someone, we are talking of a property standing in relation to a being which has the capacity to *value* things. It seems impossible to talk of a property being of *intrinsic* value for someone or something if this something lacks the capacity to value in a more or less active way. Water and light are valuable for the plant but not intrinsically so (it is hard to see how to understand the relationship in another way). Water and light are instruments or necessary conditions of the plant's growing.

So in one respect, to value something is an active process. Preliminarily I want to understand it as desiring or wanting certain things (to be the case). To value being a human for its intrinsic properties means wanting to protect the being which has this property. However, to be able to want certain things may in one sense be more active than not being able to do so, but the question is how active the capacity actually is, or rather, how active the process of valuing something really is.

4.3 Valuing as a Disposition

There is a distinction to be made between two different senses of wanting. There is an occurrent sense of wanting and there is a dispositional sense of it. Alvin Goldman says that an "occurrent want is a mental event or mental process; it is a 'going on' or 'happening' in consciousness" (1976: 86). On the other hand, a standing want is described as "a disposition or propensity to have an occurrent want" (1976: 86). Let us say that this is a distinction between an occurrent and a dispositional sense of wanting. In my view wanting (dispositionally) certain things to take place is tantamount to having

[8] Normal language is indeed fairly liberal in this regard and allows for many similar constructions, for instance between being in someone's interests and being interested in, where the former construction can be used in the case of plants as well (cf. Tom Regan, 1976: 253-4). I am not going to decide here whether or not these distinctions ought to be treated in the same way.

a disposition to try to make it the case that these things take place under certain circumstances. These circumstances include thinking it possible to make it the case that the things in question take place. Therefore, valuing (dispositionally) a property is an active process in a qualified sense—it is enough that you *would* under favourable circumstances try to protect it— which means that you may value (dispositionally) properties of which you are not thinking; you may also value (dispositionally) properties while you are asleep or for other reasons unconscious.

Now what I claim is that we may treat both the concept of wanting and that of valuing as paradigmatically being dispositional concepts. To say that a person wants p or values that p will if nothing else is said mean that she does so dispositionally. When I say that I take a dispositional view of valuing or wanting, what I say is that wanting and valuing should if nothing else is said be understood in the dispositional sense.

The simplest argument for the dispositional view is that this is how we normally treat these concepts. I need not have any actual thoughts of the object I value. Otherwise I would at every moment of my life have a pretty small repertoire of wants. And one strange consequence if we reject the dispositional view would be an inevitable and universal unstability of wants: yesterday I did not value the fact that my child is healthy, but the day before yesterday I did, for five minutes, since I was reminded of the day he broke his arm. That sounds odd; I am sure I have valued my child's health for as long as he has lived; it is one of my more stable wants.

This is an argument for *saying* that we may value things dispositionally. It is not an argument for the normative position according to which we also would make someone's life go better by satisfying her purely dispositional wants. This question will be considered in due time. In the meantime I want to consider a closely related question, namely what features of a disposition make it important *if* it is important.

Normally we seem to think that the moral weight of an experience, for instance, the mental state of feeling happiness, somehow is determined by a combination of its strength and duration. The question is whether this is true also of wanting as a disposition. This is a very difficult question, since at least in my own case there are intuitions pulling in different directions. One immediate reaction is that duration of a disposition has to count. Otherwise many of those wants we consider to be central in our lives will have to compete with more peripheral wants when their importance is determined. Many wants are considered by us to be central and important although we seldom think about them. The want concerning my child's health is a good example. I am fairly sure, however, that there might be some other in my view insignificant want that has occupied my thoughts more than or at least to the same extent as this want, for instance, the want not to have an engine failure when driving my old car.

There might be some explanations for this. For instance that I have in my life had more reasons to suspect problems with my car rather than with my child's health. But this will not change the main point—even if my thoughts for some reasons have been occupied with the engine problems of my old car on more numerous occasions than with my son's health that will not mean that it is also more important other things being equal.

Actually I have been thinking about my son's health more than about my old car, yet the example may illustrate that wants we consider to be less important after all can get a disproportionate moral weight compared to a want we consider much more important if the importance is a function of thought episodes rather than duration of dispositions. According to the dispositional analysis, the circumstances that determine which of your wants you actually think of are different compared to the circumstances that determine what kind of wants you have and what their strength is. For instance, having a child who often meets with accidents may make you think rather a lot of her or his health, but this is not what lies behind the fact that you want your child to stay healthy. It is not necessarily worse, i.e. it does not frustrate a stronger want of yours, if such a child gets seriously ill than if a child who has never met with accidents does.

The immediate consequence for the issue discussed in this book is that SA may be connected with a central and important want in most people although they normally think of other things. After all, it may be more important to a person that people refrain from torturing and killing one another in a foreign country than his car not having engine failure, although he preferably pays attention to the latter object.

4.4 Sophisticated and Primitive Wanting

If the dispositional analysis of wanting and valuing is accepted, it will be easier to claim that the property of being a human being is more or less universally valued among humans. At the beginning of the previous chapter I said that most humans probably have moral intuitions according to which there is something morally special about being human. Of course, these intuitions or whatever we call them are intimately connected with attitudes of valuing. Furthermore, we may have them without being very much aware of them; we may even have them when we deny we have them. We may be opposed to discrimination against animals in what we say but nevertheless be disposed to protect humans instead of animals in certain circumstances. And this is enough to endow the property of being human with an intrinsic value for those people.

But may *animals* then have the kind of attitude we are talking of here? That will of course depend on whether they are able to have wants in this dispositional sense. Above I specified the circumstances which would trigger off the disposition as at least thinking it possible to achieve certain things. That seems to suggest that there is a close connection between wants and beliefs and consequently that you can have wants only on condition that you can have beliefs.[9] However, I want to qualify this suggestion too.

Wanting would be a fairly high level capacity if the only way to trigger the capacity were to have thoughts about the possibility of bringing about certain things. That would exclude not only most animals from the class of wanters but also small children and many mentally retarded human beings. Therefore, we may distinguish between two cases where a being can be said to want something. In one case the being is disposed to make the appropriate intentional action and in the other case the being is disposed to show the appropriate reflex-behaviour.[10] Of course, this last case may also require a certain degree of intellectual ability, but I believe this kind of want may be found rather early in the development of a human being and also among many of the non-human animals. To have a want in the second sense will only require sensations, for instance as when you duck when you see a fast object approaching your head.

So here we have two senses of wanting which in my view will both qualify as instances of valuing. The one is sophisticated and the other more primitive; the one is tied to an intention and the other is tied merely to a reflex. These two kinds of wants may be in opposition to each other also in an agent capable of intentional behaviour, since such beings will have both the mechanisms sufficient for wanting in the two senses.

Let us now try to relate this to the issue in this chapter. What I have said so far is intended to show that things and properties might be valued by beings with fairly primitive mental capacities. Therefore, I do not think it possible to argue against this analysis with the intention to show that it is too demanding—human babies and probably very many of the animals may confer subjective value on things and properties. (I even find it plausible to think that a human foetus may confer this kind of value on certain objects, for instance, the object of being in a painless state; the requirements are merely that the foetus is capable of being aware of the pain and as a consequence of that awareness reacting with reflex-behaviour which tends to reduce the pain.)

However, even if properties according to this analysis may be valued by fairly primitive beings, we have not shown that the kind of property in which we are interested, that is, the property of belonging to a certain species, may also stand in that relation to such beings. This is an important objection, since if it turns out that it is only humans that may value the property of

[9] Many philosophers believe that there is such a connection. One of them is R. G. Frey (1980: esp. Ch. VII). Since Frey thinks that there is a link between having a language and having beliefs—"having beliefs is not compatible with the absence of language" (1980: 86)—he will also deny that animals have any wants or desires.
[10] See Ingmar Persson (1981: 95, 107).

belonging to a certain species (preferably the human species, of course), then humans might in practice be the only species with this kind of subjective value. On the other hand, if we could show that just as being a human is valued by humans, being a tiger is also valued by tigers, then it would be harder to argue for the special importance of being human, particularly if you believe that all kinds of subjective values are morally important.

Do other species have the capacity of valuing this property? I believe they have, but the question is whether they are capable of conferring *intrinsic* value on it. We all know that animals react in certain typical ways to the presence of other animals of the same species. Some of the behaviour-patterns suggest that such presence is positively valued and some that it is negatively valued. But for humans, as we have claimed, being a human is something important *per se*.

I do not believe that animals (or foetuses or small children) value their fellow members of their own species in that way; rather they react to what *looks like* and *smells like* a member of a particular species.[11] I am fairly sure, at least as long as we do not speak of animals very high on the phylogenetic scale, that these reactions would be displayed also *vis-à-vis* dummies, provided they had the right kind of look and smell. And therefore, I believe that to most of the non-human animals (if not all) belonging to a particular species may only be indirectly valued, i.e. valued for the sake of those properties with which it is typically associated.[12]

So one big difference between humans and non-humans in this regard seems to be that only the former may confer intrinsic value on belonging to a certain species. The reason for claiming this is obviously that only humans may have a concept of what it is to belong to a certain species over and above having a certain physical appearance, a certain smell, displaying certain behaviour-patterns, and so on. I find it difficult to imagine what it would be like to bestow intrinsic value on belonging to a certain species—that is, to value such a property for what it is in itself and not for what it may lead to or for the other properties that may come with it—without having the

---

[11] Steven R. L. Clark says that the "altruist responds [...] to the familiar cues of sight, smell, and evocative posture. Other creatures can 'exploit' this fact, as do cuckoos. Put it differently: altruists can be concerned for creatures not of their own species, if only they are familiar or sufficiently like what is familiar" (1983: 181). However, I claim that though this is true of both humans and non-humans, the difference between them is that the former kind of being can discriminate on the basis of genetic difference as well.

[12] Some thinkers have questioned whether these animals have the capacity of conceptual thought at all. Thus agreeing with Locke, Michael P. T. Leahy writes: "That an animal reacts to white objects (or spherical, moving or only inanimate ones) would, for Locke, be a tribute to its powers of discrimination but would in no way be evidence that it was aware of, or understood, what it was doing" (1991: 94; see also John Locke 1964: 127–31). However, my point here is not that animals *do* have a concept of for instance certain visual features of their fellow members of a species, but instead that they do *not* have a concept of species membership if this is interpreted biologically or genetically.

appropriate concepts. It seems that the property of belonging to a species *is not in itself anything* for a being which lacks knowledge of the theoretical concept of species membership, which—in this study—is a concept of something more than mere superficial physical resemblance.

If this is true, it will be an important fact to consider, since it means that there seems to be one sense in which being human actually is something morally special—such beings are able to confer subjective value on each other in a way that for other kinds of beings would be impossible. This is a morally important fact provided you believe that this kind of subjective value has moral importance. Of course, if you are a utilitarian this is what you believe, but I would like to think that you may accept the moral significance of this kind of value whether or not you accept utilitarianism as an overall norm. So this is a question which may be cut off from the question of utilitarianism.

4.5 The Intrinsic Value of Being Non-Human

It deserves to be mentioned that even if we acknowledge the presence of a subjective and intrinsic value, for instance the value of the fact that a being belongs to a certain species, this is one value among others. And I believe this is true whether or not you are a utilitarian. To say that being a human is morally significant is only, according to this thought, to say that you have to weigh the fact that a being is human against other values, whatever these may be. For instance, we have not claimed that being of direct or intrinsic subjective value is *superior* to being of indirect subjective value. What I have claimed so far is only that the property of being human seems to have a value that is *unique* among similar properties, namely that it may be subjectively valued in itself.

This too has to be qualified. What we have said so far does not exclude the possibility that a human also confers value on membership of other species, nor the possibility that a human being in an extreme case confers value exclusively on other non-human species memberships. What I have said so far is only that the extreme case probably occurs very seldom, since it seems to be almost a universal feature of us humans that we believe that being human is something morally special.

But to be morally special is something relative, and even if it should turn out that we humans, as far as the subjective and intrinsic values are concerned, are morally special compared to the rest of creation, that will not mean that all other species are on equal moral footing.

In fact I believe that we normally make a moral difference within the class of non-human animals. Some animals, in virtue of belonging to a certain species, are regarded as being more valuable than others. For instance, many people who like cats will be upset to hear about the sufferings of a cat in a way that they will not be to hear about the sufferings of some other animal, even if it can be shown that it has about the same mental capacities as the cat. Furthermore, a hunter knows that people dislike the killing of a deer more than they dislike the killing of a wild boar. Other kinds of animals with a very special standing in our eyes are dogs and horses—many people refuse to eat horse meat, and I do not think that the reason is purely gastronomic in the same way as for instance most people at least in the West refuse to eat snakes.[13]

It might be objected that these kinds of phenomena do not necessarily prove that we are also prepared to give value to membership of other kinds of species. It is true that many people find the hunting of deer repugnant, you may say, but the reason is not that these animals are deer *per se*, but rather that they have the kind of physical appearance they actually have. If this is correct, these people would not necessarily criticize killing a deer which for some reason looked exactly like a wild boar. (Given the concept of species membership chosen in Chapter 2 this kind of thought experiment will at least be logically possible.) So actually, we do not seem to have a case where membership of non-human species is directly valued by us humans— we like deer for the sake of those properties which members of that kind of species normally have.

I think there is some truth in this, but I do not think that will refute our point. Rather we will have to look for better examples of intrinsic values conferred on non-human animals as well. A bird-watcher and lover of nature is probably a better example. I assume that this person not only wants it to be the case that there are in nature birds and other animals with a certain physical appearance. She has (normally) also wants concerning the genetic structure of these animals. For instance, if you as a bird-watcher want it to be the case that a certain kind of rare bird does not become extinct, I suppose you would not be content to know that it might be possible to breed birds of another species the physical appearance of which would be identical with the rare bird's. This shows, if I am right in my assumption, that here species membership is something important in itself—you as a bird-watcher do not only want to look at birds with a certain kind of physical look, you want them to be of a certain species as well.[14]

---

[13] This can be seen as examples of what Thomas L. Benson (1983: 85) in a slightly different context has called "species favoritism", which, I think, is a better term than "speciesism", at least when differences within the animal kingdom are under consideration.

[14] An intriguing question is whether something important ought to be added here, namely that it is species membership as a result of an evolutionary process that is important in itself. When Dworkin discusses the phenomenology of nature's sacredness he says: "Geneticists have created plants that we find instrumentally valuable: they produce food and may save lives. But we do not think that these artificially produced species are intrinsically valuable in the way that naturally produced species are" (1993: 78–9). This may give rise to the following question. Suppose a species becomes extinct but that geneticists in the future may create an animal with exactly the same genetic structure as that of the extinct species, would the created animal be as

One might object that if this is what you want, we have a case where non-human species membership is indirectly valued rather than directly valued— you want there to exist birds of a certain species in order to be able to watch them. But also here I believe it possible to point to examples where this is not the end of the matter. Lovers of nature may not only want a certain species to exist for the sake of the pleasure of watching it, they may also want it to exist independently of *any* pleasure that it could produce in humans, directly or indirectly.

At least this sounds very realistic in my own ears. If I heard of a very rare and shy owl never directly observed by any human, I might spontaneously want it to be preserved. And that would not be because of the possibility of observing the owl in the future. On the contrary, it would be better if the owl also in the future remains the mysterious kind of animal it has been in the past. And the same kind of thought experiment will work for other kinds of animals—deep-sea fish, beetles and so on. And since I do not think I am unique in this respect, this means we have examples where intrinsic value is conferred subjectively also on non-human species of animals.

So, I am not denying that the property of being human remains something special and important also when we take this importance to be an effect of our capacity to confer intrinsic value on objects. However, it does not seem to be a *unique* value which only humans have—what is special about us humans is rather that we probably have this value to a greater extent and to a higher degree than non-humans. The only thing that seems unique as far as this value is concerned is that humans probably are the only beings able to *confer* it upon objects.

4.6 Two Assumptions

Let me comment also on the condition under which subjective value is conferred upon a property. This is a vexed and complicated question and

---

valuable as the original one? Here I have supposed that we have a species concept that would allow us to say that the original and the created animal were of the same species (this is an assumption that could be called into question of course, i.e. whether or not some kind of continuity also is necessary for the identity of a species). We will have to guess, and my guess is that many people would think that something valuable *is* lost in the created animal, and if that is true we have to admit that species membership of a certain being may be important in itself, as long as we talk of an individual which is not created by genetic modification. At least, to be a result of such a process will make one's value as a member of a certain species less than it would have been if the genetic make-up was instead the result of a "natural" process. I believe that Paul W. Taylor's Rule of Noninterference (1989: 173 ff.) both agrees and disagrees with some of the thoughts expressed here. On the one hand he believes that we can derive a respect for what evolution has produced from our attitude of respect for nature. On the other hand we can also, he believes, derive a principle of species-impartiality from the same attitude, a principle which "serves as a counterweight to the dispositions of people to favor certain species over others and to want to intervene in behalf of their favorites" (1989: 178).

there are many aspects of it that could be penetrated. Here I just want to mention one, namely whether the subjects conferring value on a property have to exist in order for this property to have value. This may sound like a crazy question, but I think it is not so crazy after all. And what is more, discussing it will also bring us to some other intriguing and interesting questions in ethical theory.

The question could be formulated as a question upon which we already have touched, namely what degree of activity should be required for a subject to be able to confer subjective value on something. I shall make two preliminary assumptions, one fairly weak and one stronger. I am not going to argue directly for the stronger one; I will only mention one argument against the assumption which at first glance appears to be stronger than it really is.

The modest proposal was made earlier, namely that we regard valuing or wanting as a disposition. To value X is to be disposed in certain circumstances to try to get X. So wanting in this view is not so much an activity; instead it is to be *prepared* to act. This was also qualified—to act here may mean acting intentionally or acting only on reflex. And observe that this kind of preparedness may in itself be something fairly inactive. It is enough that you actually *would* act or react in a certain way in the appropriate circumstances. You do not have to *believe* you would or *regard* yourself as being prepared to do what you actually are prepared to do.

4.7 On the Existence of the Wanter

Let us consider the second assumption. In the first assumption we argued that wanting is a state of an individual and furthermore that a want may exist in an individual independently of whether or not it is manifested in actions or registered in the thoughts of the individual. In the second assumption I will try to show (with some hesitation) that a want may be morally relevant even when the individual which once embraced the want has ceased to exist.

There is a connection between the two assumptions although not an automatic one. It seems that a person who wants to say that satisfying a want which does not depend on particular mental states counts, will also more easily allow for the moral significance of wants which do not depend on the existence of the wanter. The only difference is that the second assumption is more liberal, since it will remove the wants even farther from activity.

If we say that a person's wants may confer value on a thing even after the person has died, we will actually make two claims.

(1) First, that what Hare calls "now-for-then"[15] preferences have moral importance in the sense that it may be of value to a person to satisfy a want

---

[15] As far as I know this term was introduced in (1981: 101 f.).

which this person no longer has (I assume here that dead people have no present wants, although they may have had wants concerning the present time).

This may strike some persons as somewhat metaphysically queer—how could we satisfy an attitude which no longer exists?[16] In general terms, how could we possibly do *anything* to something which does not (and will not) exist? Of course, in certain ways non-existence excludes the possibility of being affected, for instance, just as Socrates observed, we cannot hit a person who does not exist. But existence is not always a requirement for the possibility of being affected.

We may distinguish between three different questions. The first one is the ontological question concerning the existence of the wants of persons who do not exist. The second question is whether or not these kinds of wants can be satisfied (independently of whether or not they exist). The third question is whether there is a moral value in satisfying them. The second and third question are connected—if an attitude *cannot* be satisfied then it would not be normatively interesting to consider the value of satisfying it (given that "ought" in this case implies "can"). However, these questions may be disconnected from the ontological question (at least, it is not obvious to me why a want has to exist in order to be fulfilled) and therefore, if the important thing is whether or not a want should be considered after the death of the person who embraced it, then we may disregard the question of existence.

I just want to retain one point, namely that if we may show that there is a value in satisfying a preference of a person who is dead, we should be allowed to say that things could still be done *to* this person, although she does not exist any longer.[17] The reason is that I take this expression to be about the morally relevant question—can the person's well-being be affected after she has ceased to exist?[18]

(2) Let us look at the second claim. The first claim said that "now-for-then" preferences have moral importance. If these "now-for-then" preferences extend beyond the lifetime of the wanter and if they are morally important

[16] Of course, we may distinguish between different senses of "exist", where in some (formal) sense a want of a dead person still exists, whereas in another more substantial sense it does not. For a discussion of the formal senses of "exist", see Hare (1985: 41).
[17] What I have said so far may suggest that a person who is dead does not exist any longer. This is what Fred Feldman has called "the termination thesis", i.e. "If a person dies at a time, then he or she ceases to exist at that time" (1992: 89). Feldman is a survivalist, which means that he denies the termination thesis. However, I mention this problem only to sidestep it. I do not feel obliged to take a definite standpoint on this matter here.
[18] John Harris would not agree with this. He would say that the interests of past people may be affected without these people being affected. He says: "There is of course a legitimate though somewhat artificial sense in which we may talk of the dead having interests which persist. [...] But while such persisting interests may be damaged, the people whose interests they are cannot be harmed once they are dead" (1993: 100). Harris seems in this quotation to accept what Jeff McMahan has called "*The Existence Requirement.*—A person can be the subject of some misfortune only if he exists at the time the misfortune occurs" (1988: 33).

(because of it being valuable to the wanter that they are satisfied) then the second claim will follow directly from the first one, namely that "external preferences", that is, preferences about other objects than experiences of the wanter, are morally important.

4.8 Dworkin on External Preferences

The term "external preference" comes from Ronald Dworkin (1977: 234), although he defines it as a preference "for the assignment of goods and opportunities to others". It should, according to Dworkin, be contrasted with a personal preference which is about the wanter's "own enjoyment of some goods or opportunities" (1977: 234). My definition is instead taken from Hare (1989b).[19] The difference between these definitions is that Hare's is more general in that it concentrates on only one aspect of a preference—whether or not it is for some experience of the preferrer, whereas Dworkin's can preliminarily be taken to be about two aspects—whether or not it is for an experience of the preferrer and whether this experience is an experience of (personal) enjoyment.

The explanation of this difference is that the definitions are used to illustrate different problems of preference utilitarianism. Dworkin wants to argue that preference utilitarianism, when counting these external preferences, fails to show equal concern and respect to all individuals. Consider the following example:

Suppose many citizens, who themselves do not swim, prefer the pool to the theater because they approve of sports and admire athletes, or because they think that the theater is immoral and ought to be repressed. If the altruistic preferences are counted, so as to reinforce the personal preferences of swimmers, the result will be a form of double counting: each swimmer will have the benefit not only of his own preference, but also of the preference of someone else who takes pleasure in his success (1977: 235).

This argument can of course be directly applied to our issue. The Standard Attitude (SA) says that a human being has a special value in virtue of being a human being. And there seems to be an intimate connection with this belief and wanting a being to have certain privileges in virtue of being a human being. (Sometimes, however, it might be a question of privileges within quotation marks, see Chapter 1.) For instance, you may say that since SA is a kind of moral judgement, you would not be serious in this judgement unless you also were prepared to act on it (and acting on it would require wants on your part, assuming that moral beliefs are unable to motivate independently of any desire or pro-attitude). Alternatively, you may say that this is how we come to know about SA in the first place—not all of us

[19] Hare takes the class of external preferences "as consisting of those preferences which are for things other than experiences of the preferrer" (p. 177).

embrace it knowingly, but our actions and other attitudes show that the belief in question could be ascribed to us.[20] So there are obviously connections between believing that humans are especially valuable and wanting them to have privileges.

Therefore, if SA in some way implies an altruistic desire, Dworkin would say that a preference of a human being concerning the privileges SA is about would be counted twice in a utilitarian calculus—we would have to consider partly the individual's own preference for this object and then also the preference of the rest of humanity that this individual should have these privileges.

In reply to this—a reply which does not assume that preference utilitarianism is the correct moral theory—we may distinguish between two questions. Will this really mean double counting? And will it be morally objectionable whether or not it should be described as double counting?

There is actually a kind of double counting taking place when we also count altruistic desires, but you may claim this is a rather innocent kind of double counting, for it is not the case that primarily the same *preference* is counted twice, which H. L. A. Hart has also observed (1986: 315), but instead that the same *object* is considered twice, i.e. as an object of two different preferences. The object considered in our example is that human beings should have privileges over other kinds of beings. Let us for a moment assume that this is something that each human being wants to be the case as far as she herself is concerned and also wants to be the case as far as everyone else is concerned (since that is the way we have described SA). Therefore, the fact that a particular human being should have this kind of moral privilege is an object of both the individual's own preferences and the preferences of everyone else who embraces SA.

It is true that the same preference in one way is counted twice (or rather more than that, in proportion to the number of embracers of SA), namely the preference in terms of which the privilege might be defined, but this is so only secondarily, since this preference happens to be the *object* of more than one preference. Perhaps this is exactly what Dworkin has in mind when he accuses preference utilitarianism of double counting. The preference to be saved before a non-human animal's life in a concrete situation is counted twice, since this is both what this individual herself wants to be the case (since it follows from SA) and what virtually all other human beings want to be the case. In this way some kind of double counting is indeed made. And Dworkin may then say that this is not an innocent kind of double counting.

---

[20] This alternative could fit also externalists about moral motivation, I think, which denies that moral judgements entail motivation (see, for instance, David O. Brink, 1994) and those who embrace cognitive theories of motivation.

4.9 Is Double Counting Morally Objectionable?

Let us distinguish between two cases.

Let us first ask whether we generally would regard it to be more valuable, other things being equal, that a state of affairs exists which is the object of a larger number of preferences, compared to a state of affairs that is the object of just a few preferences. Unless we are particularly hostile to the utilitarian way of counting numbers of preferences, I believe most of us would answer this question in the affirmative. This is probably the reason or at least one of the reasons why we believe it more valuable that Venice is saved than a slum district in Mexico City, even if people also regretted the destruction of the slum. It is true that there are many reasons for saving Venice instead of a slum district—historical, aesthetic, and others, but the principal reason is that *more* people want to save Venice for these reasons than the slum district.

Let us consider a case where the state of affairs valued by the larger number of people involves the satisfaction of some desire. Suppose for instance that a large number of people want some person to have her preferences for life satisfied. Will the fact that there are *many* people who want this be a morally relevant fact?

One way of answering this question will be to say that we would have a strange discontinuity if the preferences of the larger number were morally relevant in all other cases except when the object concerned another person's satisfaction of preferences. Of course, there exists one well-known objection to utilitarianism concentrating on the fact that it will ascribe value to preference satisfaction whatever kind of object the preference is directed to, i.e. preference utilitarianism does not satisfactorily discriminate between different kinds of preferences. But normally this objection wants to show that *evil* desires have to be morally discounted. What we have in mind here is instead a case where an *altruistic* desire would have to be discounted, if we could show that the larger number of preferences directed to another person's well-being have no moral relevance.

Another argument to show that (innocent) preferences of third parties count is to point to the strange moral picture we would get if they did not count—we would have to say that sometimes frustration of an innocent preference is not negative: if we very much want another person to fare well and if she does not do so, the fact that our desire in this case is frustrated is not something negative for us.

To me that seems to be blatantly false. If I have a strong preference that another person should fare well and if this preference is frustrated, this is something negative not only for the person who is the object of my concern but also for me. I am worse off if a person I very much want to be happy is unhappy. And the main reason for this seems to be that not counting my external preference is failing to show my person appropriate respect. So in the end *not* counting the external preferences will have the very consequences which Dworkin says that *counting* them would have.[21]

Dworkin's example is about preferences concerning people to whom one does not seem to stand in a special relationship. However, if all external preferences can be discounted it would not make any difference even if we tested our intuitions against a case where we *did* have an intimate relationship, for instance if we asked ourselves whether we also may disregard a mother's external preference concerning the well-being of her own children. I guess many of us would think that this is a paradigm case of something being of importance to someone and consequently of something being of value for someone and therefore being of moral significance. For instance, when children are killed the effects of this on the parents are often reported as the most tragic feature of the case. But all this would be false if the reactions of the parents actually had no moral significance; if *all* external preferences lack this kind of significance. This, I would say, is a counter-intuitive result.

One might try to defend Dworkin by claiming that the reason why we find this counter-intuitive, if that is what we do, is that we have a case where a person normally would *suffer* from the fact that her external preference is frustrated—what is tragic in a case where a child gets killed is that this is something which feels terrible for the parents. Therefore, the *feelings* of the parents have negative value, not the fact in itself that their external preferences are frustrated.

But if we take a closer look at Dworkin's example from the swimmers, he seems to claim that external preferences should be discounted even when we take into account the feelings that come with these preferences. When he talks about a person having an external preference with regard to the swimmer he refers to this person as someone who "takes pleasure" in the swimmer's success. And of course, if he is prepared to say that this kind of pleasure should have no moral importance, then it is also natural to assume he would say the same as far as the suffering of a parent with a frustrated external preference is concerned—if the positive feelings that come with a satisfied external

---

[21] Hart's point concerning Dworkin's example above is similar: "*not* to count the neighbour's disinterested preference on this issue would be to fail to treat the two as equals. It would be 'undercounting' and presumably as bad as double counting" (1986: 315). Cf. also F. M. Kamm, who says: "If our policy results in counting only objects of preferences [...], then a person's preference will be superfluous whenever one other person shares it. When we toss the coin, we 'count each person's preference' only in the minimal sense that we examine his preference to see what it is—whether it is different from that of others. If his preference differs from anyone else's, then the state of affairs that is its object will be among those given an equal chance" (1993: 114). What is suggested is of course that not counting each person's preference, but only counting its object, may be seen as a failure if one aims at treating people as equals. However, observe that Kamm, just like Dworkin, is against the counting of external preferences: "The system of counting preferences that has a chance of being correct must count only (internal) preferences a person has for his own fate" (1993: 115).

preference can be morally disregarded then why not also the negative feelings that come with a frustrated external preference?[22] Of course, there might be an asymmetry between pleasure and pain here but, as far as I know, Dworkin does not rely on this idea in his criticism of external preferences.

I conclude that Dworkin has failed to show that taking into account also altruistic desires, which is one form which external desires can take, will mean a kind of double counting. Furthermore, whatever we call this process of taking into account preferences concerning others' well-being, Dworkin has not succeeded in showing that there is anything morally objectionable in it either. On the contrary, counting these preferences will be in accordance with the intuitions of most people. At least this is my guess.

Before leaving Dworkin's objection, I just want to say something briefly about what consequences this will yield for our issue. One immediate effect of considering SA as an external preference for the well-being of all beings of our species[23] is that the value of a human being seems to grow larger the more people there are to embrace SA. In a world of five billion people the value which each of us will have in virtue of being a human being is larger compared to what it is in a world of three billion people. This may strike some as rather peculiar—will the twentieth-century human being be more worth than the nineteenth-century human being; and will she have doubled her worth when the world has doubled its population?

I believe we have to give a qualified answer to this question. On the condition that SA has the same content also when the population increases, my answer will be in the affirmative—we may say that the value of each human being increases with the number of people in the world. The reason is the same as for holding that Venice is more valuable than a slum district in Mexico City just in virtue of the fact that more people value Venice compared to the slum district. I can see no reason not to treat the two cases as similar.

But I would also think that it is unlikely that our attitudes to the worth of other human beings are totally unaffected by the fact that we live in a more and more overpopulated world. The bigger the world's population is and the more of those problems we have which are an effect of overpopulation—e.g. starvation—the less value will probably be ascribed to each individual human

---

[22] There is no reason to believe that Dworkin is talking about external preferences isolated from the feelings of having them satisfied or frustrated. In another context he writes: "These are external preferences, but, once again, they are no less genuine, nor less a source of pleasure when satisfied and displeasure when ignored, than purely personal preferences" (1986: 304).

[23] Actually I do not know if it is correct to describe SA simply as an altruistic preference concerning (almost) every human being. That seems to suggest too much, since I assume that we may hold SA without being glad to hear that other persons fare well. The concern for other human beings implied by SA is something which will be displayed in rather special situations, like for instance, as we shall see, when we have to choose between saving a human being and an animal from a burning house. These are the kind of dispositions SA may be about, and they can be part of a person independently of whether the person is a full-blood egoist or not.

being. These are only guesses from my part, but they seem to be reasonable, and if true it would mean that the force of the many people embracing SA in an overpopulated world will be counterbalanced by the fact that SA in such a world tends to be about a lower moral status of humans beings compared to a less populated world.[24]

With this guess I leave Dworkin's account of external preferences.

4.10 Hare on External Preferences

Let me make some comments on Hare's definition of what characterizes an external want. The problems Hare discusses are a bit different from Dworkin's, since they concern generally whether there is value in a state of affairs which satisfies a preference of a person without this person having any knowledge of it. For example, Hare writes:

> So far we have allowed into our reckoning all now-for-now and then-for-then preferences. But some of these will be for states of affairs which are not presently within the experience of the person having the preference. I may for example prefer that my apples not be stolen, but not know whether they are being stolen or not. In the examples we have been considering so far, we have been concentrating on preferences with regard to experiences which the preferrer is currently having. Ought we to extend our account to cover what have been called "external" preferences (1981: 104)?

Here it is asked not only whether there is value in the fact that your apples are not stolen but also whether a present preference may endow a future experience with value. If it may do so we get the following problem: "we may have strong antecedent now-for-then preferences which lead to actions which, then, we would very much prefer not to have been taken, because they lead to the non-satisfaction of our then-for-then preferences" (1981: 105). Now, Hare requires that our preferences be rational, which means that they have to be submitted to logic and facts, which in turn means that some of these now-for-then preferences may be disregarded because they are irrational, i.e. they will not survive a rationality test. But if they survive, we get the problem of the *autofanatic* person, which is "somebody who allows strong antecedent now-for-then preferences to override fully represented then-for-then preferences" (1981: 105).

Although I believe that it is of the utmost importance to give a satisfactory solution to the problem Hare points to (especially if you are a utilitarian and favour the preference version rather than the classical one) I am not so sure that this question will have as interesting an application to our main issue as

---

[24] Observe that there is no automatic connection between increase in population and increase in problems of overpopulation. As time passes there will also normally be an increase in scientific knowledge, which means that we probably will be able to use at least some of the world's resources more efficiently. More food can be produced in a given area today than one hundred years ago, which also naturally means that more people can be fed today compared to then.

the question which I take to be the more fundamental one, i.e. whether states of affairs in themselves, apart from experiences of them, may have value for a subject. Therefore, let us first of all concentrate on this question.[25]

Generally, if external preferences (in Hare's sense) are not allowed to be taken into account, not even when directed at purely selfish concerns (which Hare's definition will allow for) most people (or at least very many of them) I have met will actually be wrong about what kinds of things are valuable for them. In my experience, many people will say that they value not being deceived even secretly; they value that adultery is not being committed by their partner in marriage even if they never will come to know about it. Are they mistaken about this? If we say they are and act on that judgement, we may once again be accused of failing to show appropriate respect to these persons. The difference now is that we will have to say that their mistake is much greater than if it concerned just whether the (unfelt) satisfaction of their altruistic preferences had value for them.[26]

The problem you have to face if you believe that it is a mistake to think that unfelt preference satisfaction may be valuable is how to explain how that may be so. One possibility would be to say that preferences for other things than experiences would not survive critical reflection and exposure to facts. However, I find it hard to believe that our external preferences really *are* irrational. I cannot imagine what kind of reflection would make my want that I am not secretly deceived go away.

The only mistake I can think of being committed when I have this want is that, when believing that a secret deception would be something bad, I actually have in mind the risk that this deception would be revealed. If this hypothesis is true, I am not valuing not being deceived *per se* but only not having the bad experiences of realizing that I am being deceived. I mistakenly believe that the object of not being deceived is intrinsic when it actually is something bad in virtue of what may come out of it.

This may be so in some cases, but it is almost definitely wrong to think that *all* external wants suffer from this mistake. Deciding whether a want

---

[25] The problem of autofanaticism is solved by Hare by his requirement of prudence, which says "that we should always have a dominant or overriding preference now that the satisfaction of our now-for-now and then-for-then preferences should be maximized" (1981: 105). The nature of this requirement seems to be a bit mysterious. But according to Wlodek Rabinowicz it is a demand of rationality which says that "we should adjust our now-for-then preferences to the then-for-then preferences that we know we are going to have" (1989: 146). It has to be distinguished from the well-known principle which says that knowledge of preferences entails preferences and which Hare claims is a conceptual truth. See also Hare's reply to Rabinowicz (1989a).

[26] You may think that this argument is a two-edged sword. Do we not have to say that those people who do *not* value states of affairs apart from experiences of them are mistaken? No, there is an asymmetry here, since if we also take into account external wants, we will do justice both to those people who value states of affairs *per se* and to those valuing only the experiences of them (provided we do not talk of these experiences as states of affairs). If a person values only experiences, then these are the only things valuable for her, also according to the idea that external wants have moral importance.

really will pass a rationality test will to a certain degree be guesswork—unless we really undergo some kind of cognitive psychotherapy to test our wants—but I am fairly confident that my own want not to be secretly deceived would remain pretty unaffected by this kind of reflection.

So the main problem, if you claim that external wants ought not to be taken into account, is to explain *why not*, when people actually value the objects of these external wants. I am not going to pursue this general discussion here, but I believe that the only way to claim that external wants should not count is to point to the *counter-intuitive* consequences of doing so. Allowing that things which we do not experience have value for us opens the door to various unacceptable ideas, you may claim.[27]

For instance, one such consequence, already mentioned, is that counting external wants seems to allow for counting also then-for-now preferences (i.e. antecedent now-for-then preferences) which conflict with now-for-now preferences,[28] which is the case referred to by Hare in the quotations earlier (although Hare was not trying to show that taking these preferences into account would yield counter-intuitive results—Hare does not accept appeals to intuitions[29]). A person who knowingly lets his now-for-then preferences

---

[27] Peter Carruthers has constructed the following thought experiment: "Suppose that Astrid is a very rich woman, who has become tired of life on earth with its squalor and constant violence. Accordingly, she buys herself a space-rocket, and takes off on a trajectory that is set irreversibly to carry her out of our solar system, and forever out of contact with her fellow humans. She does not even carry with her a radio with which she can be contacted. Now suppose that before leaving earth she had erected a statue in memory of her beloved late husband, and one of her most cherished desires is that the statue should outlast her. But within months of her departure the statue is struck by lightning and destroyed. Is Astrid harmed? It seems to me plain that she is not, since she can never know. Yet her desire has been objectively frustrated" (1992: 80–1). It is true that I have argued against this kind of attitude before, but I want nevertheless to make a comment on the kind of example used by Carruthers. The reason is that it is typical in a certain respect, namely in that the preference in question is rather queer. The problem with such preferences is that we are inclined also to assign less importance to their *subjective* satisfaction. I therefore believe that if we want to test our intuitions against a case where a person's desires are satisfied merely in an objective sense, then we have to choose desires which we under normal conditions find important. For instance, suppose instead that Carruthers had designed his example in the following way: Astrid has for some reason been forced to leave earth alone in a space-rocket. Before leaving earth she had deposited all her savings with Adam in order to let him be responsible for the care of her only and beloved daughter. However, soon after Astrid has left earth it turns out that Adam has embezzled the money Astrid left to him, which will have the consequence that Astrid's daughter cannot get the kind of proper care that Astrid very much wants her to get. Is Astrid harmed? Well, it seems to me that it is easier to answer this question in a positive direction compared to the original example, and the reason is, I think, that we have to do with wants of a kind which we tend to respect.

[28] A prerequisite is that one of our previous arguments was successful, i.e. that it is *possible* to satisfy a past attitude.

[29] Sometimes he seems to give *some* weight to moral intuitions, however. For instance, concerning "past-held" preferences, he writes: "But have I, because of universalizability, any duty in

override his now-for-now preferences was called an autofanatic by Hare. And it may be true that in some cases taking into account autofanaticism will be unacceptable. But not generally I think, since we may also describe the *ideals* we have about how to live our life as some kind of autofanaticism— having ideals may imply a preparedness to live in a certain way in the future whether or not this is what you then want to do.

And then of course another alleged repugnant possibility is the one which initiated this discussion, namely of taking into account not only past preferences of existing persons but also such preferences of non-existing and past persons.

4.11 An Argument Against Counting Past Preferences

If we count past people's preferences, it seems that the importance of being a human will grow larger the longer the history of humanity lasts. The value of being a human today will be larger than it was one hundred years ago thanks to the fact that our history contains a greater number of people who have accepted SA. The difference between this argument and the argument considered above is that we are now considering the effect of taking into account past preferences which will work independently of whether the world's population will increase or decrease.

One possible solution could be stated as follows. If it really is sensible to take into account past people's prospective preferences (apart from the alleged consequence under consideration) would it not also be sensible to take into account *future* people's *retrospective* preferences? If you believe that there is something special about being human, and if one aspect of this is that you also want the future humans to have a special kind of protection, would you not welcome or regret the fact that people in the past have been or have not been given this kind of special protection?

The result of this would be that the worth of a human being at any given point of time was about the same as far as the external preferences of past and future people were concerned, since the more external preferences of past people of whom you would have the pleasure of being the object, the less such preferences of future people there would be to count, since naturally the number of future people decreases as the number of past people increases.

This reply rests on a supposition which can be discussed, viz. that people in the future will continue to have the same attitude to the value of being human as people have had in the past. I am in no position to estimate the probability of that supposition, and therefore I also think it problematic to

---

moral thinking to listen to the voice of that small boy that I once was? Our intuitions go against this—not that we ought to give much weight to intuitions. But they are perhaps worth exploring, and seem to me to pull in opposite directions" (1989: 156).

base an argument on it. For all I know, it may be false, although I spontaneously think we probably will retain SA also in a reasonable near future.
One reason for saying so is that I think we are genetically constructed to
have such a disposition. Another reason is that I believe religion will continue
to have almost the same grip on people in the future as it has had in the past,
and at least in some of the big religions SA (or an interpretation of this
belief) plays a major role.

We may ask whether we would accept that SA should have influence on
our lives even after people had ceased to embrace it, *if we make the assumption
that SA will disappear in the future*. Most people would *not* accept this, I
guess.

But what is the difference between this and the case where we had a
conflict in one person between a then-for-now preference and a now-for-now
preference, and where I tried to claim that perhaps we should accept the
moral weight of the then-for-now preference after all? The big difference is
that we cannot in the present case draw parallels to ideals. An ideal that a
person has, as we said, is an attitude which, among other things, can manifest
itself in a wish to continue to live in a certain way whether or not one will
feel for it in the future. It is manifested in a want which is not, in Parfit's
terminology, conditional on its own persistence.[30]

It does not sound natural to speak of one generation having *ideals* for
another generation. And I consider this difference not only a semantic one—
it is not only a problem about the application of the term "ideal". I also
believe we have a different attitude to whether or not we may reasonably

---

[30] This parallel to ideals may seem a bit problematic, since it appears that it may tell both for
and against taking into account past wants. An ideal is a want built on a value judgement which
you also wish to satisfy in situations where you have ceased to have it. (I am not sure whether
this really should be described as two distinct things. Maybe being unconditional in this way is
merely a manifestation of a value judgement. However, to retain the possibility that some wants
may be unconditional without in any sense being built on value judgements I will treat the two
parts as separate elements in the description of what an ideal is.) Therefore, from the perspective
of your present ideals it seems perfectly sensible to claim that there is value in having them
satisfied also in the future when you perhaps do not have them any longer but instead have
ideals which you consider today to be inferior compared to your present one. On the other
hand, from the perspective of these new ideals—when they come into being—it will seem
strange to continue being morally tied to the *former* ideals. At the same time we could not
possibly accept as a general truth that past ideals can be ignored, since that would have a
negative effect on the very meaning of embracing our present ideals unconditionally—to have
ideals is *per definition* to regard certain things as valuable independently of our own changing
attitudes. We may therefore conclude that looking backward from the perspective of an ideal
will tend to undermine the idea that past ideals matter morally while looking forward from the
same perspective will tend to support it. And when I tried to draw attention to the ideals in
order to show that maybe we have to accept those conflicts between preferences then-for-now
and now-for-now (or from another angle: preferences now-for-then *versus* then-for-then), i.e.
accept that they are genuine moral conflicts between different values, I was obviously appealing
to the first kind of aspect or perspective. I mention this complication—that appealing to ideals
might be double-edged only to note it.

demand that preferences should be complied with even in conflict with preferences held in the future. I believe we will more easily understand and accept that future generations will ignore the plans we have had for them.

And this is, I assume, what lies behind the counter-intuitiveness of a proposal to let preferences of past people matter morally. But I stubbornly insist that for many people it will seem counter-intuitive also *not* to take these preferences into account at all, since that would mean that the moral relevance of death-bed wishes could be reduced to considerations about the side-effects of complying with or ignoring such wishes.

So we seem to have a conflict between different intuitions here. This much can be said about my own intuitive reactions to the questions we have considered in the latter part of this chapter, which has been about past and external preferences: I am very firmly convinced that things have value for me even when I am not aware of the existence of these things, which means that I find it intuitively very plausible to attach value to preferences which are external in Hare's meaning of this term. I also find it very plausible to assign moral importance to preferences which are external in Dworkin's sense, that is, which are *impersonal*, which may regard other people's well-being.[31]

When it comes to past wants of still existing persons I am convinced also here, although less so compared to the external preferences, that they should be considered morally. What supported this conviction was the reasoning about ideals. Lastly, concerning past preferences of past people, I am not sure as to what to say about them. The relevance for this on the effects of SA has already been outlined.

To sum up, in this chapter we have considered a couple of distinctions in connection with a property being of direct moral importance. One sense in which I believe the property of being human has such importance is the subjective one—the property is important in other people's eyes.[32] This is therefore one sense to give to the idea of a human dignity, although many defenders of this idea have had in mind some kind of objective value, a value independent of any valuing subject. The reason why I have preferred to develop the subjective aspect is that I believe there is a sense to be given to the idea of human dignity also when you are not an objectivist.

In the next chapter I intend to make some comments on the more precise content of SA and then I want to assess it. Is it true or false, does it conflict with other attitudes? (Some of the arguments considered will be applicable whether you are a subjectivist or an objectivist about the value of being human.)

---

[31] Some of these points have been further developed in Dan Egonsson (1990: esp. Ch. 2).

[32] Stephen R. L. Clark has formulated a similar thought in the following way: "Speciesists need not claim that all human beings are objectively different (save, of course, in species) from all nonhuman beings, but only that they are subjectively different: they matter more to *us*, not always to the universe" (1983: 178).

CHAPTER 5

SA EXAMINED

[Most] of those who say they believe in the sanctity of life are not vegetarians.

Helga Kuhse & Peter Singer *Should the Baby Live?*

[It] might be more reliable to accept what they actually practised as indicating less than complete confidence in what they preached.

Michael P. T. Leahy *Against Liberation*

In Sweden there was an investigation carried out in 1986-7, led by Anders Jeffner, which attracted rather a great deal of attention. The investigation concerned, among other things, what I have called SA, i.e. whether people think there is a moral difference between human and non-human beings.

When asked whether one ought to show more respect to a human being than to other living beings, 43% answered "no", 37% "yes" and the rest did not know how to answer the question. This was of course surprising, but a follow-up investigation seemed to confirm that two Swedes out of three believe that humans and non-humans are equally valuable, which is an even stronger conclusion![1]

This is astonishing and it *seems* like a direct contradiction of what I have said above. An attitude is not the standard one and it is definitely not universally embraced when found only in one person out of three.[2]

Now, we could always qualify SA and call it something else and then claim that we may found the idea of a human dignity also on an attitude which is not universally embraced. For something to have a subjective and

[1] See Jeffner (1988). A question has been raised concerning the scientific value of the study, and therefore concerning whether any reliable conclusions can be based on it (see Birgitta Forsman, 1996: 53–71). I do not share this opinion. For one thing, I am not capable of determining the scientific value of the investigation, but I believe it records a spontaneous reaction that is fairly widespread. In that sense it is interesting as a take-off for further reflections concerning, for instance, the content and seriousness of a moral opinion. It is true that the investigation does not say very much about *why* people answer the way they do. But that is not a fatal flaw in this context.

[2] We have no reason not to believe that we would get a similar picture if the investigation was carried out in another (Western) country. If nothing else is said I confine the discussion to what is the case in our own part of the world—so "universal", when I talk of a universal Standard Attitude (SA), means "universal in the Western countries". My hypothesis is that SA actually *is* universally embraced, which does not necessarily mean that I expect to find it literally in *all* subjects, but rather in the overwhelming majority.

intrinsic value we do not have to show that this kind of value emanates from *all* subjects of a certain kind and not even that it emanates from the majority of subjects of a certain kind (i.e. human ones). If it should turn out that only 30% of us humans embrace SA that would mean that the value of a human compared to another being was less than it would have been if it was embraced by all humans, and not that the two kinds of beings were equally valuable.

For the idea of a unique value in virtue of a being belonging to the species *Homo sapiens* to prevail, it is enough that some of us believe in this value to such an extent that it does not have any counterpart as far as other species are concerned.

5.1 Is the Denial of SA Serious?

Many of those who have discussed Jeffner's investigation have had difficulties in reconciling the fact that only about 30% believe that a human being ought to be shown more respect than other kinds of living beings with the fact that a majority of us certainly do not act as if this is what we actually believe. For instance, one common reaction is to point to the fact that most of us eat meat without protesting and to the fact that it might be difficult to believe that someone who is serious in her denial of a difference in worth between humans and animals really would continue to do that (unless *ex hypothesi* the idea was that humans and animals where equally *worthless*). It is true that we have formed habits which might be difficult to extinguish, but the point is that it seems troublesome to claim that humans and animals are of equal value against the background of these habits.[3] It is also true that we have other attitudes that might conflict with SA—for instance, a taste for meat—but we seem to have no behavioural evidence that there really is such a conflict. Our meat-eating habits appear fairly unproblematic.

But the picture is even more complicated. When asked why they regard humans and animals as equally valuable, 93% in the investigation answered that they believe that everything which is alive is equally valuable. I certainly do not know of a single person who in practical life behaves as if there is no value difference between different kinds of living organisms. That attitude would not only prescribe a radical change in our treatment of animals and nature but would also prescribe reverence for micro-organisms such as viruses. In choosing whether to save from a burning house our neighbour's ten-year-old daughter or an invisible micro-organism (for instance an AIDS virus) in a test tube, you would, if you had the belief in question, consider the choice to be morally indifferent—you could just as well save the micro-organism. (If you prefer not to call the virus a living organism, a comparison can be made instead between a human being and, for instance, a potted geranium.)

---

[3] Part of the explanation why we continue with these habits may of course be suppression and ignorance (cf. John Robbins, 1987: esp. Ch. 5). But I do not think this is the whole truth.

I am absolutely sure that the majority of Swedes would reject such a conclusion (even if it would have saved them from the accusations of not being vegetarians).

These examples are enough to show that we have reason to question the *seriousness* of the attitude expressed in Jeffner's investigation. We have to distinguish between what we *say* about the values we embrace and what values we *actually* embrace. There has to be some connection between our values and our actions.

If we look upon SA as a moral intuition we might regard it as both a want and a belief, or alternatively as a kind of attitude which has both a cognitive and a conative aspect.[4]

We can also say that for some people the cognitive aspect is the most prominent one and for some others the conative aspect is, which means that some people will treat SA as a part of their explicitly articulated conviction whereas others will not, but instead display SA by their actions, or at least by their dispositions to act in certain ways in real or imagined situations where some hard choices have to be made. I think we may treat SA and even moral intuitions generally in this vague way whatever meta-ethical decisions we want to make in the end. Once again, my account of moral intuitions will be meta-ethically innocent. This talk of aspects of intuitions can be taken literally, or as another way of expressing an uncertainty as to what exact analysis to choose in the end.

Now, one might claim that the investigations referred to above are only about this *cognitive* aspect of a fundamental moral intuition. However, there has to be some way of distinguishing between a sincere and an insincere belief and it is hard to imagine a criterion which is not at all sensitive to the practical life of the believer. So whether we prefer to concentrate on the cognitive or conative aspect of a moral intuition, it seems difficult to escape the conclusion that if there is a conflict between these aspects, that will be a sign as good as any that we may doubt whether the moral belief really is serious. (And observe that this is not necessarily the same as saying that beliefs should be defined in terms of wants. Neither is it to deny the possibility of weakness of will.)

The upshot of this is that even if we admit that there are different aspects of such fundamental moral intuitions as SA and the denial of it (referred to

---

[4] No doubt, the word "attitude" is vague enough to be able to apply to both beliefs and wants. See, for instance, Gilbert Harman (1977: 48), G. E. Moore (1966: 116), L. W. Sumner (1995: 776) and Alfred R. Mele who writes that "attitudes are at least partially constituted by a psychological orientation toward a representational content" (1996: 740). However, see also Anne Maclean, who makes a distinction between a belief or opinion and an attitude—"the sort of attitude that is a matter of the way we instinctively behave" (1993: 35–6). A moral intuition— for instance the one saying that it is generally wrong to kill babies—seems to be more like an attitude than an opinion in her eyes.

in the investigation) and also admit that for some people these intuitions in question are more like beliefs than preferences, it seems difficult to make sense of the idea that we hold these beliefs seriously when our way of living obviously speaks another language. Therefore, the way most of us actually treat animals and non-human organisms tells against the idea that we believe that non-humans ought to be shown the same respect as we show humans.

5.2 A Third Aspect of a Moral Intuition

We have distinguished between two aspects of a moral intuition, but a third aspect may be the *emotional* character of a moral intuition. This is probably the aspect we have in mind when we talk of a moral sentiment or a moral feeling.

Now, one idea could be to interpret the result of the investigation as expressing these moral sentiments rather than beliefs or preferences. The denial of a special value of being human would then reflect one's moral emotions.[5] Of course, this in turn could be interpreted in many different ways, for instance negatively, which means that those who deny a moral difference between humans and non-humans thereby deny only that they feel morally attached to a being just in virtue of the fact that it is a human one, i.e. as a denial of a special (moral) emotion directed towards humanity *per se*. It could also be given a more positive interpretation; perhaps the majority of people react with the same kind of moral emotions when someone fails to show respect to an animal and when someone fails to show respect to a human being. The exact character of these emotions may be different depending on the context. Naturally, the brutal killing of a being will arouse more violent emotions than less brutal behaviour. But if the investigation is reliable it means that there will be no emotional difference depending only on whether the victim is a human or a non-human being. (Let us in the following ignore the case of viruses, plants and things like that.) I assume that the investigation is particularly about feelings of this positive kind and not only about the absence of a special feeling towards humanity.

We may ask two questions here. First, does it make sense to claim that a majority actually display these emotions in the way the investigation says? Second, if the investigation gives a true picture of our emotional reactions, what should we say about the fact that we live as if we after all thought there *were* a big difference between humans and non-humans? Do we have to call into question whether these emotions are serious, or what?

---

[5] For the moment I disregard the relation between these emotions and the other aspects of a moral intuition. But compare Samuel Scheffler who talks of "the range of powerful human emotions and attitudes that seem both to be capable of spurring us to action and, in their central forms at least, to presuppose moral beliefs, in the sense that they could not be experienced by someone who had no such beliefs. Guilt, remorse, indignation, resentment, conscientiousness, and a sense of indebtedness all seem to fall into this category, for example" (1992: 68).

I am not sure how to answer the first question. If we talk of emotional reactions which are rather spontaneous and superficial I think the proposal may well make sense. For instance, I believe people may be as upset by seeing on television that animals are mistreated as they get by watching mistreatment of human beings. At least, I have noticed such a tendency in myself without being able fully to explain it. And actually, it seems that aggression against animals may often arouse even stronger emotions in us than aggression against human beings, since people are often more upset after watching these kinds of television programmes about animals.

There can be many good explanations for this, for instance that we are much more used to watching human beings suffer as a result of natural catastrophes and wars, and so on—as regards human suffering (at least in other parts of the world) we are simply to some extent blunted. And this is perhaps not yet the case concerning animal suffering.

Furthermore, one very important moral sentiment is a guilty conscience. If it really were true that we had the same emotional attitude to the suffering and mistreatment of humans and animals, then it seems that this should also be reflected in our conscience. But I am quite sure that we nevertheless feel less bad about having, for instance, killed or indirectly participated in the killing of an animal compared to a human.

Let us for the sake of argument assume that I am wrong in this and consider the second question. Could we possibly accept what the investigation suggests, that is, an emotional insensitivity to a moral difference between humans and non-humans in the majority of people, in spite of the fact that this majority live the way they do? This could be interpreted in different ways.

It could be interpreted as a logical question: is it conceptually possible to have moral sentiments in direct opposition to one's displayed behaviour or even to one's disposition to behave in a certain way? And we could distinguish several elements in this question too. Is it logically possible to have certain specific moral sentiments without also acting or being disposed to act in certain ways? For instance, is it possible to react with moral indignation to something without at the same time having a tendency to avoid it? Maybe some moral emotions are more tightly connected to behaviour than some other emotions? We may also put a general question about the conceptual connections between emotions and behaviour. Do we ever have an emotion of which it is true that it has to be linked with a certain kind of behaviour in order to be an emotion of that kind?

Some philosophers think so. For instance, O. H. Green says that it "is necessary that emotion-terms are defined by reference to a person's behaviour in certain circumstances" and that the "[b]ehaviour which is described in defining emotion-terms must be typical" (1970: 552). Now, this could easily be misinterpreted as suggesting that there is a conceptual tie of this kind only sometimes, only for some emotions in some circumstances. However, as

I interpret Green, this kind of tie is supposed to be general and the reason is that there is no other way of recognizing emotions in others than by their behaviour. Merely a causal connection is not enough—a definite sort of behaviour has to be part of the definition of every emotion, according to Green.

If we accept this we will definitely have problems with adjusting the fact that we report some moral emotions (presupposing that this is what we actually do in the investigation referred to) with the fact that we behave the way we do, since it will be difficult to claim that there exists some behaviour pattern that is more typical of such emotions than avoidance behaviour.

But should we accept it? Indeed, the claim that there is a *conceptual* connection between the emotion and the behaviour is problematic. We all have experiences of emotions which are not at all reflected in behaviour. For instance, I may feel glad that a person whom I do not like has lost his money on speculation without ever showing that I have this emotion (one of the reasons for this being of course that I know that malicious pleasure is something one should not experience).[6]

This will not prove that a slightly weaker thesis is false also, namely that there exists a conceptual tie concerning *some* of the emotions. For instance, could one possibly be passionate without this implying at least some kind of behaviour (including tendency to behave)? An even more difficult question is whether this possibility exists also in the case of *strong* passions. (The fact that the proposal is false when we talk of *violent* passions does not refute a scepticism about the kind of conceptual connection discussed here, since I take this term to be not only about a kind of emotion and its strength but also about its external effects.)

We do not have to make a decision on this general question as long as we agree on the possibility of having the moral emotions which *ex hypothesi* are expressed in the investigation without being logically committed to act in a certain way. But does this mean that these reports may *be* serious after all? Ought we to believe those people who claim that animals and humans should be shown equal respect, interpreting this as a report of these persons' moral sentiments?

We have to distinguish between what is logically possible and what is likely. What this shows is only that it may be possible to have these emotions while acting as if one did not have them as far as logic is concerned. But from this it does not follow that we may take these descriptions at their face value, since it is more *probable* that they are false or insincere when combined with a behaviour which rationally contradicts it. So the answer to our initial

---

[6] Furthermore, cf. Adrian M. S. Piper who points to the fact that "sometimes there really are no words adequate to express our gratitude for another's support, nothing we can do to demonstrate the depth of our affection, no way to express our heartfelt appreciation—and simply saying this, or doing nothing, doesn't do the trick, either. This doesn't mean that we do not have those attitudes" (1996: 530).

question will depend on how the question is interpreted. Interpreted as a logical question, we may answer "yes"—what the investigation suggests may be true. But interpreted as a question about whether or not we have factual reason to believe that the investigation reflects our most serious attitude, the answer will be "no".

Even if there is no close conceptual connection between emotions and behaviour, I believe that behaviour should be taken as an indicator or (natural) sign of what emotional state a person is in.[7] And when doing so we see that there is a strong case for doubting whether the investigation really shows that we are prepared to abandon SA even when we focus on the emotional aspect. So I have no reason to change my hypothesis which says that SA is normal, even among very many of those people supporting the animal liberation movement.[8]

[7] The fundamental idea lying behind this proposal is shared also by William Lyons: "we do look upon behaviour as an 'external' or public indicator of 'inner' or private states, the beliefs, evaluations, and in particular the wants involved in emotions. If no behaviour that could be interpreted as stemming from, say, love is ever present in a putative love relationship, and the person is rational, then there is good reason to believe that the desires which make up part of the very concept of love, and which usually lead to appropriate actions or behaviour, are not present" (1980: 155). Notice, however, that there is a problem here, which comes from the fact that Lyons wants to tie the emotion of love to desire. If the concept of a desire should be analysed as a disposition to act in certain ways, then we will of course get the kind of close connection between emotion and behaviour if we accept what Lyons says. So if you want to argue for the strong thesis that there is no conceptual connection between emotion and behaviour, you will either have to deny that desire is ever part of any emotion or choose an analysis of the concept of desire in which behaviour plays a less salient role. Another alternative is to claim that there does not necessarily exist a close conceptual connection between emotion and *actual* behaviour although there does exist such a connection between emotion and a *disposition* to behave in certain ways, at least for some emotions. This is perhaps what Lyons wants to say. And if you are disposed to act in certain ways, then actual behaviour will of course be a sign that you have this kind of disposition. But notice that we have been considering an even stronger thesis, namely that there does not even exist a conceptual connection between having an emotion and being disposed to act in certain ways.

[8] Peter Carruthers has a similar idea. He says: "Our common-sense, pre-theoretical, view is that it would be very wrong to place the lives of many dogs over the life of a single (albeit old and friendless) human. This belief is probably too firmly held, in the case of most of us, to be shaken by theoretical argument. (Recall from Chapter 1, indeed, that it is a belief shared even by those philosophers who have been most vociferous in defence of animals, namely Regan and Singer.)" (1992: 96) However, what Singer says is not that the life of a human being is more valuable *per se*, only that it would be judged more valuable from an impartial standpoint, and "In general it does seem that the more highly developed the conscious life of the being, the greater the degree of self-awareness and rationality, the more one would prefer that kind of life, if one were choosing between it and a being at a lower level of awareness" (1979: 90). Singer certainly does not in this passage support the idea that there is something intrinsically special in being a member of the species *Homo sapiens*, only that there is something special about having the mental capacities that human beings commonly have. We will return to Singer's argument in a coming chapter. Turning to Regan, I also believe that he would protest against Carruthers' accusation, since what Regan says is that a belief that the life of a human being should be placed before the life of a dog is justified by appeal to the worse-off principle, i.e. killing the

So far we have considered three alternative views on the nature of a moral intuition, or if one prefers, three aspects of this kind of attitude. It may express a belief or a preference or an emotion, or all these things at the same time. I have tried to show that whatever aspect of SA we are talking of, it is difficult to prove that the attitude is present when the behavioural evidence we have speaks another language.

5.3 Taking into Account People's Moral Attitudes

What I have tried to do is to argue roughly that we should take into account the actual values of people when trying to settle what things are valuable— some things have a kind of subjective value in virtue of being valued by people.

I have assumed that when we talk of seriously valuing here we are also talking of a practical attitude in one way or another, since it does not really make sense to claim that a person actually values something—that p is true—unless she tends to make it the case that p is true. So in whatever way we understand a moral intuition or attitude it will get its moral relevance in virtue of being connected with our preferences.

This is not necessarily a utilitarian reasoning (once again, I am not assuming a utilitarian approach). But it could be, and some philosophers have called into question whether utilitarianism really is capable of doing justice to the moral attitudes of ordinary people. For example, Mary Warnock says (her example is about our attitudes towards embryos, but it will have a general application):

> In particular, there remains the question how far, in the calculus of pleasures and pains, one ought to take into account, not, doubtless, the pains of the embryos (for they will not experience any) but the feelings of outrage suffered by those who think it simply morally wrong to use human embryos for research at all. If someone is a utilitarian, and therefore committed to the view that right action is that which gives rise to more benefit than harm, is he or she obliged to weigh in the balance the moral outrage or distress caused to people, where a practice they deeply and sincerely believe to be wrong is permitted, and perhaps even encouraged? (1987: 7)

Notice that Warnock does not here ask whether a utilitarian will take into account what we in the previous chapter discussed under the label external

---

human would cause that individual a greater harm than the harm that would be done to the dog if we killed it instead (cf. 1984: 324). On the other hand, what Carruthers says about the content of the common-sense intuition is the following: "our common-sense intuition in the case of Saul, the sadist, is not simply that it would be wrong to rescue an animal before the human [...], but that it is wrong to weight the suffering of an animal equally with the *equal* suffering of a human being" (1992: 72, my emphasis). Surely this is not what Regan says in the passage referred to by Carruthers. However, my idea, which I have expressed several times in this study, is that it may be true that a person somehow embraces SA, although she would declare something else when asked.

wants in Dworkin's sense, i.e. wants concerning the well-being (positive or negative) of other beings. The problem with embryos is that they probably have no well-being, whether this is defined in terms of sensations, emotions or wants. However, many of us will nevertheless have strong moral opinions about how to treat embryos. And Warnock's question seems to be whether or not the effects of taking into account these moral opinions should be included in the utilitarian calculus.

But *why* should not these reactions be taken into account in such a calculus? If there is something intrinsically bad about preference frustration, which is one of the basic values in utilitarianism, and if it is true that we frustrate someone's preference concerning the embryo by doing experiments on it, then it seems to follow trivially that doing this experiment will be something bad, other things being equal. (Nothing will change if we instead choose a hedonistic version of utilitarianism, which seems to be the version that Warnock has in mind, talking as she does about a calculus of pleasure and pain.)[9]

One may decide not to include these morality-related harms in the utilitarian calculus,[10] but then one will *abandon* utilitarianism in order to solve a well-known problem of it, for instance the possibility of giving a utilitarian sanction to the majority oppressing the minority. Even if this possibility is indeed a problem, it seems to require some kind of non-utilitarian solution. Therefore, from utilitarianism alone, i.e. from an unrestricted utilitarianism, it seems plain that the effects of offending someone's moral sentiments should be taken into account.

The problem is that Warnock seems to think that one has to mix some non-utilitarian elements in one's theory in order to be able *to account for* these moral sentiments. We have claimed that *not* taking into account these opinions will be a departure from the utilitarian path, whereas Warnock seems to claim the very opposite. She says that "as soon as the criterion of right and wrong moves from a plain calculation of benefits and harms, and begins to take into account people's *moral sentiments*, then I believe it becomes a different theory" (1987: 8).

This is a bit strange, since to take into account sentiments whether they are moral, aesthetic, egoistic, and so on, is what the fundamental idea of utilitarianism is about, at least the hedonistic versions of it. Warnock says,

---

[9] Compare Ted Honderich: "Morality-dependent harm, as we can call it, is typified by the distress of the Sabbatarians, or by the state of feeling of the ordinary families which has to do with the homosexual commune being established in, as they say, their block of flats. [...] If it really were true that the distress to be caused by a contemplated action was of great magnitude although via moral beliefs, it would surely be absurd *not* to take this into account" (1982: 504, 508). Cf. also Anthony Ellis (1995), who believes we have no right not to be caused moral indignation. This does not mean, however, that we have no right not to be caused any kind of belief-mediated distress (which J. J. Thomson has claimed, 1990).

[10] For some reason, which is not apparent to me, Warnock calls the result of excluding these kinds of harms "Strict Utilitarianism", and she ascribes it to John Harris (1983).

furthermore, that taking into account such sentiments, utilitarianism will be "in the much messier, less tidy, business of compromise" (1987: 8). But making compromises between different feelings of different people seems to be exactly what utilitarianism is about. Therefore, I suspect that Warnock slides between two different questions.

The two questions concern whether a utilitarian should take into account people's moral opinions in so far as they are expressions of what they *believe* and whether she should take them into account in so far as they are expressions of what they *value* or prefer or feel. That Warnock does not properly distinguish between these questions is confirmed in passages like this one:

For I would argue that when we begin to take moral beliefs into account and to weigh them in the balance against future good, we are beginning to move away from Utilitarianism, towards a different moral theory altogether, perhaps towards a form of intuitionism (1983: 245).[11]

What Warnock says here is strictly speaking true, since I can see no reason to take into account a moral belief *qua* belief in the utilitarian calculus. It is true that one may combine utilitarianism with many different kinds of axiologies and one may well designate a moral theory which exhorts us to maximize the number of true beliefs as utilitarianism. But since this is not what utilitarians in general would say, there is no reason to reckon with this possibility.

However, what Warnock says is true only because she seems to think exclusively of this single aspect of a moral opinion or normative conviction, namely the cognitive one. And that is the reason why she thinks that this attitude may come into conflict with the utilitarian calculus of the future good. She has to say that a normative conviction is an attitude which in its nature is different from the attitudes utilitarianism normally deals with. But look at the kind of concrete example Warnock discusses—experiments on embryos. We have strong reasons to suppose that those who are opposed will also have negative emotions when they hear that such experiments are carried out.

Therefore, I conclude that Warnock is wrong in thinking that utilitarianism cannot, without becoming some kind of mixed theory, account for people's moral convictions. Warnock slides between different questions—whether there are utilitarian reasons to reckon with sentiments on the one hand and beliefs on the other.[12]

---

[11] Notice that this quotation is taken from an earlier article. But since she discusses the same subject and even brings forward the same argument in the two articles referred to, I can see no reason not to compare them in this way.

[12] Hare has directed a similar argument against Warnock's proposal that normal people's sentiments have to be taken into account and that utilitarianism will become a mixed theory if they are. He says: "The main point, however, is that, although we ought to have regard to the fact that people think what they do think, it does not for a moment follow that *what* they think ought to be given any weight in our moral reasoning, in the sense of providing premises for our arguments. We may, indeed, argue 'All those people think it wrong, so they will be shocked if

5.4 A Brief Summary

Let us sum up what has been said in this chapter so far. I have claimed that an apparent belief that something is or is not especially valuable will not be very trustworthy in the absence of behavioural evidence to the same effect, let alone in the presence of behavioural evidence which speaks a completely different language. However, this is not necessarily to say that behaviour which rationally contradicts an expressed belief logically would entail that the belief in question is not serious. It is better to be careful and claim that *we have reason to believe* that a belief which is contradicted by behaviour is not serious. The same is true of the emotional aspect of the belief—behaviour is a sign of emotions.

And these considerations lie behind the conclusion that we may doubt whether the alleged denial of SA by the majority of people really is a serious denial. We have also discussed the moral implications of this.

What reasons are there for saying that human beings have got a special worth? Notice that we have to distinguish between several questions carefully. One distinction concerns what reason we may have for saying that there is something special about being a human being in a broadly utilitarian framework and what reason we have for embracing SA. To say that there are good reasons to reckon with SA and let it determine what is valuable is not to say that we have good reasons for embracing SA. I have tried to claim that given the way we actually work, given that we seem to attach a very special importance to the fact that someone is a human being, we have a utilitarian reason to reckon with at least certain aspects of this attitude, since there is a value in doing what will satisfy this attitude. If we are utilitarians the reasons for this claim are fairly direct, which I tried to argue for in the previous section, and that seems to be true whatever version (hedonic or non-hedonic) of utilitarianism we choose.

However, I have also tried not to presuppose utilitarianism in these arguments. I believe there is a case for saying that you may have reason to attach importance to SA whether or not you are a devoted utilitarian. Of course, it goes without saying that some people would deny this, just as some people would deny that we have reason to comply with death-bed wishes after the one who expressed them is dead. Furthermore, many people would also deny that we may benefit someone by satisfying one of her preferences concerning the well-being of another person (possibly with the

---

you don't stop it, and you shouldn't cause them that distress'. But we cannot cogently argue 'All those people think it wrong; so it must be wrong; so it ought to be stopped'" (1987: 177). This is a more elegant way of expressing the same idea as I tried to explain above. According to Hare there is an ambiguity between these two ways of reasoning, and actually Warnock seems to reason in the second way. That would be a kind of intuitionism which of course Hare will reject.

exception of the well-being of relatives and friends). The point is, however, that you *may* attach importance to both kinds of preferences whether or not you are a utilitarian, and it is difficult to claim that these preferences have direct moral importance without claiming that the same is true also of SA.

5.5 The Rationality of Attitudes

Let us pause to consider how you reason when you claim that we have direct moral reasons to comply with death-bed wishes. (The relevance of this question will soon be revealed.) What demands, if any, do you put on these wishes? In putting this question I want to use certain elements discussed in previous chapters: ought the wisher to be rational, that is, ought the wishes to be held on rational grounds? Will it harm the wisher to disregard an irrational wish as well?

Consider a classical type of case where your best friend is going to die and now she asks you to make sure that her money after she has died goes to the church where she was confirmed. She believes that this is what God wants her to do, but since you do not believe in God you think that her belief is false. Now, the question is whether your belief about the irrationality of her wish should make you less inclined to comply with it. In some cases I believe that is so, even if we suppose that you believe all the time that a person can be harmed by things which happen after her death and without her knowledge.

In this example I guess we tend to believe that this is a kind of wish there is less reason to comply with in virtue of its being an *instrumental* want. Your friend wants the money to go to the church to please God, and this is what is important to her (maybe the important thing is what will happen to her when God finds out that she has pleased him, but that is a complication which can be ignored). Here I assume that common sense says that if your friend falsely believes that A is a means towards B and if what she values is primarily B, then getting A will (in itself) be of no value for her.

Then look at SA. If it works in the way described in the previous chapter, then it seems to be immune to this kind of criticism. If what one values is the prospering of a human being for no other reason than that she is human, then the object of one's want has intrinsic value, or in other words, one has an intrinsic want towards the prospering of human beings. That is how SA was described, which means that those kinds of wants which one may consider to be morally important whether or not one is a utilitarian—death-bed wishes, etc.—seem to be more vulnerable than the wants which come from SA. Nevertheless I claim that the very fact that one is prepared to consider death-bed wishes morally important will also make one inclined to regard SA as morally important.

One example considered above was W. E. May's, who at a glance seemed to be a proponent of the idea of human beings having moral value in themselves. It turned out, however, that they had such a value in virtue of having a spirit, according to May. Therefore, even if all members of *Homo sapiens* and no other members actually had a spirit it would not *in itself* be important whether or not someone was such a member, but instead being a human being would be important for the sake of those properties *associated with* being a human being. (See Chapter 3.)

But if this is how to describe our attitude towards humanity, then we also have to admit that it will display the same kind of vulnerability as the death-bed wish considered above, namely it matters a great deal whether we share this belief, i.e. whether we believe that all human beings have the kind of spirit May is talking about. If not, I can see no obvious reason—besides the indirect one—to pay any regard to the attitude in question.

So here we seem to have a common-sense principle which says that if you falsely believe that A is an attendant property to B and if what you value ultimately is B, which means that you would not value A if it were not for the fact that it was associated with B, then getting A will (in itself) be of no value to you.

Unfortunately, things are more complicated than this. In Chapter 3 we discussed a psychological principle according to which there is a tendency in us to regard things which initially had an exclusively indirect value as directly valuable as well. In other words, there is a tendency to confuse what is directly and indirectly valuable. Furthermore, I also expressed a suspicion in Chapter 3 that at least part of SA is a result of this kind of confusion, either in ourselves or in those people who gave us our upbringing (or in someone else).

If you are able to *give reason* for claiming that human beings have a special kind of value, then there is a risk that you embrace an attitude according to which humans beings have their value on indirect grounds (which is to embrace something else than SA). Moreover, if it occurred to you that these reasons rest on some belief which in your opinion is false (for instance, that human beings have a special kind of spirit), then common sense will prescribe that you ignore this attitude (while paying attention to the side-effects of doing so). So, it will make a moral difference whether or not your attitude to the importance of being a human is irrational in the sense that it attaches indirect importance to a species membership on false grounds.

5.6 Irrational Preferences in Preference Utilitarianism

Until now I have discussed the question of irrational attitudes in common-sense terms. I have tried to show what our reactions would be independently of our moral theory. Let me also briefly state what reason a utilitarian will have for denying an attitude moral importance if it rests on a false belief concerning either means and ends or attendant properties.

In my view the fundamental aim of utilitarianism should be to maximize what is *intrinsically* valuable, understood as satisfying intrinsic desires. What is valuable both personally and impersonally is nothing but the satisfaction of such desires. Now, suppose you have a false belief concerning what is a means towards something valuable; suppose you falsely believe that A is a means towards B, and that you value A exclusively for the fact that it in your opinion is a means towards B. Making it the case that you get B will *not*, then, lead to the satisfaction of an intrinsic want and is therefore, other things being equal, according to this theory worthless.

This is easy to illustrate. Suppose you want to be remembered as a great artist and believe that building an enormous tower of motor-car tyres actually will give you a place in the history of art. Suppose furthermore that I am absolutely sure that you are wrong in this belief. Instead I am confident that building the tower at the most can place you in the Guinness Book of Records, and that is not what you strive for. Obviously I have no preference utilitarian reason to help you in your project, since I realize that what you actually value will not be the case even if you succeed in building the tower. To build the tower is an instrumental want of yours, i.e. a want derived from your intrinsic want to be a great artist together with your false belief that building the tower will make you so.

And this situation is exactly similar to the question of human dignity. If what you ultimately want is to respect beings with a certain kind of spirit and if you falsely believe that human beings have got this spirit, which explains your instrumental want about respecting human beings, then on the condition that only satisfaction of intrinsic interests counts, there will be no utilitarian value in respecting humans.

5.7 A Serious Objection

I have claimed that human beings *are* special in so far as they *think* they are. There is a widespread attitude to this effect and I have tried to show that this attitude has to be accounted for. I have also tried to show that this is an attitude which is reasonable to consider whether or not you are a utilitarian— ignoring a preference is something we spontaneously think will call for arguments, especially ignoring a preference which is almost universally held.

But—and that is the problem—this reasoning seems to be applicable to other subjects where most of us would hesitate to draw this kind of conclusion. For instance, what are we to say if many people of a certain race regard people of another race as inferior?

The idea is of course that if an attitude according to which belonging to a certain *species* is morally important should have any weight, then why not also an attitude according to which belonging to a certain human *race* is important?[13] What I have invented here seems to be a perfect defence of racism. Especially problematic seems to be the situation where very many people have negative attitudes towards a smaller number of people, which in history has been the case concerning for instance the Jews.

I believe that several replies are possible here. Let us look at two of them.

(1) The most important explanation why our reasoning will not support racism is that I believe that more preferences will be frustrated in the long run if racism is encouraged than if anti-racism is. This is of course a guess, but I think it is a qualified one, since I find it hard to believe that humanity in the long run has any use for this kind of attitude. On the contrary, it seems to be the cause of much of the world's misery, such as wars and hostility.

Furthermore, we have to remember that nowadays there is an almost world-wide and strong opinion against racism and that is of course an attitude which should be weighed *against* every kind of preference *for* racism. If I am correct in what I claimed in the previous chapter, then a person who dislikes racism is harmed if racial persecution takes place, even if these actions will not in *physical* terms affect her at all. And that is a kind of harm which is morally relevant. Therefore, my thesis about counting various kinds of attitudes morally will not be a potential argument for supporting racism.

This reply is somewhat dangerous, since you may ask why the same is not also true concerning the attitude that humans are special. We may ask whether SA really in the long run will create more happiness than unhappiness. And remember now that we are talking not only of the effects for human beings but instead of the effects for all those beings which have moral standing according to our theory.

Can we really claim that the total effects of SA can be defended in utilitarian terms, i.e. that we have utilitarian reasons to encourage people to retain this attitude instead of radically changing it towards an outlook in which human beings and other animals are more equal? Think of the factory farms and think of all the experiments performed on animals—can we really believe that more happiness than suffering has resulted from these things *if we also count the effects on the animals*?

We must, however, distinguish between two things, namely between (a) whether the way we have treated the animals can be defended in utilitarian terms, and (b) whether we can give a utilitarian defence of treating human beings and animals differently. To say that we have mistreated the animals is not to say that we should treat them as if they were just as morally important as human beings. To say that we cannot defend the way experiments have been performed on animals in history is not to say that we should stop all

---

[13] This objection is formulated by, among others, Helga Kuhse (1987: 212–3).

experiments on animals. It is true that SA has been historically devastating in utilitarian terms, but that is not to condemn the attitude in itself. I believe that some kind of attitude according to which humans are more valuable in themselves may have a utilitarian justification, on condition that it does not express itself in action the way it has done in the past.

And that is one of the big differences between SA and for instance racism. We have no reason to believe that the latter kind of attitude can be justified in this way. What kind of good consequences will follow from the fact that people believe that skin colour has moral importance? Concerning SA it is easier to imagine a situation where people breed animals, for instance by keeping sheep on dry and poor land, and where everybody including the animals will gain by this arrangement. Therefore, even if it *is* true that SA in the past has had consequences which might be comparable to the bad consequences of racist attitudes, the big difference is that we can imagine a morally acceptable situation where SA could have a place.

(2) The second reply concentrates on the distinction between properties which have an intrinsic importance and properties which have an importance in virtue of what they are associated with.

Suppose that Jews are persecuted because non-Jews believe that Jews kill Christian children (which once was a widespread belief). The difference between this attitude and SA is that it is founded on a belief about the properties of some of the individuals in the group which the attitude is directed at. One type of reply is to ask for an explanation why someone who has this belief persecutes *all* Jews (if that is what he does). If a group of people is valued (positively or negatively) not for what they are in themselves—e.g. Jews— but for the sake of a property which is associated with the group, then there seems to be no reason to attach the value in question to a member of this group who lacks this attendant property.

There is an even more important reply. If one has a negative attitude towards the Jews because of some kind of property which one believes can be associated with them, and if this belief is false, then there will be no reason to take this attitude into account. The explanation is what we said about preference utilitarianism: it is reasonable to assign value only to what will lead to the satisfaction of an *intrinsic* desire, and what the racist in our example seems to value intrinsically is that someone who kills Christian children should be persecuted. But if it is false that Jews do that, then by persecuting the Jews the racist will not have his intrinsic want satisfied.

This is a reply which I believe has got a wide application, since I guess that racism is very often founded on false beliefs in this way. Take for instance the idea of the chosen people, which in Popper's words

assumes that God has chosen one people to function as the selected instrument of His will, and that this people will inherit the earth. In this doctrine, the law of historical development is laid down by the Will of God (1966: 8).

If all this is false, then we will not achieve what this people believes will be achieved by satisfying their wants. To let this people dominate another will *not* be to please God—for several reasons—and to please him seems to be the important thing.

Now, I am well aware that this kind of reply also is potentially dangerous for my thesis that SA concerns the *intrinsic* value of being a living human.[14] What I have said above is that racism often is not an intrinsic attitude. What makes me believe that the same is not true of SA? Well, I do not believe that SA will include all kinds of partiality towards the human species, or, if you prefer, I do not believe that SA is *only* about the intrinsic value of being a living human. There are probably certain aspects of our treatment of non-humans that are to be explained as a result of false beliefs (concerning, for instance, capacity for having pain sensations). What I want to do in coming chapters (starting with Chapter 7) is to show that there is also a case for claiming that SA to a large extent is an intrinsic attitude. Whether or not I am successful in these plans will have to be judged then.

5.8 Conclusion

The upshot of this discussion is that it will be important to consider the reason behind SA in order to be sure that we have a reason to take it into account in our moral thinking. (And I believe that this is true whether or not we are preference utilitarians.) We have already discussed the possibility that SA might be irrational in the sense that we have confused what is indirectly important with what is directly important. The origin of our attitude is that we believe that human beings are important in virtue of some property or some complex of properties which humans typically have over and above simply being human. However, this attitude can be transformed into an attitude in which human beings are important *per se* without it being possible for those who embrace the attitude to give reasons for this.

From the intuitionist perspective it might be relevant to consider what changes you would undergo in certain hypothetical circumstances (realizing certain facts about the origin of your attitudes). From the utilitarian perspective on the other hand it is only relevant to consider actual changes of your attitudes. You have the attitudes you have and as long as you have them you have to reckon with them, and there is no place, in my view, for attitudes you would have in certain circumstances unless these circumstances actually materialize.

Things are different when we talk of an attitude that is built on a false belief, since in this case it might also from a preference utilitarian perspective be negligible, although the attitude is there whatever we do to eliminate it. Satisfying it will never lead to satisfaction of an *intrinsic* want anyway (which

---

[14] I owe this objection to Ingmar Persson.

is just another way of saying that it *cannot* be satisfied). So in a sense, it is more risky to have an attitude which you are able to give some reasons for— the risk is that your reasons are defective, whereas if you are unable to give any reasons for your attitude that will prove that the object of your attitude is intrinsically valued.

This means that we may have to look into the reasons for claiming that human beings are morally special, even when it is claimed that humans have their value solely in virtue of being human. Therefore, I will devote one coming chapter (Chapter 9) to investigate some well-known defences of SA.

CHAPTER 6

ELEMENTS IN THE PHENOMENOLOGY OF SA

The idea of a human dignity may in many cases be described as an idea of a moral privilege. And indeed it is normally a privilege to be placed before another kind of being when resources are allocated. In the same sense it can be a privilege to know that there are moral reasons not to kill someone who belongs to the kind of species to which one happens to belong oneself. These privileges are fairly general and there are reasons to believe that there is more to say about their content. To be able to do so we have to give a more detailed account of what SA prescribes.

Let us now consider some of the elements in (the phenomenology of) SA.

6.1 Objectivity

The first element is about the *objective* value of being a human, that is, the value which is to be attached to every human being in virtue of her species membership is independent of her value for others.[1] In Dworkin's terminology this is what it means to be *intrinsically* valuable in contrast to being *subjectively* valuable. An object is valuable in this sense, he says,

if its value is *independent* of what people happen to enjoy or want or need or what is good for them. Most of us treat at least some objects or events as intrinsically valuable in that way: we think we should admire and protect them because they are important in themselves, and not just if or because we or others want or enjoy them. Many people think that great paintings, for example, are intrinsically valuable (1993: 71–2).

But the belief in the objective value of being a human is, I believe, much more widespread than the belief in the objective value of great works of art. This is of course not philosophically important in itself. But it may give rise to some interesting points. For instance, I believe that SA in fact is one of the most widespread evaluative attitudes, and this is why it has been important to me to analyse SA and to draw moral conclusions from the fact that SA is that widespread. Furthermore, what I have tried to do is to show that SA is for most people one of their most *important* evaluative attitudes. This does not automatically mean that SA is a particularly *strong* attitude. For some people—preferably devout Christians—SA is indeed a very important part of

---

[1] Observe that we discussed a related idea in Chapter 4. However, the present discussion concerns a phenomenal question—what kinds of values something has in people's eyes—whereas the discussion in Chapter 4 concerned the meta-ethical question whether this should be the general understanding of values.

their conception of the world. And actually, the idea of human dignity seems to be most vigorously defended by these people. This can be seen from the philosophical discussions of the subject but also in public debates concerning, for instance, abortion and euthanasia. But how strong is SA normally?

Actually I believe that an art-lover might value the preservation of a great painting more than most embracers of SA will value the fact that a human being is not killed. One seldom reads in newspapers about murders taking place in foreign countries unless they are extreme in some way, but if someone should cut a great painting into pieces, this would probably make an echo in the rest of the world.

I do not think there is a value in claiming that SA necessarily is a particularly *strong* attitude and that this is what lies behind its importance for normal people. The importance of SA has instead to do with what we said before, i.e. its universality, and furthermore with its *centrality*, i.e. to many people it is an attitude which is tied to very many of their moral opinions in such issues as abortion, practical solidarity, animal rights, and so on. This too is something I have tried to illustrate in this text.

Objective value is to be contrasted with *subjective* value. Dworkin defines this in the following way:

Something is *subjectively* valuable only to people who happen to desire it. Scotch whiskey, watching football games, and lying in the sun are valuable only for people, like me, who happen to enjoy them. I do not think that others who detest them are making any kind of mistake or failing to show proper respect for what is truly valuable. They just happen not to like or want what I do (1993: 71).[2]

The contrast with this kind of subjective value is obvious both in connection with the value of human life and the value of great works of art. If someone does not share SA, we tend to regard her as morally insensitive or defective in some sense and similarly, if someone does not share our high opinion of a work of art we tend to regard her as in some sense aesthetically unqualified.

Many aesthetic judgements are subjective. For instance, I do not believe that other people have a defect if they are unable to appreciate the same kinds of flowers as I do. I know that the reason why I find some flowers beautiful is the kind of associations they arouse in me—concerning, for instance, memories from my childhood—associations which I hardly expect other people to get.

I also think it is fairly common that *all* aesthetic values of a person are subjective. And that is the reason why, as we said above, it probably is much more common to assign objective value to human life compared to assigning this kind of value to aesthetic objects.

---

[2] Compare Vinit Haksar: "You can pursue certain personal ideals (such as living the life of a monk) without thinking that others are wrong in not pursuing these ideals, but you cannot show similar tolerance in the sphere of human rights" (1979: 92).

I think there are other important disanalogies between SA and aesthetic values. One is that you will feel much more uncomfortable or upset[3] about others lacking SA if you embrace it yourself compared to what you will feel when discovering that other people do not share your aesthetic attitudes (about what has objective value). Hand in hand with this difference goes another one: I believe we have a much stronger tendency to try to change other people's attitudes towards the objective value of human life than to try to change their attitudes concerning the objective value of Rembrandt's self-portraits or some other aesthetic object.

This also has to be qualified. It seems that this discrepancy exists particularly when you are not directly affected. For instance, if your neighbour is busy destroying his old house which in your opinion is objectively valuable (for its aesthetic properties), then you might feel forced to try to stop him, just as you will feel forced to try to stop him from seriously maltreating his child. By contrast, if the same combination of actions takes place in another part of your town, you might probably feel obliged only to try to stop the person from maltreating his child. (I am not going to decide here on a definition of "moral", but I am sure that one of the distinctive properties of such an attitude is its imperative character, which means that you will naturally want and strive to change those attitudes which do not harmonize with your own.)

6.2 Objective Values and Utilitarianism

We may also consider whether these objective values are important from a utilitarian perspective. In one sense they are not, but in another sense they are. Since, according to utilitarianism, no objective values exist, a utilitarian cannot possibly reckon on their existence. Therefore, in a sense the element considered here is directly anti-utilitarian—it affirms exactly what utilitarianism denies. However, one point made in this study is that there is no utilitarian restriction concerning the content of an attitude as long as satisfaction is generated by the fact that we pay regard to it. In this sense there will be a utilitarian value also in satisfying an anti-utilitarian attitude, on condition that satisfying it does not demand for instance significant frustration of other attitudes.

But it will always be interesting for a utilitarian to know not only what will happen if a certain attitude is satisfied compared to if it is not, but also compared to if another possible attitude is encouraged and satisfied instead. Strictly speaking, this means that every attitude has to be compared to what is optimal from a utilitarian perspective, and it may be the case that the kind of objective value discussed here fails in this regard.

---

[3] According to Gibbard (1990) *anger* has together with guilt a central role in morality.

The practical bearing of this is not clear. A utilitarian has to strive for the ideal whatever she does, whether this means satisfying a preference or trying to change it. But it is also a truism that not all preferences can be changed and that those which can, cannot be changed to the extent required by the ideal utilitarian picture of the world. Therefore, we cannot escape the fact that most attitudes *are there* whatever we may think of them, and that the decision will concern whether or not to *satisfy* them, and will not concern whether or not to *change* them.

Within these existing attitudes we must try to satisfy only those which come closest to the ideal, and therefore we have to ask ourselves what will happen if we take into account objective evaluations instead of some other existing evaluation in the case of a conflict. Furthermore, we have to put the question whether we want to encourage people to stick to these kinds of values in the future as well.

The kind of attitudes to consider in a utilitarian calculation will be manifold, ranging from broadly utilitarian (altruistic) ones to different forms of anti-utilitarian ones. For instance, a utilitarian has to count with egoistic desires despite the fact that this kind of desire affirms what utilitarianism denies, namely that there is a special importance to be attached to the fact that I am I. So there is no paradox involved in the fact that utilitarianism reckons with anti-utilitarian attitudes.

6.3 Inviolability

The second element in the phenomenology of SA is that it assigns an *inviolable* value to their objects. This element too is described by Dworkin:

We must notice a further and crucial distinction: between what we value incrementally—what we want more of, no matter how much we already have—and what we value only once it already exists. [...] The hallmark of the sacred as distinct from the incrementally valuable is that the sacred is intrinsically valuable because—and therefore only once—it exists. It is inviolable because of what it represents or embodies. It is not important that there be more people. But once a human life has begun, it is very important that it flourish and not be wasted (1993: 73–4).

In my view the distinction concerns a difference which is normally less clear-cut than what is suggested by the quotation. For instance, let us look at a typical example of an object which is valued incrementally: money.

No doubt we would value money even if we had never had any. So there is a value not only in protecting an existing fortune, but also in obtaining one and in increasing an existing one. However, this does not necessarily mean that we want to increase our fortune beyond all limits. Dworkin says that an incremental value is something we want more of, no matter how much we already have. But to be sure, very few things in life are valued in that way. Normally there is a point where we think we have got enough of some object which is valued not only because we already have it.

I believe one might say that normally an object is regarded as having incremental value *within certain limits*. And I also believe that for some objects which are incrementally valuable, when the point is reached where one ceases to value having even more of them, one starts to regard them as inviolable to a certain extent. For instance, I may not wish (i.e. it may be the case that I lack such a wish) to have more money but nevertheless be sad to lose the money I already have—I value the protection of what I have in my bank account more than increasing the sum of money there.[4]

Now, my example concerns an object which typically has no intrinsic value (although we have also discussed the transition from being instrumentally to being intrinsically valued). As I interpret Dworkin, however, his distinction between what is incrementally valuable and what is inviolable (or sacred, which is the same thing) is a distinction within the class of intrinsic values. He writes:

Some things are not only intrinsically but incrementally valuable. We tend to treat knowledge that way, for example. Our culture wants to know about archaeology and cosmology and galaxies many millions of light-years away—even though little of that knowledge is likely to be of any practical benefit—and we want to know as much of all that as we can (1993: 73).

I think that two different distinctions figure in this discussion. Dworkin has distinguished between intrinsic (in our terminology objective) and subjective value, where an object has intrinsic value independently of the value it has for some subject, whereas this is not true of an object which is subjectively valuable. Now, Dworkin also distinguishes between these values and instrumental ones. For instance, he asks: "Is human life subjectively or instrumentally or intrinsically valuable?" (1993: 72) I believe that something may be valuable *in itself* but nevertheless *for some subject*, which means that I can see no natural contrast between subjective and intrinsic values, i.e. values as ends instead of means. So it seems as if Dworkin is sliding between two different senses of intrinsic value, one being the sense one naturally gets when contrasting it with subjective value, whereas the other is what one gets when contrasting it with instrumental value. (I have used the terms "objective" and "intrinsic" value to make this distinction.)

I would not say that knowledge has objective value. It is true that knowledge may be intrinsically valued in contrast with instrumentally valued, but when we discuss the value of human life (phenomenologically) this is to be contrasted with both instrumental and subjective value. I claim, therefore, that knowledge is treated as something valuable only on condition that it is somehow valuable for someone. There is no other explanation why we, for instance, would not be prepared to finance a project which aimed at counting the leaves on all the trees in Hyde Park for no other reason than obtaining this knowledge.

---

[4] This can perhaps be seen as an instance of a principle which Robin M. Hogarth describes in the following way: "'losses loom larger than gains'. [...] For most people the displeasure of a loss is experienced more intensely than the pleasure of an objectively equivalent gain" (1987: 100).

We support the kind of knowledge which we believe may interest people (in the short or long run), even when we affirm the value of knowledge independently of its practical value.

The example from knowledge will also illustrate another point which I tried to make above, namely that even when an object has incremental value, there are limits to how much we want to have of an object with this kind of value. At least, there is normally a point where more knowledge becomes less valuable. For instance, it might be interesting to know whether some historical person used to eat pea soup for lunch, but not what temperature this soup usually had (unless her preferences were extreme in some sense). There is therefore a limit to what we value knowing about historical persons and events, and I believe that is true whatever branch of knowledge we look at.

One might object that Dworkin is not talking of particular branches of knowledge, but instead of knowledge generally, just as he talks of human life generally, and after having made this distinction we may well claim that knowledge generally has an incremental value in Dworkin's sense. But I doubt this. I doubt that we would value getting more knowledge (generally) however much we already have. I find it strange to believe that there is a limit as far as every particular branch is concerned but no limit as far as knowledge generally is concerned, since what is knowledge generally if not the sum of all the branches of knowledge?

I claim that objects which are valued incrementally seem to be valued in that way only within certain limits. I now want to propose that a similar kind of reservation should be made concerning objects which are inviolably valuable. First of all, I believe we tend to treat a human life as something less inviolable if there already is a vast number of people; the strength of SA will probably be affected by the number of people one has to compete with for the bare necessities of life.

The second kind of reservation is that we must not think that an object which in our eyes is inviolably valuable has value *only* when it exists and not at all when it does not exist (and never has existed). Of course, many people value not only the fact that we refrain from killing the people who already exist, but also the fact that there will exist people in the future. Therefore, many of us believe that it is valuable that there be more people and indeed valuable that the human race does not end. Some of us, and I guess there are quite a number of them, even believe that ending the human race, for instance by taking a drug which would render us infertile, would be about the worst thing it would be possible to do.[5]

And I actually think this is true not only when the object concerns human lives, but also when it concerns other things, for instance works of art. This

---

[5] Cf. Jonathan Glover (1977: 69–70).

is suggested by what Dworkin says: "We attach great value to works of art once they exist, even though we care less about whether more of them are produced. Of course we may believe that the continued production of *great art* is tremendously important [...]" (1993: 74). Here Dworkin seems to allow for the possibility that sacred objects are valuable not only once they exist, but also that we may value very much that there exists a certain minimum amount of them (whether or not they have existed before) and furthermore that we may value having more of them even when we already have this minimum amount.

6.4 Irreplaceability

The third feature in the phenomenology of attitudes like SA is that objects which have an objective and inviolable value are *irreplaceable*. I mention this as a separate element, but actually I believe we may show it to be derived from the element discussed in 6.3, which concerned inviolability.

Let me illustrate by referring to the vegetarianism issue. Many people who defend meat eating do so by claiming that there is nothing wrong in itself in killing animals, at least not animals with fairly small mental capacities. Frey describes the argument in the following way:

> though the killing of food animals does diminish the amount of pleasure (happiness, utility) in the world, this loss is made good by the creation of additional food animals, who lead lives roughly as pleasant as those of the animals consumed. Thus, just as the level of water in a glass falls but is made up again, if, after a drink, the glass is replenished, so, while replacement remains possible, the loss in the amount of pleasure in the world is constantly made good; accordingly, there can be nothing wrong in killing, say, chickens for food (1983: 161).

Of course, we have to make certain assumptions here, for instance that the chickens we eat really are animals that have lived a pleasant life and that they are replaced by other chickens that will live equally pleasant lives, and furthermore that the killing takes place painlessly. We have reason to doubt that these conditions are fulfilled in modern chicken factories. But *if* they are, then killing and eating these chickens will seem to be morally unproblematic—the chickens are *replaceable*.

Now, what SA says is that human beings do not have this kind of property. And this is intimately related to what we said above. How intimate the relationship is will of course depend on the way we choose to define the property of being irreplaceable and also how we choose to formulate the element discussed in 6.3, i.e. whether inviolable is taken to mean absolutely inviolable or if we just mean inviolable within certain limits, and furthermore how we understand what that would mean in turn.

Let us first consider what it means more precisely to say that human beings are not replaceable. The content of such an attitude will depend on what it means to say that a being *is* replaceable. There seem to be some alternatives. We have already seen Frey's suggestion, where being replaceable means that one's death may be compensated for by the creation of additional beings. Compare this with Singer's description:

> Even when the animal killed would have lived pleasantly, it is at least arguable that no wrong is done if the animal killed will, as a result of the killing, be replaced by another animal living an equally pleasant life. Taking this view involves holding that a wrong done to an existing being can be made up for by a benefit conferred on an as yet non-existent being (1993: 132–3).[6]

I actually believe that Frey and Singer have fairly similar opinions on what it means to treat a being as replaceable, but I want to use an opportunity created by a difference in their formulations, in order to point to one distinction.

There is a seed to a strong formulation of a denial of replaceability in connection with humans, if we start out from Frey's quotation on replaceability. Frey does not in this quotation say anything explicit about the condition for compensating for the killing of a certain being. What would it take—the creation of another being which leads an equally pleasurable life, or the creation of a being which leads a more pleasurable life (or the creation of more than one being which leads an equally happy life)? What Frey says is merely that it takes additional animals, according to the replaceability thesis, to make good for the killing of animals.

Frey talks about a level of water in a glass which falls but is made up again, and that may naturally be interpreted as a suggestion that the loss of a certain amount of pleasure would be made good with the same amount of additional pleasure. But depending on what animal one is talking of—for instance pigs or chickens—the number of animals it takes to reach this amount may differ. Therefore, the picture used by Frey does not automatically determine the conditions of replaceability.

The question now is whether SA contains a strong or a weak denial of the replaceability of human beings, where the strong one would deny that the death of one human being could be made good by the creation of any number of beings and the weak one only denies that it could be made good by the creation of another equally happy being.

The only way of settling this question is to listen to one's intuitions, since they are the very source of all the elements in SA. What kind of denial will be the most attractive one intuitively speaking? Well, that depends of course also on how we understand the weak denial more exactly—does it take just a few human beings to make up for the killing of one, or does it take very many? Suppose the killing of one happy human could be made good by creating a whole new world of happy people.

---

[6] Singer's position is that there is a difference between self-conscious and non-self-conscious beings in that it is only the latter kind of being that is replaceable. This is a suggestion which will be considered in a coming chapter, where we discuss some attempts to show that being a human is morally important in an indirect way.

Such a case might be hard to judge, because we may have conflicting intuitions. To be sure, many of us have some kind of utilitarian intuitions in which there is a value in the creation of additional people. But since we embrace SA as well, we will not gladly regard people as replaceable, since if my proposal concerning the universality and content of SA is correct, we will also have a tendency to deny that one human being might be justifiably killed for the creation of others. So uncertainty in connection with an extreme example like this does not automatically mean that SA contains a weak denial of the replaceability thesis, but may instead mean a conflict between intuitions pulling in different directions, that is to say, between intuitions stemming from SA and intuitions stemming from somewhere else.

There might also be certain tensions within SA concerning examples like this one, since how could it be rational to regard a certain object as very valuable once it exists but not valuable at all before (unless it will exist whatever decision about its existence we make)? The conjunction of these proposals is strange, since once the human being who replaces another human being exists, then she will be equally valuable as the one she replaced. How could we be wholly insensitive to this fact before she exists? Furthermore, how could there be a value in the preservation of an object without there being any value in the *mere* existence of that object? And if there is a value in the mere existence of an object, how come there is no value in making it the case that an object the mere existence of which is valuable will exist in the future?

Suppose the third element in SA is about a strong denial of replaceability for humans. Let us continue our discussion of whether or not this is a reasonable assumption by comparing it with inviolability. What is the relationship between inviolability and irreplaceability? May we derive irreplaceability from inviolability?

That will of course also depend on what sense we decide to give to inviolability. Remember that we considered whether the thesis about the inviolability of human lives should be given a strong or a weak interpretation. Dworkin suggests a strong interpretation. Recall what he says: "It is not important that there be more people. But once a human life has begun, it is very important that it flourish and not be wasted". Here there seems to be no value *at all* in the creation of more people, but value only in the protection of those who exist. He also says that "the sacred is intrinsically valuable because—and therefore only once—it exists".

With a strong interpretation of inviolability, the strong interpretation of irreplaceability will follow directly. If a human life is valuable only once it exists and if there is no value at all in creating a human life, then of course we could never justify the killing of one being with the creation of other human beings, no matter how many. The irreplaceability of a human life would follow from its inviolability.

I tried to show that a weaker interpretation is much more plausible, that is to say, there is *more* value in the protection of a human life than in the creation of it. You may express this thought in different ways. Either you may say that inviolability is not the only kind of value which human life has—it is also to a certain extent incrementally valuable (which seems to be what is meant by saying that human life is inviolable within certain limits). Or you may say that the sacredness or inviolability of human life means that there is value *particularly* in the protection of it. And I guess that this (the second alternative) is also what Dworkin would say. For instance, when he makes an analogy between the sacredness of human life and works of art, he says: "We attach great value to works of art once they exist, even though we care *less* about whether more of them are produced" (1993: 74, my emphasis).[7] This seems to suggest that inviolability only concerns the proportionately stronger value in preservation than in creation.

But if we decide to understand inviolability in this weak sense, then we could not possibly understand irreplaceability in a strong sense, since that would be a contradiction. Irreplaceability would deny that there is a value in creating additional humans, whereas inviolability would claim that there is such a value.

Since we are not here considering a philosophical system but instead a pre-theoretic attitude, we might indeed admit that it contains contradictions. But I believe that a better strategy will be to try to regard SA as a more or less coherent attitude, especially since there is plenty of room left for interpretation. SA is vague enough to allow for a decision in these matters, and therefore I prefer the weak interpretation of irreplaceability as well as the weak interpretation of inviolability.

6.5 Dignity

To call the fourth element in SA "dignity" is an oversimplification. It is not the same thing as saying that this element is the central and most important one in SA. But often when we talk of human dignity we think of Kant's injunction to treat people always as ends and never merely as means. This is perhaps the most well-known conception of human dignity.

F. M. Kamm writes:

---

[7] It seems that Dworkin makes a normative distinction here between works of art and great works of art. He continues in the following way: "Of course we may believe that the continued production of *great* art is tremendously important—that the more truly wonderful objects a culture produces the better [...]" (1993:74). I have not made this distinction in my discussion. But if Dworkin is right I believe he would say that the value of good works of art is similar to that of human life, whereas bad works of art are valueless and great works of art are both incrementally and inviolably valuable.

Consider a family who conceives for the sake of having a child whose marrow might be able to save their other child. They are quite willing to give this child a happy life and love it even if its marrow does not match their first child's. Does this mean there is no problem? Rather than having the child for its own sake, they create it for the sake of another (1992: 135).

Suppose the new child's marrow does *not* match their first child and that the child is given a happy life nevertheless. Then the case will not be so problematic, I think, since treating someone as a means only, will in most people's eyes require that we let this someone endure something which is negative or at least not positive from her perspective in order for someone else to receive something that is positive from *his* perspective. As Kamm notes: "we may treat them as means as long as we also treat them as ends. One way of doing this is to intentionally use them as long as this does not conflict with their interests and in fact promotes their interests" (1992: 136). But if one does not even *use* the child's marrow, then one might question whether it is treated as a means in any sense of that word.

Therefore, the principle of dignity will be more easily applied to cases where someone is *harmed* in order to benefit another.[8]

But this can be questioned. It is a fact that many people believe that taking tissue and organs from aborted foetuses is morally problematic. There might be several ways of explaining this, but I do believe that one of the reasons is precisely what the fourth element is about: one must not treat a human being *merely* as a means, which will be the case if we take tissue and organs from these foetuses, notwithstanding their mental level. And it goes without saying that in doing so we will not in any sense harm these foetuses, if the tissue and organs are taken when the abortion already has taken place and when the foetus is therefore dead.

6.6 Equality

We could preliminarily describe the fifth element in a very simple way, namely that all human beings are equally valuable, i.e. that all humans have the values considered above to the same extent. As Michael Meyer puts it: "One's human dignity, if it is a mark of anything, is a mark of one's equality on some fundamental level with other human beings" (1989: 524).[9]

This is an extremely problematic standpoint. For instance, consider once again what Dworkin says about the sacredness of a human life, namely that it means that "once a human life has begun, it is very important that it flourish and not be wasted". One very natural question is: suppose we have a human life that does not flourish and that could not possibly be made to

---

[8] For instance, as Kasper Lippert-Rasmussen notes: "it is not permissible, according to commonsense morality, to kill one to save five others" (1994: 1).

[9] In a similar vein Michael S. Pritchard claims that human dignity "is something shared by all men regardless of the offices they may hold or the social standing they may have" (1971–2: 301).

flourish. Would that life be equally valuable as a life that does flourish and would it therefore be equally important to protect? According to one interpretation, Dworkin says it is important that a human life flourish and not be wasted on condition that it could be made to flourish, but less or not at all important if it could *not* be made to flourish. But at the same time, that would intuitively seem be too cynical an attitude. The idea of a human dignity seems to be an idea of something that does not disappear when you become unhappy.

What do we say about a human being who no longer wants to live, perhaps because of a terminal and painful illness?[10] In the introduction I claimed that the notion of dignity applies to this being whether or not she wants it. One solution could be to make a distinction between human dignity and the value of protecting a human being. Accordingly, the humans in these situations have human dignity although there is less value in protecting their lives, at least if we make the important assumption that these people do not consider their life to be worth living any longer. However, this is a very problematic thought, since in what, then, does their dignity consist? What does it mean to claim that all human beings have an equal part in the human dignity, if it turns out that this does not mean that all humans should be protected to the same degree?

Perhaps the thought *is* simply that human dignity means having a right to be respected, i.e. having one's wishes respected. That would naturally mean that we should not protect someone's life against her own wish. But observe that this is a completely new understanding of SA and it does not seem to have anything to do with the elements considered above. SA denies that human dignity varies with the strength of our desires to go on with life; a happy existence does not have a human dignity to a higher degree than a less happy existence.

Indeed, we have considered one kind of variation in the value of a human life, namely that this value probably is dependent upon the degree of overpopulation, which means that a human life presumably will be considered as something less valuable for a person who has to fight against the great disadvantages of living in an overpopulated area of the world. This will not necessarily contradict the equality thesis, however, since what this element says is only that whatever value you are prepared to give to a human life, SA prescribes that you should give it *equally* to all human beings.

But there is a problem here, a problem that ought to be discussed also in connection with the other elements. If we can find these elements in the *phenomenology* of SA, that is to say, if the special value assigned to human beings has this very appearance for us, that is not the same thing as claiming that these elements are included in our actual evaluations of other human beings. Here too we may question the seriousness of an attitude, and I

---

[10] See, for instance, Paul Ramsey (1970: 115–7).

believe that the fifth element has a special standing, since it is hard to make sense of the idea that we would put into practice an equality principle. In what sense can we be said to live as if we believe that all human beings are equally valuable?[11]

It is very hard, of course, to investigate the question as to whether a certain universally embraced attitude is serious or not, and neither is that the task of an ethicist. But I guess we can more easily find practical evidence of the first four elements, and therefore I prefer not to put any emphasis on the fifth one concerning equality. Besides, as we shall see in the coming chapters, when we turn to practical tests of SA, we will be concerned more with simple gut feelings than with their exact mental content.

To sum up this chapter, I have tried to examine what it means more exactly to say that a being has a special *value* in virtue of being human. Using what Dworkin has written on the subject as a basis for my examination of the phenomenological elements in SA, I found four such elements. In the next chapter I want to examine in more detail whether we really believe that being human is something valuable *in itself*.

---

[11] See also Helga Kuhse (1987: 15–6).

CHAPTER 7

TOOLEY'S ARGUMENTS AGAINST SA

[It] is an open question whether genetic determination can be fine-grained enough to preset a particular belief. Maybe heredity can only mildly affect the probability with which a belief is formed.

Roy A. Sorensen *Thought Experiments*

Recall how Wertheimer described SA: "most people believe that being human has *moral cachet*: viz., a human being has human status in virtue of being a human being". Remember also that we had certain difficulties when we tried to determine what this really means. The quotation can be given stronger or weaker interpretations.

We may ask whether every kind of human life is sacred in the way spelled out in the previous chapter or if only the life of human *beings* is. What Wertheimer says in the first part of the quotation supports a strong interpretation and what he says in the latter part of it seems to support a weaker one. The difference between these interpretations is shown in our attitudes to newly fertilized eggs. If we support the view that we may treat such an egg in whatever way we want; if we believe that the special worth of being human will be found merely in human organisms which have developed beyond a certain stage, if we, for instance, believe that they must have at least a certain shape (e.g. vestiges of arms, legs and a head), then we support a weaker interpretation.

There are many things that might be human, and naturally we do not want to endow them all with a special moral significance. For instance, I do not want to say that a piece of my fingernail is of any importance whatsoever. And I assume that the same could be said about a drop of my blood or a single (living) cell from my finger, etc. But what about gametes, i.e. the unfertilized egg and the sperm? Are they proper objects of SA?

There is one simple and one more complicated answer. The simple one is to say that although human beings have a special worth and although the gamete is a potential human being, this will not be enough to endow the gamete with moral significance. And this has to do with the elements discussed in the previous chapter. For instance, irreplaceability is a direct consequence of a denial of a principle saying that a potential being, i.e. a being which you could produce in order to replace an already existing being, has the same value as a being who already exists.

There is also a more complicated answer. Suppose you have a gamete which you know will develop into a human being whatever action you take.

Suppose furthermore that you may do certain things with the gamete now that might affect the well-being of the human being who develops out of it. Will these facts affect the value of the gamete, i.e. will it affect its protection value, will it make you believe that it ought to have certain privileges that will not accrue to gametes of some other species?

Evidently, we all tend to say that this gamete has a special status. We do not feel free to do whatever we want to the gamete if we know that there will some day be a full-fledged human being whose life-conditions could be influenced by our present treatment of the gamete. But I also figure that for many people the reason for this has to do exclusively with how this treatment would affect the full-fledged human being and not at all with how it would affect the gamete itself. Strictly speaking, therefore, the gamete still lacks moral standing in its own right. Something would not be a proper object of SA unless we could term the action morally right or wrong in virtue of what happened to this particular object.

Therefore, let us forget about the value of the gamete henceforth in this study.

The question from which we started remains however, namely whether Wertheimer's quotation should be given a weaker or a stronger interpretation in the following sense: is human life sacred from the moment of conception or is it necessary that a *being* in some more qualified sense is the bearer of this life in order for it to be sacred? I am not sure that we can settle this question conclusively, but I will give it a more thorough treatment in the next chapter.

Another difference in the direct-indirect dimension which we have considered in previous chapters is the difference between a *property* of an object being important either intrinsically or instrumentally. We have defined SA as an attitude according to which being human is *intrinsically* important. This must now be questioned. It should be noted once again that this issue cannot be decided conclusively. I want to show, however, that there is a case for the idea of an intrinsic importance of species membership (and against what José Luis Bermúdez calls "The Moral Irrelevance of Species Membership Principle", 1996: 379).

Many philosophers with whom I have discussed this subject have been sceptical of this idea. James Rachels expresses this scepticism in the following way:

Unqualified speciesism is the view that mere species alone is morally important. On this view, the bare fact that an individual is a member of a certain species, unsupplemented by any other consideration, is enough to make a difference in how that individual should be treated. This is not a very plausible way of understanding the relation between species and morality, and generally it is not accepted even by those who defend traditional morality (1991: 183).

Although we have not used the term "speciesism", SA is clearly speciesistic in our interpretation, at least if it is added that the certain species in question is the human one. Commonly the term "speciesism" is used derogatorily[1] to draw attention to the kinship between this attitude and such attitudes as racism, sexism, nepotism, etc. I am at this moment not interested either in the emotive tone or in what kind of arguments usually support the rejection of the attitude.

7.1 Tooley's First Counter-Argument

Michael Tooley gives three counter-examples to show that membership of the human species has no intrinsic importance. His first example is this:

Some human beings have suffered brain damage that, while so extensive as to destroy completely the neurological basis of consciousness, memory, personality, thinking, and all of the higher mental functions, has left the brain stem intact and functioning. As the brain stem controls basic bodily functions such as circulation, respiration, digestion, etc., such a human can remain alive, even without artificial life-support systems. Now if the damage is irreparable, not merely at the present stage of technology, but in principle, it seems plausible to hold that although a human organism lingers on, the conscious individual once associated with that body no longer exists, and hence that it is not even prima facie wrong to kill the human organism that remains (1983: 64).

First of all, this example will probably not convince someone who believes that there is a special value in being human, since this person typically believes that euthanasia *is* morally problematic. The example will appeal particularly to someone who already has decided to say that there is no special value in protecting human life just because it is human and who therefore, as it seems, will consider the euthanasia question to be uncontroversial.

The best kind of evidence of this is people's actual attitudes to euthanasia. It is often in cases which look exactly like this example that the question of euthanasia is raised—the *person* is irreversibly dead and what is left is only the basic biological functions of the body. And why would someone who is against (active) euthanasia in such a case be influenced by Tooley's example? It describes essentially the normal state of affairs for many chronically comatose patients. And if you are against (active) euthanasia, then typically you are against the killing of this kind of patient.

You may believe in a special worth of human beings, but nevertheless be for active euthanasia. As we noted before, it is hard to say what kind of privilege SA dictates, but if we preliminarily say that it consists of something like a right to live and have one's life protected, it does not follow from this that one has a right to have one's life protected *by any means*.

---

[1] The term is originally Richard Ryder's, who says that he "promulgated the awkward word *speciesism* to describe mankind's arrogant prejudice against other species [...] *Speciesism*, a pamphlet published in 1970. My first published comments in this field were letters to the *Daily Telegraph*, April 7th, May 2nd/3rd, and May 20th, 1969" (1979: 4, 219). See also (1989).

And the point is precisely this: not killing this being (or at least letting it die) *would* have a price, namely the price we would have to pay to take care of it. And that is a feature which does, I believe, explain why we may consider it all right to kill such a being, whether or not we like the thought of an intrinsic value in being human. (Of course, the normal thing will be to claim that letting it die would be better than killing it. But in a situation where letting the being die would be difficult—it might be painful or just take too long—I think killing would normally be preferred after all.)

Another very important feature which might influence our verdict is that persons normally have some kind of attitude towards the possibility of being in such a state described in Tooley's example. Very many people, including me, do not want to live under such circumstances, that is to say, we do not want our bodies to live in a situation like this. And I would say that is also a price that has to be taken into account.

It is true that Tooley claims it would not even be *prima facie* wrong to kill the body. But it is notoriously hard to know what features to include in a prima facie judgement of a case. It seems that we at least have to place it in some context, and then we automatically will bring in other features suggested but not explicitly mentioned in the example. Even if we try to consider a case distinct from its normal context, we have to confess that we tend to be influenced by this context in our judgements.

What is more important is that we may call into question whether it *is* true that many people would consider the fact that this being was human to be morally irrelevant. There are many distinctions to keep in mind when considering the example. One distinction concerns the content of an intuition in contrast with the strength with which we embrace it.

Suppose one agrees that it does not even seem prima facie wrong to kill the kind of being described by Tooley. In my view that may support the conclusion that "the property of being an action of killing a member of the species *Homo sapiens* cannot itself be a wrong-making characteristic of actions" (1983: 64) to a certain extent. But it will not establish a conclusion to the effect that being a member of the species *Homo sapiens* is morally *irrelevant* in connection with these thought experiments, unless we had exactly the same intuitive reactions when faced with a case where only members of other species were involved. And by "the same" is meant both content and strength.

What about a situation where one would be prepared to say with a light heart that killing a chronically comatose animal would not be prima facie wrong, whereas one would be prepared with hesitation to say the same of a human being? If there is any sense in listening to our intuitions, then it seems that we have to listen not only to *what* they say but also to how *loud* they say it.

My guess is that the person who claims that it would not be prima facie wrong to kill the human organism[2] that remains, would find it even easier to accept that conclusion, *mutatis mutandis*, if the being or organism in question had been a member of *another* species. If so, that would be enough to conclude that some kind of special worth after all pertains to human beings.

Returning to the question of the content of the intuition Tooley appeals to, I believe that we may also question whether we are serious when we claim—if that is what we do—that it is not even prima facie wrong to kill the human being in Tooley's example. Would we truly claim that it is morally speaking absolutely *indifferent* whether or not these beings are killed? Would we be prepared to do the killing ourselves? And if so, would we do it with a light heart, just as if we merely blew out a candle? Would we be prepared to kill a large number of these beings; would we be prepared to work as a professional terminator of those beings?[3]

One might reply "No, but neither would I be prepared to be a professional killer of non-human animals". One cannot argue against Tooley's example by pointing to the instinctive reactions one would have against killing the human being in the example, unless there is a *difference* in the reactions that pertains to killing humans compared to killing other (particularly higher) animals. It is true that you may describe a situation where most people would find it repugnant to carry out the killing of a large number of human beings in a purely vegetative state, but it is also true that you can describe a case in which the killing of non-humans as well would rouse aversive feelings. The intrinsic value of being human, therefore, has to be established via intuitions concerning a *difference* between cases where humans and non-humans figure.

This is a reasonable reply. However, it does not establish the kind of conclusion which Tooley wants us to draw unless it also shows that there is *no intuitive difference at all* between killing humans and non-humans in these situations. One can admit that we have an instinctive aversion against killing both comatose humans and non-humans but yet insist that there is a difference in these reactions.

Suppose there are only two jobs available and that you for several reasons very much want to have a job. One job is like the one described above— your primary function is to kill chronically comatose human beings in hospitals (let us suppose you know that they would not have protested against this and also that their friends and relatives will raise no objections). You will

---

[2] Notice that Tooley uses the term "*organism*" to refer to the humans in the example. This is a bit misleading since it may lead the thoughts to existences which are even more primitive than those in the example. Even a chronically comatose human is a *being*. By calling it an "organism" one places it in the same category as many of those forms of human life of which it is more controversial whether they are the proper object of SA, for instance newly fertilized eggs.

[3] An answer in the negative would certainly not *prove* that we believe the property of being a living human to be *intrinsically* valuable. There are alternative analyses. One will be considered at the end of the next chapter—but until then I am satisfied with claiming that a negative answer here at least *supports* my analysis of SA in terms of intrinsic importance.

have to kill, say, one patient every working day and the killing will be completely undramatic—you just inject a lethal dose of some drug. The other job involves exactly the same assignments except for the fact that now your patients are non-human animals—you have to kill one animal patient each working day. Which job would you prefer? I am pretty sure that most of us would prefer the second job and that seems to suggest that we sense a difference which is due only to membership of the human species.

It is true that there is one difference between the two jobs which cannot be eliminated very easily if we want the example to be life-like, namely a difference in appearance. A human being looks like a human person even when she is comatose, while a comatose animal of course does *not* normally look like a human person. And then you may claim that the basis for an intuitive difference between the two cases is not purely species related but is also related to some accidental overt characteristics particularly of members of our own species.

Therefore, we have not yet established an intuitive support for the idea that being human is important in itself. At the most, we have provided intuitive support for the idea that being human is morally important, and this is another thing. The question of physical appearance will have some role to play also in connection with Tooley's other examples, but in the meantime I will refrain from taking a definite standpoint on how to judge the first example.

7.2 Tooley's Second Counter-Argument

Consider then Tooley's second example:

Suppose that a disease arises that alters the genetic make-up of human beings, so that all future offspring, rather than having the sort of mental life and skills possessed by normal adult human beings today, enjoy a mental life comparable to that of chickens. If, at some point in time, all present and future humans were of this sort, would it still be seriously wrong for any non-human persons who happen to exist to kill human beings? It seems to me that it would not (1983: 66).

I might deny that it would be *seriously* wrong to kill the humans but yet claim that it would be wrong. I might claim that one (the future non-human person) is allowed to kill these human beings *in certain circumstances*, which means that killing them is allowed when one is able to give a reason for it, for example, in terms of scarcity of resources. If one kills without being able to cite these kinds of reasons, the killing is wrong, but not necessarily *seriously* so. Therefore, even with a *ceteris paribus* clause one might claim that killing these humans is wrong.

This will not enable one to establish that the biological property of being human also has intrinsic importance, unless one claims that there is a *difference* in the degree of wrongness in killing these humans compared to killing other beings, for instance chickens. And if what I claimed in connection with Tooley's first example is correct, then it is not impossible to imagine that there exists such a difference, even if it of course will be more difficult to find a realistic example to test one's intuitions against. Would we not after all see a moral difference between an act of killing a vast number of these human beings (at least if Tooley also makes the assumption that they still look like human beings)[4] and killing a vast number of chickens? That is to say, would we not have a spontaneous reaction to this effect? Consider once again the forced choice between being a terminator of either these human beings or the chickens—what would cause you more moral troubles?

Therefore, even if it *were* true that few people would be prepared to say that killing these human beings would be seriously wrong, that would not prove Tooley's point, unless he also shows that there is no intuitive difference *at all* in how we judge killing these humans compared to killing some non-human animals with comparable mental capacities, for instance, chickens.

However, things are more complicated. In the quotation, Tooley asks whether it would be *seriously* wrong to kill the resulting human beings, and my reply was built on that interpretation. But he also uses formulations which suggest a different interpretation. For instance, he asserts: "So if it would not be wrong to kill such beings, the property of being an action that kills an innocent human being cannot be a wrong-making characteristic" (1983: 66).

As one interprets Tooley here he claims that if it is not *at all* wrong to kill a being on a mental level comparable to that of a chicken, then neither will it be wrong to kill human beings whose genetic make-up is changed. Explicated in this way I believe very many of us will have less firm intuitions when judging the example.

Tooley seems to believe that killing chickens is morally uncontroversial. But surely it is not.[5] Many people who are vegetarians do not believe it to be right to kill chickens even painlessly. Furthermore, a hedonist might claim—whether or not she is also a vegetarian—that killing a chicken which otherwise would be able to derive pleasure from its life is wrong, other things being equal. In a coming chapter these questions will be considered in more detail, but what the hedonist claims here is that an action might be wrong not only in virtue of the positive harm it causes but also in virtue of the benefits of which a being might be deprived in the future.

This problem too can be solved. Tooley can make a slight modification of his example and substitute a more primitive being for the chickens. What we have to search for is a kind of organism which lacks both the capacity to feel pain and pleasure. This is not an uncontroversial question, but I believe that

---

[4] I think that this is tacitly assumed, since Tooley's example is only about a change in mental capacities.

[5] This point is made also by Christian Munthe (1992: 98).

there might be examples of some animals which very few people would be prepared to award these capacities—for instance plant lice.

If we consider our intuitions concerning a case where we substitute plant lice for the chickens in Tooley's original example, I believe that many people would see a moral difference between killing these humans and killing plant lice. I am not claiming that the difference will be significant, only that it can be sensed, and that seems to suggest that the property of being an action that kills an innocent human being can for some people be a wrong-making characteristic.

7.3 Tooley's Third Counter-Argument

The first two examples were designed to show that we can imagine a situation where there is no moral advantage for a being in the fact that she is human. The third example, on the other hand, wants to show that we can imagine a situation where there is no moral *dis*advantage for a being in the fact that she is *not* human. The thought experiment is constructed as follows:

> There might exist on some other planet, such as Mars, non-human animals that speak languages, have highly developed cultures, that have advanced further scientifically, technologically, and aesthetically than humans have, and that both enjoy sensations, thoughts, feelings, beliefs, and desires, and attribute such mental states both to us and to themselves. Would it not be wrong to kill such Martians? And wrong for precisely the same reason that it is wrong to kill normal adult human beings? (1983: 67)[6]

To eliminate the problem which was discussed in connection with the second example, we would have to imagine that these Martians look exactly like human beings. So the principal difference between these Martians and human beings turns out to be genetic—they are different species genetically speaking.

I want to make some comments on this example.

First, Tooley wants us to decide not only whether or not it would be wrong to kill these Martians, but also whether or not it would be wrong to kill them for the same reason that it would be wrong to kill normal adult human beings. I believe that this is a bit tricky. Suppose that you decide to say that it *would* be wrong to kill these Martians, does that mean that you also know *why* it would be wrong? Of course not. One of the main tasks of these thought experiments is to *detect* what kind of reason one has for one's moral judgements. The supposition is therefore that this is something one might be mistaken about. Therefore, I suggest that we start by asking the simple question about what one's spontaneous reactions to the wrongness of this kind of killing would be.

---

[6] Of course, this is a classical example which many other philosophers have used to prove the same point as Tooley wants to do. See for instance Vinit Haksar (1979: 43).

Second, if that is what we do, we have to make sure that we concentrate on the *comparative* wrongness of killing these Martians and killing human beings, since the conclusion Tooley wants us to draw will not follow from the sole fact that it would be wrong to kill these Martians, unless it were wrong *to the same extent* that it would be wrong to kill a human being (assuming that it makes sense to talk of different degrees of moral wrongness). This point was also stressed in connection with Tooley's previous example.

Third, there is one strangeness in Tooley's example. I said above that the principal difference between the Martians and the humans was genetic. However, if we take a closer look at the example, we see that there is also another difference. The Martians' intellectual achievements *exceed* the human ones—their cultures have advanced *further* than human cultures have. This might be an important difference, since if one believes that it would be wrong to kill these Martians, equally wrong as killing human beings, then this could be explained in the following way.

There are (at least) two factors which might be relevant when deciding the moral status of the act of killing a certain being. Species membership can be important in itself, which follows directly from what we have said about SA. But the degree of intellectual capacity might also be important. In a coming chapter the rationale for asserting a thing like this will be considered. Here I just want to point to one reason why it might be so. For instance, John Rawls proposes a principle which he calls *the Aristotelian Principle*; it runs as follows:

other things equal, human beings enjoy the exercise of their realized capacities (their innate or trained abilities), and this enjoyment increases the more the capacity is realized, or the greater its complexity. The intuitive idea here is that human beings take more pleasure in doing something as they become more proficient at it, and of two activities they do equally well, they prefer the one calling on a larger repertoire of more intricate and subtle discriminations (1972: 426).

Certain things have to be assumed. One thing is that this Aristotelian Principle also applies to the Martians, so that it is not true only of human beings that their pleasure in doing certain activities increases as the complexity of the activity increases. Given this assumption and given that the Martian culture is *more* advanced than the human one, it follows fairly naturally that a Martian gets *more* pleasure out of practising the Martian culture. Of course, one cannot be sure as to whether the Martian one kills really is an active participant in the Martian culture, but I believe that this will not damage the main point, since the idea is just that other things being equal, the probability that a Martian will enjoy a life containing deep cultural pleasure if not killed is higher than the probability that a human being will do so.[7]

[7] By the way, I assume that some kind of Aristotelian Principle applies also to the *passive* participation in cultural activities. That is to say, it does not merely apply to the *writing* of books, for example, but also to the *reading* of them, which means that the greater their complexity, the more profound will or may the pleasure of reading them be. This consideration would mean that the probability that a Martian experiences the deep pleasures from participating in the Martian culture increases still more.

The upshot of this is that there might be a difference in the moral status of killing a human being and a Martian based on the fact that the human being belongs to a superior species, something which in this case is *outweighed* by the fact that the Martians' cultural capacities exceed the human ones. And given the Aristotelian principle we also see how this can be the case—the thought is not that rationality or intelligence has some kind of intrinsic importance, but rather that a high cultural level means richer opportunities to have pleasurable experiences. And there is nothing strange at all in the thought that there might be other factors besides the fact that a being is a human one that are important for the moral status of the act of killing this being.[8]

Suppose that we eliminate this difference, which I believe we would have to do if we want to construct a case in which we test whether or not we are prepared to award intrinsic importance to species membership, will we then believe that there is a moral difference between the action of killing a Martian and an action of killing a human being, that is to say, given that there does not exist any important intellectual difference between them?

Tooley considers one argument for saying that there is a moral difference between these two actions. He says:

> Most people believe that it is wrong to kill humans, but they also believe that it is more wrong to kill one's parents. If this view is right, why may it not also be more wrong for humans to kill other humans, than for humans to kill Martians? In short, even if there are general moral principles, concerning killing, that do not refer to particular species, why can there not be other principles as well, that do involve reference to species, and that supply what might be referred to as *agent-relative* reasons for not killing (1983: 68–9)

This is an interesting possibility. We are here considering whether it makes any moral difference who *judges* the killing, and the main idea is to draw a parallel between a human being's sensitivity to what happens to members of her own family and what happens to members of her own species. If she is sensitive in the one way, why not believe that she may be sensitive in the other way as well? There is also a question of *agent*-relativity, i.e. whether in the eyes of the one who judges the killing it makes a moral difference who performs the killing. (The argument from agent-relativity or what some philosophers have called "the family argument"[9] will be further considered in a coming chapter.)

Tooley does not accept a special kind of loyalty or sensitivity founded on a common membership of a certain species. It is true that these feelings exist

---

[8] I am not here saying that the Aristotelian Principle is true or uncontroversial. On the contrary, in a coming chapter on Singer I will question a principle very similar to it. Instead I have pointed to a possible line of argument that might explain why we react the way we do to Tooley's example.

[9] I believe the term is Vinit Haksar's and he describes the argument in the following way: "human beings have special obligations and loyalties to people who are members of the human family" (1979: 38).

when we talk of family members, but it is important, Tooley says, to consider the basis for these feelings:

> I suggest that when this is done, it turns out that what is relevant, at least for most people, is not some biological relation, but shared experiences and social interaction over an extended period of time. Consider, for example, a case of artificial insemination by a donor. Would most people really feel that it is more wrong to kill one's biological father, in such a case, than to kill some other individual? It seems to me that they would not (1983: 69).

Now suppose that Tooley does not only take an interest in agent-relativity but that he also wants to consider the more general question whether the fact that you are biologically related to another being will have any effect on your reactions to what happens to this being. This talk of reactions is of course vague, but I have in mind the different kinds of reactions which we claimed before were intimately connected with moral beliefs—for instance, various kinds of emotional reactions, such as anger at the person who deliberately causes suffering to the person with whom one is biologically related.

I think that if we specify the question in this way, Tooley is wrong in believing that biological relatedness does not in itself play any important role for us.

7.4 The Intuitive Importance of Biological Ties

No doubt, being biologically related to another person can be very important to one quite apart from the social ties one has (or lacks) to this person. We may hear this from time to time from persons who have been adopted or who have been conceived as a result of a sperm donation.

Obviously, Tooley is talking of what is true of most people. And one reply could therefore be to claim that it *happens* that people spend time and efforts on this question, but it is not normally so. However, I find this hard to believe. Since it can be an extremely important question for some people, I find it hard to think that it is a question which does not matter at all for the majority. Think of what your own reactions would be if you were told that you had actually been adopted. Would not the question of who your biological parents were interest you at all? Would you not want to know whether they were still alive? Would they not have a special status in your eyes, even if you may find it hard to define this status?

From a biological perspective, it would be very strange if we lacked this kind of sensitivity to biological ties. If what is important biologically for an individual is to spread one's genes (which includes those genes which resemble one's own), then there should be some mechanism which makes it possible to react to the presence of these genes. Since it would be biologically useful to have this kind of sensibility, it would not, at least, be far-fetched to assume that it exists in us.

The crucial question, however, is on what level it operates, if it exists. One possibility is to argue in the following way. Suppose the normal state of affairs is that a human being grows up in intimate social contact with those persons with whom she is closely biologically related. Then one's capacity to detect biological ties could operate on the social level, just as Tooley argues. If the persons with whom one shares one's experiences and with whom one has close social interactions over an extended period of time very often are the persons with whom one is biologically linked, then the useful mechanism could be simply to feel a special loyalty to the persons to whom one has this social relation. It seems that there would be no urgent need for another mechanism.

An alternative way of arguing is the following one. It is true that Tooley's social explanation might be one important explanation for some of the loyalties one feels, but that does not exclude the possibility of explaining loyalties in other ways too. Human beings are mostly rational and a mechanism which worked on a cognitive level, that is to say, which was triggered off by mere beliefs, would no doubt be evolutionary advantageous. For instance, we normally live in close contact with other humans than those with whom we have close biological links (for instance with the mothers or fathers of our children) and it lies in our strict biological interest to care for our offspring more than we care for these other persons (at least when these other people are not important for the welfare of our offspring). So biologically speaking we might gain from retaining the capacity to distinguish between those people in our social vicinity who are and those who are not biologically related to us.

Therefore, we seem to have at least two reasons to believe that it may somehow be important to us to learn that we are closely tied to a certain person biologically.

First, we have some experience of cases where this question has played a very important role, and it seems reasonable to assume that this question would be at least of *some* interest to most of us. If we have doubts concerning this, the reasons may be that the question has never been actualized in our own lives—most people, I figure, do not have an unknown biological parent, brother, sister or child, and therefore most of us have to trust our imagination when we ask ourselves whether or not a person to whom we only had a biological relation would have a special moral status in our eyes. Personally, I find it hard to believe that the biological question would be *totally* uninteresting morally speaking.

Second, we also have a biological explanation why this is so. If our primary biological interest is to spread our genes, then it seems natural to suppose that one has some kind of sensitivity which makes a difference between those people who have and those who do not have genes which are identical or very similar to one's own. And why not assume that this sensitivity is founded on our beliefs? There exists a genetic sensitiveness in us which is at least partly triggered by beliefs concerning biological relatedness.

An alternative analysis would say that there need be no sensitivity to genes *per se*—there need only be sensitivity to some apparent characteristic connected with the genetic, for instance to morphological or psychological features.[10] I realize that this would in a sense be a simpler analysis, since it makes no assumptions of our concept of biological ties. Nevertheless, I believe that it will not catch the whole truth, since, if this analysis is correct, how come we take a special interest (which I believe we do) in persons to whom we know that we are closely related biologically, but who display neither outer nor inner similarities to us? I even believe that most of us have practical experience of the opposite mechanism—we may have *negative* feelings towards persons who are very similar to us in their inner and outer characteristics but to whom we know that we have no close biological ties.

And the biological explanation proposed here will also, I believe, support our interpretation of the argument which Tooley describes. If genetic sensitivity is biologically useful, then I can see no reason to make any fundamental difference between the killing of a relative performed by oneself and the killing performed by someone else, since the prospect of one's genes spreading would be equally damaged by both these sorts of killing. Of course, one might expect a difference in how one judges the fact that one has killed a close relative and the fact that one has killed someone else, but if the biological meaning of this sensitivity is to protect one's genes, one ought to be equally eager to protect them against the aggression of someone else as against oneself.

The upshot of this is that I believe there is a case for saying that one has a capacity to react emotionally to biological ties, whether or not they are also connected with social ones. First, we have fairly extensive experiential evidence for this belief, and second, we can also give a biological explanation for it. Furthermore, considering the biological explanation we claimed that it will support the thought that we react emotionally to the harming of an individual to whom we are biologically related whoever performs the action which causes the harm.

7.5 Are Biological Ties Important in Tooley's Third Counter-Argument?

Of course one cannot go directly from a claim that there seems to exist an intuitive sensitivity to very close biological ties, to a claim that we also have this kind of sensitivity to more remote ties, that is to say, the fact that we have a special feeling for those human beings who are as close to us genetically as our parents and children and siblings founded on knowledge of genes alone, does not also mean that we have a special feeling for human beings generally in contrast to non-human beings.[11]

[10] I owe this argument to Ingmar Persson.
[11] Cf. Rosemary Rodd's discussion of "species loyalty" (1990: Ch. 8).

But the explanation for the first feeling seems to be applicable to this second kind of feeling as well. If one's principal biological task is to spread genes which are either identical with or (very?) similar to one's own, that would not only mean that there is a biological point in being disposed to protect one's children rather than other human beings, but also in being disposed to protect another human being (regardless of whether or not she is a close relative) rather than a non-human animal. For in comparative terms there seems to be as much genetic difference between a human being and an animal as between a sibling and another (non-relative) human being. The difference will be even *bigger* in the former case: compared to an animal one shares more genes with a human being just in virtue of her being human than one does with a sibling compared to another human being. Therefore, other things being equal, in view of genetic egoism, the difference between a human and a non-human is more important than that between a sibling and another human being. And I feel safe in saying so, even against the background that we human beings share very many of our genes with other primates.[12] Furthermore, in Tooley's example we are not told to compare the killing of a human being with the killing of a great ape but instead with the killing of a Martian which for all we know may be more genetically different from us than the primates. Therefore, considering whether it is morally more serious to kill a human being compared to a Martian, who by hypothesis has a very different genetic make-up than our own, it seems that other things being equal, from the perspective of a human being it is more serious if another human being gets killed than if a non-human being does.

There are serious problems in this picture. First of all, I have simplified the evolutionary argument by presupposing a *ceteris paribus* condition. The problem is that in real life all other things are never equal. It may seem safe to conclude that if we are biologically programmed to spread genes which are identical with or similar to our own, then we should be disposed to favour a human being before a non-human. However, as far as I understand, the evolutionary value of doing so will depend on what the other conditions are. In the present world, for instance, there does not seem to be much of a threat from non-human animals against a human being's chances of spreading her genes, but instead the threat comes from other human beings, and that is of course relevant from an evolutionary perspective. That is to say, given certain facts about the difference in power between mankind and the rest of creation—that there is no real non-human threat against mankind—from an evolutionary perspective it seems more important for the individual to guard

---

[12] Jared Diamond, a physiologist, writes that "humans differ from both common chimps and pygmy chimps in about 1.6 per cent of their (our) DNA, and share 98.4 per cent. Gorillas differ somewhat more, by about 2.3 per cent, from us and from both of the chimps" (1993: 95). Singer concludes: "In other words, we—not the gorillas—are the chimpanzees' nearest relatives" (1995: 177).

against the threat from other human beings. i.e. to try to spread genes which are *identical* with her own, rather than similar to them, since the spreading of these latter kinds of genes seems guaranteed anyway (by the fact that mankind has such a dominating position in creation).[13]

Furthermore, there are other problems with the thesis we are considering. One problem is of course that there exists *no* clear intuitive difference in the example from Martians, even if we believe there *would* be an explanation for it. I guess that most people would not be prepared to say that there is a clear difference between killing the Martians in Tooley's example and killing human beings. I am less sure, however, whether a majority of people would say that there is absolutely no intuitive difference at all.

One might claim that *if* there is an intuitive difference, the difference is yet too small or indistinct to be the foundation of a conclusion concerning a moral difference between human and non-human beings which is due to the genetic difference alone. Therefore, let us instead see whether we might explain our reaction to Tooley's example in a way that will make us able to resist the kind of general conclusion Tooley wants us to draw.

7.6 Seeing As

One possibility is that we simply cannot see the Martians as beings of a completely different kind. The suggestion is that in some sense these Martians appear in our eyes to be humans, and the explanation is of course that they are so extremely similar to human beings. I believe that an analysis of the concept of "seeing as" might be useful to capture the phenomenon we are talking about here.

Göran Hermerén has distinguished two senses of the concept:

> If I walk in a dark forest, I might see a juniper bush as a hostile man. I am confronted with a juniper bush, but I have not—in one sense—seen a juniper bush, since it appears to be a man and I mistakenly believe that I am seeing a hostile man. Since I have these beliefs, I am disposed to behave as if a hostile man were present (1969: 34–5).

This first sense, which is called the "deception" sense of "see as" is distinguished from the second sense, which is called the "as-if" sense:

> The phenomenon I have in mind is familiar to everybody. Who has not at some time seen a cloud as a face or as a big animal? When a person is looking at clouds on a sunny summer day and sees a cloud as a big animal, say a bear, he does not mistakenly believe that he is seeing a bear; and he is not disposed to act as if a bear were present. Nor does he mistakenly believe that he is seeing a representation of a bear; he simply sees a cloud as a bear (1969: 36).

---

[13] A more sophisticated picture of the implications the theory of evolution will have for our treatment of animals is given by Rachels in (1991). A summary of Rachels' position can be found in (1993a). As will be evident from the rest of my text, however, I do not wholly agree with Rachels' ideas.

Now I want to claim that there are cases which fall somewhere between these two senses. For instance, when I watch a good film based on the life of some real person, I have a strong tendency to believe that the real person looked like the person who plays him or her in the film. This tendency is especially strong, I have recognized, concerning historical persons the appearance of whom we know fairly little. In one sense we know that the person in question (almost certainly) did not have the appearance he or she has in the film, but in another sense we will (perhaps for the rest of our life) think of him or her as the person with the very appearance he or she has in the film. And much of the magic in good films can be explained in the same way—in one sense we believe that what we see is true, in another sense we do not; some of our tendencies support the one interpretation (for instance, we may cry when seeing a sad scene) and the non-existence of some tendencies supports the other interpretation (for instance, we do not actively try to help a hero or a heroine in trouble).

We can express what happens here by saying that *we know that we are deceived* when we watch a good film. So we seem to have a phenomenon which is a combination of the two important elements in the distinction Hermerén describes—there is a deception element, but there is also the cognitive element of knowing what is the truth behind the appearance. Maybe the phenomenon could be described as an instance of "half-believing", that is, as the presence of some but not all of those characteristics which distinguish believing from not believing, or alternatively, as the presence of these characteristics only to a certain degree, which yields something other than full-fledged believing (Coleridge spoke of a "willing suspension of disbelief", which I believe amounts to the same).[14]

Now my theory is that a similar phenomenon happens when we are asked what to say morally about the killing of Martians in Tooley's example. Are we really capable of treating these Martians as Martians? Well, it seems to me that in one sense we are and in another we are not, or more exactly, in one sense one knows that the comparison is between humans and non-humans, but in another sense one fails to do so, since there is a strong and irresistible tendency in us to regard the Martians as human beings. Their intellectual capacities and their appearance so to speak fool us into thinking that they are human beings—the similarities between the Martians and the humans are too great for us to be able to see them as two different kinds of beings, although on another intellectual level one knows very well that they are.

A possible reply would be to call into question the phenomenon of half-believing. There are two ways of doing this. We may either question its general existence or its existence in connection with Tooley's example. Is

[14] Compare H. H. Price's analysis of "half-believing" (1964) and (1969: 307 ff.). Compare also R. B. Braithwaite (1964) and Oswald Hanfling (1983).

there a sense of "seeing as" which lies somewhere between what Hermerén calls the "deception" sense and the "as-if" sense? The only proof I had was some examples: for instance, watching a good film or, we may add, "flying" in a simulator.

The very fact that the phenomenon exists and can be detected in some areas will not prove that it also lies behind the fact that we see no difference between the moral standing of the humans and Martians in Tooley's example. We have to find an independent argument. One way to argue could be to try to find the phenomena in areas very close to Tooley's example.

One such area concerns adopted children, where just as in Tooley's example I believe people may realize that there is a genetic difference which underlies the fact that the child is not biologically related to its parents, but where the attitudes of the parents often cannot be distinguished from the attitudes of a biological parent. That is to say, I believe we have the phenomenon of half-believing here too. Where the adoption has occurred very early in the child's life I believe that one will have some difficulties in realizing that the child is not flesh of one's flesh. One will see the child *as* one's own after a while, and whatever that may mean I believe that there is a biological reference in this kind of attitude.

I can only prove this claim by what I have heard and read about adoption. But I figure that the new reproduction techniques will give rise to the phenomenon to an even greater extent. I have in mind the techniques of *in vitro* fertilization which have made possible, among other things, "egg or embryo donation", where, in John Harris's words, "a woman will donate an egg or embryo so that another woman may carry, give birth to and bring up a child of her 'own'" (1985: 137). This is just a guess, but I believe it can be supported empirically. The mothers to whom the egg or embryo is donated will probably have a very strong tendency to regard the children as children of their own flesh and blood. They will have some kind of an intellectual understanding of the fact that the child is genetically different, but this thought will have a very small impact, since in many different respects they will regard themselves as the *real* mothers. What this means more exactly can be disputed, but I believe that as a rule, the term carries with it a reference to biological ties.

Therefore I conclude that we have some indirect and independent evidence that the phenomenon of half-believing can occur in the kind of situation which Tooley's example describes, which is to say that if we do not judge the killing of a human being as worse than the killing of a Martian, that may mean that we fail to see them as two different kinds of beings. We tend to see the Martians as humans.

7.7 Half-Believing and Vividness

Unfortunately I do not think that this will also amount to a rejection Tooley's conclusion. It is *possible* that my explanation is true, but I do not know how *likely* it is.

First, when supporting my explanation I referred to some instances where the phenomenon in question is likely to occur. But there is a difference between Tooley's example and these instances. One might claim that the phenomenon presupposes real life or concrete situations or at least situations very similar to that (like watching a film). That is to say, one might claim that there would exist a tendency to regard the Martians as human beings if we were brought face to face with the Martians in a concrete situation. The evidence I cited is at the most evidence for that. This is not to say also that we have this phenomenon of seeing-as in a situation where we are to judge what is better or worse and where an example like Tooley's will constitute our point of departure. On the contrary, in this kind of thought experiment we normally have a clear intellectual apprehension of the prerequisites and it is as a rule also on the basis of this apprehension that we make our judgement.

This may be so. But then the question will be whether we should be satisfied with this state of affairs, i.e. with the fact that we judge a case on the basis of pale propositional knowledge and not instead on the basis of vivid knowledge. Is not lack of vivid beliefs a cognitive defect in connection with thought experiments? This is of course once again a question of whether or not we should put a requirement of rationality on our intuitions. But I believe that this question might be of special interest in this particular case.

F. M. Kamm has expressed some scepticism concerning a requirement of vividness in a context (concerning reason for action) which is similar to the one we are discussing here. She makes the following reflections:

suppose vivid knowledge *did* cause us to act when pale propositional knowledge alone did not. It might not be better appreciation of the reasons that require action that would then be the cause of our acting. Rather, it might be psychological pressure resulting from the vividness; this is something we should often resist. Indeed, exposure to vivid knowledge—for example, via pictures and on-site visits—often gives us the sense that we are being manipulated psychologically, that reason is being overridden by feeling. Suppose this were how vivid knowledge affected us. Then even if we were cognitively imperfect in not having vivid knowledge, this would not necessarily render our knowledge imperfect for purposes of moral action (1992a: 361).

Spontaneously it seems that vividness adds to the value of the experiment, which also means that there is a value in choosing realistic examples other things being equal.[15] At the same time, a demand for vividness is also problematic. One problem concerns what degree of vividness should be

[15] In her book *Morality, Mortality*, Kamm observes that there might instead be a value in choosing examples concerning unfamiliar situations—"one advantage of considering somewhat bizarre cases is that our responses to them are less likely to be merely the application of principles we have been taught, and the novelty of the principles we derive from them suggests that our investigation is going beyond the conventional" (1993: 8). Of course, it might be

demanded and another that it opens up the possibility for rejection of a person's reactions to a particular example with the reason that she did not represent the facts in it vividly enough.

Therefore, I believe there are things to be said both for and against the demand of vividness in this particular context.

What can be said for it is the kind of authority that we generally ascribe to a higher degree of vividness. As I have said before, if we believe that there is some connection between an intuitive conviction and action tendency, one's behaviour in real-life situations has to be more important than one's reactions in an armchair when reading a philosophy book, since action tendency is tendency to act particularly in concrete situations.

And I believe we will argue in exactly the same way when considering our own intuitive reactions. If in a process of judging the moral status of a state of affairs we change our judgement as the vividness of our imagination increases, then we tend to regard the judgement founded on the more vivid imagination as authoritative. However, even if things could be said for preferring the greater vividness generally, we must also remember that the particular case we are discussing here is special if my suspicions about seeing these Martians as Martians is correct, since then the greater vividness will actually *disturb* one's capacity to imagine the case as it is actually described— what would a judgement about a moral distinction between humans and non-humans be if one fails to see any distinction between them *at all*?

There is of course something to be said against a demand of vividness *in this particular case*. If there is a risk of not being able to see the various features of the case we want to judge and if this risk increases with an increasing degree of vividness, then this very fact seems to tell against imagining the case with a great degree of vividness.

The problem is that *not* imagining the case in a vivid manner may *also* contribute to one's failure to see the various features of the case to judge, and I suppose that this is one of the reasons why the demand is put forward in the first place. Imagining a situation vividly is (normally) a guarantee that some important features of the situation have not been overlooked. Even propositional knowledge may presuppose vividness in order to be veracious, which means that *pale* propositional knowledge may often be equivalent to *incomplete* knowledge. For instance, will it be (empirically) possible to have

---

valuable to go beyond the conventional to investigate the structure of our intuitive responses, but I think one should bear in mind that the risk of choosing bizarre examples is that we cannot imagine what it would be like if they were real and therefore we cannot know for sure what our responses would be if we were to be confronted by the situation in real life. Furthermore, one should also keep in mind that conventional morality in one sense might be a part of oneself, in that one seriously holds the very moral principles that one has been taught. On the other hand, if the principles one applies are conventional in the sense that one embraces them from mere habit and not out of firm conviction, then investigating them will be less interesting from a normative point of view.

complete pale propositional knowledge of the emotional experiences of a parent who loses a beloved child in an accident?

This question has many aspects. The question may be about our intellectual capacity. Will it be empirically possible to have a propositional grasp of all the experiences of a parent who loses a child? But the question might be also about epistemology in general: will it be possible to so speak to *translate* an emotional experience into some information which could be grasped in pale propositional knowledge?

One might claim in a similar fashion that knowledge of others' emotional reactions has to be represented in concepts of which one has first-person understanding. This is the philosophical point. The psychological point is that it might be very hard to make use of these concepts in an objective fashion, i.e. without representing for instance emotional experiences with life and force. And I believe that these ideas have a general application also, that is to say, beyond the range of emotions.

We need not settle these questions here, since I believe that in the end it is wiser to disregard the psychological phenomenon which initiated this discussion, namely the impossibility of regarding a being which has all the human attributes as something other than human. The reason is the very fact that we have discussed above; it seems hard to *prove* the existence of the phenomenon.

Indeed, I tried to deliver some independent arguments for my thesis. I tried to argue for the existence of the phenomenon generally and I pointed to areas which have a fairly close relationship to the situation described in Tooley's example, areas where, just as in the example, we tend to disregard a genetic difference—as when we have grown up with parents who have adopted us when we were very young. We tend to half-believe that these are our biological parents. This may be so even if it is true also that we lay stress on knowing the identity of our actual biological parents. Remember that this was also one of the ideas argued for in this chapter—it is important for us to learn that we have close biological ties to a certain person.

This may sound paradoxical. On the one hand I claim that the social factor plays an important role when determining our loyalties and on the other hand I claim that we lay stress on knowledge of biological ties. But I do not think that these ideas necessarily contradict each other, since what I have claimed is that the importance of the social factor might be explained partly by the existence of the phenomenon in question—we tend to regard the parents who have brought us up as our biological parents. And the explanation why we do so may be biological—normally our social parents are also our biological ones. This does not exclude the possibility that *if* we were to learn that our actual biological ties were elsewhere, then that would be an important piece of knowledge for us. This possibility would follow fairly naturally from the first suggestion, since its main point was that at least one aspect of our loyalty will be founded on our beliefs about biological ties. Furthermore, the fact that we tend to half-believe that a certain person is our biological parent will not exclude that we learn that our biological ties are with a completely different person. It will not even exclude, I believe, that we continue to half-believe that we are biologically tied to the first person after we have learned where our real biological ties are.

But even if these considerations may function as some kind of an independent support for a claim about the existence of the phenomenon, one might doubt whether these situations and Tooley's example are similar enough to deserve the same treatment. Indeed certain dissimilarities are striking.

First, in the adoption case the phenomenon is a result of a slow and gradual process. It takes time. If it were present also in Tooley's example, we would have it there right from the start.

Second, in these examples what triggers the phenomenon is a *social* process, whereas in Tooley's example we would have to suppose that it might be present without any social ties existing in advance.

Third, in these examples it works on a level where we are talking of very close biological ties. We tend to see someone as our biological *parent* or *child* or *sibling*, and so on. And even if there existed a mechanism in us which would have this result, that will not mean that there would also exist a mechanism which worked on a similar level where we are talking about humans versus other animals.

In view of these differences I conclude with some hesitation that Tooley has probably succeeded in showing that there does not exist a moral difference between the Martians in his example and human beings, and that we therefore have reason to believe that being human lacks intrinsic importance in his example. Of course, he wants us to draw a much stronger conclusion, namely that being human always lacks intrinsic importance, since it does so in his example. In the next chapter I am going to claim that we may resist such a strong conclusion.

7.8 Summing up this Chapter

Let me recapitulate the main points in this chapter. We have considered three arguments against SA delivered in the form of three examples by Tooley, i.e. three arguments against the idea that being human has intrinsic moral importance.

In his first example Tooley exhorts us to consider the case of a "human vegetable", that is a case where the basic bodily functions of a human being still remain but where she lacks a capacity for conscious life. Would it be wrong to kill such a being? One of the problems, as I see it, is that a negative answer will not be able to tell us anything about the worth of a human life unless one compares one's responses in this case with a case which involves a non-human animal. Even if we *were* inclined to think that it is not wrong to kill the human beings in Tooley's example, that would not show that species membership is intrinsically unimportant to judge from our intuitions, unless there were no difference between this inclination and the inclination to make the same judgement in a case where only non-humans figured. This means that Tooley's first example does not touch the general idea behind SA.

In his second example Tooley asks us to imagine a disease which will change the genetic make-up of the human species and eventually give its members a mental life comparable to that of chickens. Would it, as Tooley says, be seriously wrong for any non-human persons who happen to exist after this change to kill the human beings? Generally, the same consideration applies to this second case; it is not enough to consider what our responses would be to this particular case. These responses have to be compared with our responses to a case where non-humans figure. And given certain modifications to Tooley's example, modifications which I claimed that we would have very good reasons to make, I stated that when such a comparison is made, we may well end up with an intuitive difference between killing humans and killing other beings. It is important to note that I made no claims about the significance of this intuitive difference, only that it could be sensed by very many of us. That is enough to undermine Tooley's argument. I shall not at this stage say that it supports the truth of SA. I shall restrict myself to the more careful negative conclusion: Tooley has not yet been able to show that SA is false.

In his third example Tooley wants us to imagine what it would be like if there existed non-human inhabitants of some other planet, such as Mars, who were mentally, intellectually and culturally on a level with mankind. In fact, one gets the impression that these Martians have developed capacities which *exceed* the human ones. Anyway, Tooley wants us to consider whether it would be wrong to kill these Martians and wrong for the same reason, as he puts it, that it would be wrong to kill normal adult human beings. I simplified this and interpreted it as a question as to whether it would be equally wrong to kill these Martians and humans beings.

Suppose we tend to regard the killing of these Martians and human beings as morally equivalent. I claimed that this does not automatically undermine the idea of an intrinsic moral difference between humans and non-humans.

First, since there is a difference after all in the capacities of the humans and non-humans, we cannot say for sure whether these differences will influence our judgements. And since by hypothesis it is the non-humans which have the greater capacities, it may well be the case that our judgement is a result of an unconscious summing up of different factors, where the greater capacity of the non-humans will *compensate* for the intrinsic value difference between the non-humans and the humans. Therefore, it is still possible to claim that being human is intrinsically valuable.

Second, suppose that the tendency will exist even after we have removed the first problem (by modifying the example). We may try to resist the conclusion nevertheless. With the help of Hermerén's two senses of "seeing as" I suggested that there was also an intermediate sense, which means a kind of half-believing. This might have relevance for Tooley's example, since possibly we fail to see these Martians as Martians, but see them instead as human beings (due to their similarity with human beings in the modified example). However, I concluded with some hesitancy that the evidence for this was too weak.

Consequently, the upshot of the chapter is that we seem to have an example which tells against SA: in a case where a non-human Martian person has all the attributes of a normal human person, we tend not to make any moral difference between it and a human being. This, Tooley says, supports the idea that there is no intrinsic difference between a human and a non-human.

CHAPTER 8

EXAMPLES SUPPORTING SA

> Driving instructors will tell us that if a cat or dog strays into
> our path, and we are unable to stop or otherwise avoid it in an
> orderly fashion, then we should run it down. Only a psychopath
> would include children in the instruction.
>
> Michael P. T. Leahy *Against Liberation*

In the previous chapter I considered an argument against SA which was constructed in the form of three examples. These examples were meant to show that there is no intrinsic moral difference between humans and non-humans. I concluded the chapter by saying that only one of the examples seems to support that idea.

In this chapter I want to point out some arguments which are designed to *support* SA. I will confine myself to arguments which work in the same way as Tooley's, i.e. to arguments which appeal to our intuition by means of examples or thought experiments. I believe that one *can* construct examples which support SA, although some of the attempts to do so have failed. Furthermore, I will also comment on what conclusion to draw from the fact that some examples seem to undermine and other examples seem to support SA. Is it the case that being human has intrinsic importance in some situations but not in others? In my view it is very difficult to escape that conclusion.

In one sense this chapter is merely a continuation of the previous one. We are still discussing the *intrinsicality* of SA: do we really believe that being human is important *in itself*, over and above the properties that as a rule accompany humans, such as intellectual sophistication together with a well developed capacity to feel pain and to suffer? One recurrent problem is that many of those philosophers who want to defend SA fail to keep a steady eye on this feature, and support the attitude with examples which are built on differences over and above species membership. As we have seen, this problem also pertains to examples designed to undermine SA, like for instance Tooley's.

In any case, the reason why I want to devote so much space to this very discussion has of course to do with its importance in a subjectivistic defence of human dignity. I have claimed that there is something special about being human *per se*, and the reason is simply that most of us tend to stress this property. If it might be shown that we do *not* consider the property of being a member of the human species to be intrinsically important, then of course our defence of human dignity will fail, which will be the case if Tooley is correct.

8.1 Warnock's Example

Let us start with an example delivered by Mary Warnock, which states a principle that concentrates particularly on the fifth element in the content of SA (see Chapter 6):

no human being should use another for his own ends, however noble. Therefore, suppose that embryos could be kept alive *in vitro* for so long that they became plainly human, able to experience pain, or to perceive their environment; it would immediately become wrong that they should be used for experimental or observational purposes. It would be absolutely prohibited, too, that anaesthetics should be administered to them so that, though capable of feeling pain, they did not actually feel it. Here would be an area where there would be a total difference between treatment of humans and treatment of other animals. I believe that nearly everyone would agree that this was a barrier in no circumstances to be crossed, whatever the demands of scientific knowledge (1983: 248–9).

I believe it is plain that Warnock is talking of an intuitive difference that pertains to species membership *per se*, or at least this is her intention. One of my reasons for so thinking is that she presents the example partly as a defence of speciesism. She argues that treating speciesism as a form of prejudice is absurd: "Far from being arbitrary, it is a supremely important moral principle" (1983: 242). Now, I will comment only on the example she gives in order to see whether or not it supports SA.

One thing that seems a bit confusing is that she refers to the embryo as a being that is not plainly *human* at the same time as she claims that this term is a biological one (1983: 241). This makes one wonder what she means by the term "biological".

Above we have distinguished between different species concepts, or kinds of criteria for distinguishing one species from another. Let me here compare the two versions that could be described as instances of essentialism, i.e. the morphological and the genetic criteria. It is plain that Warnock does not have in mind a genetic criterion, otherwise she would not talk about the property of being human as something that comes in degrees. The genetic make-up of an embryo does not change during its development.

The problem is that Warnock does not seem to embrace the morphological criterion either, since to be plainly human, according to her, is not only to have a human appearance, but also to be able to experience pain, perceive the environment, that is, to have a certain minimum degree of intellectual capacities. This is the way I want to interpret her, even if she describes these properties in a disjunctive sentence.

Clearly this is *not* a normal species criterion, since we do not cease to be biological humans the day we lose these capacities. We do not abuse normal language when we refer to patients in irreversible coma as humans or members of the human species, although they have lost those intellectual capacities which according to Warnock would make them plainly human.

Furthermore, suppose she is right in her guesses in the example, that is, suppose we make the value judgements she thinks we do. What will follow from that? Clearly not that being a human is something important *in itself.* Actually, it will not even follow that being a human is of any *direct* importance at all. It might be the case that our judgement of the moral status of the developed embryos is based on the fact that we lay stress on being a member of the human species *and* having these intellectual capacities. But for all we know, it might also be the case that our judgement is *exclusively* based on the presence of these capacities. To decide that question, Warnock needs to consider a case where biological species membership is absent but where the intellectual capacities are present, and that kind of example is not explicitly considered by her.[1]

The next question I want to consider concerns whether she is correct in what she states about our normal responses to her example and if her own values are reasonable. Actually she makes two claims. On the one hand that a being which is plainly human should have a very strong moral protection (*the first claim*) and on the other hand that there is a difference in the way we regard a foetus that *is* plainly human and for instance an embryo that is not (*the second claim*). The latter claim is more or less implicit.

8.2 Warnock's First Claim

The problem, as I see it, is that Warnock formulates an extremely strong view. She says that no human being should use another for his own ends, however noble, and from that principle she derives, as it appears, a moral prohibition against using some embryos for experimental and observational purposes. What exactly does this mean? Well, Warnock would certainly not prohibit observations of an embryo with a view to making the birth easier, for instance by means of ultrasound. Therefore, she has to have something else in mind.

But suppose that a person wants to study foetuses by ultrasound in order to gain some general knowledge which might be useful in the future, not necessarily for the subjects of the study but for *other* individuals.[2] Would this be wrong as well, in Warnock's opinion? According to the first part of the quotation she seems to think so, since she explicitly rejects using others

---

[1] She does indeed address the question cursorily. The problem of how to treat an intelligent being from another planet, she says, "might well turn on the new creatures' concept of the human race" (1983: 242). So she seems to claim that our treatment of these kinds of beings will depend on their treatment or at least concept of us humans. This argument will be considered in more detail in the next chapter. In the meantime I insist that Warnock by her example does not establish SA.

[2] Suppose also that there is no other way to get this knowledge. In the Warnock Report studies of disorders such as Down's syndrome and research into the process of human fertilization are mentioned as areas in which there is no *substitute* for human embryos (1985: 62).

as a means to one's own ends even if this is motivated by one's *noble* ends, and the end to diminish the problems for future human beings may definitely be termed noble. But this is clearly absurd. Very few persons would like to rule out studies of foetus development with reference to this fact. Furthermore, notice that Warnock does not rule out only observations by, for instance, ultrasound and other new techniques. To judge from what she says, *any* observation done with the purpose of gaining some information about the foetus, which will not accrue to the individual observed but to someone else, will be wrong. Again, this is an extremely strong position, and it is not, as far as I know, a view which Warnock defends in her other works.

This means that we must not make a literal interpretation of Warnock. We must not take the general principle stated about a moral prohibition against using a human being as a means to one's own end literally and regard what she says about the embryos kept alive *in vitro* merely as an application of this principle. Instead it is this very fact about embryos kept alive *in vitro* that is her main interest.

One possibility is that her conclusions are derived from a less general principle, namely that a human being kept alive *in vitro* must not be used as a means for one's own ends. That could rule out experiments and (at least certain) observations of them without ruling out experiments and observations of foetuses generally.

But this is not a plausible principle either. First, why distinguish between the moral status of some actions done to an embryo *in vitro* and to an embryo in a woman's uterus (*in vivo*)? What is the moral relevance of this difference? I can think of only one reason for believing it relevant, namely that in normal circumstances we will not keep the embryo alive *in vitro* if we are interested in letting it develop into a child. It has not been possible (at least it was not possible when Warnock wrote the article) to keep an embryo alive *in vitro* for more than a relatively short time. And the possibility of so called "ectogenesis" clearly lies in the future.

John F. Leeton *et al.* write about the technique of in vitro fertilization:

Pregnancies have developed following the transfer of one-cell to sixteen-cell human embryos. Older embryos are not used because they do not develop beyond sixteen cells in the Fallopian tube under normal circumstances. Prolonged culture is thought to promote degeneration of the embryo (1982: 7).

But if this is the fact that lies behind the distinction, then Warnock will probably have another more basic principle in mind, since the reason I cite now has nothing to do with being kept alive *in vitro* in itself. It is not the fact that one is being kept alive *in vitro* that will give one a protection against being used as a means; it is rather that being kept alive that way under normal circumstances is an indication that a being is treated *solely* as a means towards one's own ends.

One difference between making experiments on an embryo *in vivo* (which will develop into a child) and on an embryo *in vitro* (which will not develop into a child) is that in the former case the object of the experiments *may* have a share in the results of the experiments. Even if they will probably not have a direct share, they may well have an indirect one: for instance, their children may in turn profit from these results. By contrast, if the embryos kept alive *in vitro* will never develop into children, that means they may hardly profit from the results of the experiments performed on them.

Another way of understanding the principle which Warnock formulates in the quotation is that it prohibits the regarding of someone's *existence* as being solely in another being's interests. Given what we have stated above, it is not only false that these embryos will profit from the experiments made upon them, it is also false that they may profit from anything else in life. Therefore, another big difference between making experiments on these embryos and making experiments on normal embryos in a woman's uterus is that in the latter case we make use of something the existence of which is independent of our use, whereas in the former case we profit from something the existence of which *depends* on it, in the sense that it would not exist unless we could make this kind of use of it. This is not explicitly mentioned by Warnock in her example, but it could easily be read into it.

We have to assess this principle. Is it plausible to have a moral prohibition against using a plainly human being solely as a means in the sense that we keep her alive in order to let other human beings profit from this? (We do not have to state what kind of being will make the profit, but I guess that the principle will be more interesting in this formulation.)

In one sense I believe this principle has intuitive appeal, since it deals with what will for many people be considered a paradigm case of profiting from another being, and doing so in this obvious way will no doubt appear morally problematic to many people. I noted this in the discussion of the fourth element in the content of SA. It is true that Warnock also considers the administration of anaesthetics to the embryos, which means that they will never have to feel the pain which they are capable of feeling, but I guess that many people will nevertheless feel uncomfortable about keeping these embryos alive and doing the experiments. At least, I am firmly convinced that most people would think that doing so would require a *justification*. Therefore, I believe it safe to conclude that intuitively most of us would regard keeping human embryos alive in order to do experiments on them as *prima facie* wrong.

8.3 Absolute Principles

However, the problem with the quoted passage is that Warnock is claiming something much stronger; she claims that keeping embryos alive in order to do experiments on them will be *absolutely* wrong, that is to say, wrong in all circumstances and irrespective of what may come out of it. She says explicitly that such a thing must not be done "whatever the demands of scientific knowledge", and furthermore that "nearly everyone would agree" with that. Allow me to express my doubts. All kinds of absolute moral prohibitions are problematic in the sense that they will have counter-intuitive consequences.

However morally repugnant a certain action is—for instance torturing an innocent person—one may imagine a situation where the costs of refraining from it will appear even more repugnant, which might be the case if the future existence of mankind is at stake. These kinds of examples are well-known. And the pattern they follow seems to be this one: there does not exist any treatment of a single person which is bad enough to be out of the question whatever the gains to other persons ("gains" here might be the absence of something negative).[3]

Indeed, I am aware of several ways to escape this conclusion as well; some of us *do* support the thought of absolute moral principles (preferably negative ones), and some philosophers will deny the tacit assumption made in these examples, namely that the suffering of more people is *worse* than the suffering of a single person. In short, they deny that the number counts in the sense that the suffering of a number of people can be *added up* to something that may outweigh the suffering of a single person.[4]

Now if it appears morally problematic to have an absolute prohibition against using another person as a means in the sense of letting him undergo torture although innocent (in the sense that the threat against the greater number of people is not his fault), then we might expect it to be even more problematic to have an absolute prohibition against using another human being as a means in the way described in Warnock's example—namely as an object of experiments and observations which other human beings might profit from and which are not even painful. Furthermore, I do not think that this judgement will change even when we add that this human being is kept alive *merely* in order to function as such an object.

---

[3] One might possibly discern an even more general pattern here, namely the following one: there does not exist any treatment of a certain number of persons which is bad enough to be ruled out whatever the gains to a vastly greater number of persons. And this is also the reason why there is a "tendency to append a 'catastrophe clause' to familiar principles whenever the consequences of adhering to the principles are so repugnant that it seems morally perverse to refuse the exception" (Thomas E. Hill, Jr., 1992: 199).

[4] See John Taurek (1977). Notice that it is not necessary to derive an absolute prohibition against harming a single person from this very thought that the number does not count. One might believe that the number *does* count but nevertheless claim that we must not torture an innocent person in order to let others gain from this. For instance, we may believe that we ought to save the greater number of people without believing that we may use a person as a means towards this. We may think that if we have a boat and there is one person on one island and ten on another one and if all other things are equal, then we ought to save the ten persons and thereby let the one person die. However, if the only way of saving the ten persons would be to kill the one (enormously fat) person, inflate him and use him as a raft, then we might think that such an action is morally prohibited. Compare Judith Jarvis Thomson (1975).

For many philosophers there is another very important difference between the torture case and Warnock's example. Not only will a human being suffer in the first example whereas no one does so in the situation prohibited by Warnock, but also, in the first example one uses a *person* solely as a means towards one's own end whereas the embryos in Warnock's example will not qualify as persons, given a fairly common (Lockean) definition of this concept in terms of rationality and self-consciousness.[5] Having the capacity of experiencing pain and perceiving one's environment is normally not enough for personhood.

It is true that Warnock does not find the question whether or not we are dealing with a person morally crucial, and actually that is one of her main points in the articles we have referred to. She says, for instance, that

I would like, however, to attempt to approach the question of the embryo's rights without reference to the question whether or not it is a person. Personhood is a notoriously difficult and ambiguous concept, and if we can get on without it in this matter, so much the better (1987: 1–2).

Nevertheless, I believe that the significance of personhood has an appeal to us in this situation. And I figure that one important reason for this is that only a person might fully understand that she *is* being used merely as a means and therefore only a person may be *offended* by being the object of this kind of treatment.

And it does not make much difference that Warnock is considering subjects to whom anaesthetics have been administered, since I as a person might of course want not to be treated in a certain way even if the treatment involves no sensations of pain. I as a person might very well rather want to die than to be kept alive solely for experimentation, no matter how effective the anaesthetics that I had access to. Such a life might have lost its personal value for me, since I as a person am capable of having attitudes towards other things than sensations. By contrast, if we eliminate the sensations of pain from the life of a non-person it is hard to see on what grounds it might protest against using it for experimental and observational purposes.

8.4 Does Warnock's Example Really Support SA?

Now I have to address an even more important question. Clearly, Warnock's example from experiments on plainly human beings can be seen as an intuitive appeal to the intrinsic importance of being a human, since it follows from being human that one is entitled to a strong protection against certain kinds of treatment. But even if I am right in my critique of her claim about the

[5] At least this definition figures in modern philosophy books. However, that there is no such thing as "the concept of a person" is made clear in an article by Amélie Oksenberg Rorty (1990: 21–38).

strength of this protection, that will not show that her example also fails to support SA.

The main thought behind SA has nothing to do with the *absolute* strength of the privileges that ought to be conferred on human beings, but instead it concerns the *relative* strength of what regulates the treatment of a human being and what regulates the treatment of a non-human being. Therefore, the principal question should not be whether or not Warnock in her example succeeds in showing that there are some absolute rules against using a plainly human being merely as a means, but rather whether or not her example will support the thought that there is a moral difference between treating a human being and a non-human being in this way.

I am well aware of the fact that Warnock's claim is stronger than that. She is talking about "an area where there would be a *total* difference between treatment of humans and treatment of other animals" (1983: 248, my emphasis). However, even if she is wrong in this, which she seems to be, that would not necessarily make her example less useful from the viewpoint of someone who wants to defend SA, since the main idea behind this attitude seems to concern the difference between the value of a human and a non-human, not essentially the size of this difference.

Does this difference exist? Will we consider it as *worse* to breed and use plainly human beings exclusively for research purposes, than to breed and use some animals, for instance mice, for the same purpose? Notice that there would not necessarily be a difference in the mental capacities between what Warnock calls plainly human beings and mice. Mice are normally not considered to be persons, but, as we have seen, neither are those human beings of which Warnock is talking in her example.

I have to guess again, but I am fairly sure that there is a much stronger presumption against using a plainly human being in this way compared to using a non-human being.

8.5 Two Cases

Imagine a case (C1) where scientists breed human embryos *in vitro* solely for research purposes. The experiments made before they are killed are totally painless but they require that the embryos (or whatever we would call them) have developed beyond the point where they are conscious and capable of feeling pain. However, in order not to offend the feelings of the persons who have to take care of these human embryos, the fertilized eggs are manipulated at an early stage of the process so that these embryos will never look human. Instead they very much look like rabbit embryos.

Compare this with a second case (C2) where instead non-human embryos are bred merely for experimentation. Just as in the first case, they are kept alive *in vitro* beyond the point where they are able to perceive their environment, and so on. In short, (C2) differ from (C1) in only one respect: the subjects of the experiments in (C2) *are* rabbit embryos.

Now the simple question is whether or not you will sense a moral difference between the two cases. Imagine what it would be like to read about the two cases in the morning paper. Would you reflect at all on (C2) if you read about it, and honestly, would you not care more about an article about (C1)? I strongly believe that very many people would sense even a considerable moral difference here.

Suppose I am right. That would definitely support SA, since we seem to sense an intuitive difference between a human and a non-human based solely on a genetic difference, which is precisely what SA is about.

Someone might raise an objection against this last statement, since for all we know there is indeed another difference between the two cases, namely in (C1) one is dealing with beings which have a *potential* for much more than the beings described in (C2), for instance they have a potential for personhood. It is true that as things work in the actual world, if one kept human embryos alive *in vitro* for a long time, then they would probably lose this potential, since there does not at the present moment exist a technique for transferring these embryos to uterus, but it is still true that such embryos *at some stage* of their development would have a potential to develop into persons. Furthermore, since our example already is somewhat science-fictional, these limitations *need* not apply to it. So we seem to have a difference between (C1) and (C2) after all.

But then let us fill in with some more fictional information about the cases. For instance that in (C1) one has used a special technique to sort out the sperms that have a very special defect. The embryos fertilized by these defective sperms cannot possibly develop into persons—they can develop an ability to experience pain and to perceive their environment, but they cannot develop the intellectual capacities which we normally associate with persons. In order to assess the intuitive importance of a potential for being a person, we might add that there exists a drug which could be injected into the rabbit embryos which makes it possible for them to develop rationality and self-consciousness. So we have the following situation: the beings described in (C1) are not potential persons, whereas the beings described in (C2) are (at least given a fairly common sense of the term "potential"). And now the question is whether this will give us reason to reconsider our first judgement to the effect that (C1) is morally worse than (C2)?

I have to confess that I am not totally uninfluenced by this difference, which means that my initial judgements seem to be based at least partly on the potentiality factor, but I still insist that this is only part of the truth, which is evident from the fact that I am not prepared to reverse my judgement in view of the added information that the rabbit embryos but not the human embryos have a potential to develop into persons. I do not consider (C2) to be morally worse than (C1). Furthermore, I still feel inclined to say that (C1) is morally worse than (C2), although perhaps a little bit less so, when the information concerning potentiality is added. The upshot is that potentiality may have some moral significance (I say this although I am fully aware of the theoretical problems that pertain to such a position), but it is not a decisive factor in judging between the comparative moral status of (C1) and (C2). There will remain an intuitive difference which can be explained only as something that is based on the genetic distinction in itself, i.e. on the fact that the subjects in (C1) are humans whereas the subjects in (C2) are not.

Some comments on what we might learn from this: I have claimed that we learn that there is some truth in SA. But this does not automatically mean that there is some truth in Warnock's claims as well, since what she says can be given an interpretation that is quite different from SA (even apart from the fact that in contrast to SA she wants to defend an *absolute* principle), and this has to do with what we did find a bit mysterious at the beginning of this chapter, namely the way Warnock uses the term "human". She claims that it is a biological concept, yet she seems to think that the property comes gradually. And in the end what she wants to do is merely to protect *plainly* human beings against being used for another person's ends.

Are the beings described in (C1) plainly human, according to Warnock? I am not sure that we can settle this question, simply because she does not, as far as I know, directly address the question of a demarcation criterion in her articles and books. She does discuss a distinction between being a collection of human cells and being a human individual. And this, among other things, is what she says about that distinction:

We, the majority of the Inquiry, recommend that research on the human embryo should be brought to an end on the fourteenth day because of the development then of the primitive streak. Up to that time, it is difficult to think of the embryo as an individual, because it might still become two individuals (1987: 11).

As I interpret Warnock, this is not exactly the same distinction as the one in the quotation which states an absolute prohibition against using a plainly human being for one's own ends merely. I may be wrong in this, but the reason for my interpretation is partly that she presents this concept of a plainly human being together with fairly high-level capacities such as the capabilities of experiencing pain and perceiving one's environment, and it seems that such capacities have nothing to do with the distinction above between merely being human and being a human individual.

A second reason for believing that she has another distinction in mind when she talks about being plainly human, is the way she denies that the potentiality principle should apply to early embryos. She says: "The question whether or not they may be used in research must be answered, not with regard to their potentiality, but with regard to what they are ... how far they are along the long road to becoming fully human" (1987: 12). I take this as indirect evidence of the fact that Warnock is appealing to more sophisticated properties than merely being a human individual, since fourteen days is hardly "a long road".[6]

My third reason for thinking that to be plainly human in Warnock's eyes is to be something more than merely a human individual is the way she formulates her example. She exhorts us to "suppose that embryos could be kept alive *in vitro* for so long that they became plainly human, able to experience pain, or to perceive their environment" (I am not really sure whether she states a disjunction or a conjunction or both). It seems to me that if by being "plainly human" she only had in mind being a human individual, then she would not have to appeal to our imagination in this way, since the possibility exists already. On the other hand, suppose she wants us to imagine that embryos could be kept alive until they became plainly human *and* able to experience pain. Then the first part of the conjunction seems to be redundant if she has in mind merely being a human individual, since it is hard to imagine an organism which is capable of feeling pain but which is not an individual, but instead a mere collection of cells.

I am not sure that Warnock is prepared to formulate any precise criteria, and neither am I sure that this would be a reasonable demand.[7] I am prepared to admit that Warnock possibly defends an idea which is quite different from SA, but that her example might function as a springboard for a defence of SA.

Now we have already slid into Warnock's second claim. Remember that Warnock made two proposals (in the example from human embryos kept alive *in vitro*). First, that a being which is plainly human should have a strong moral protection and second that there is a moral difference between a human organism which is plainly human and one that is not. I now turn to the second claim.

---

[6] Notice that Warnock in a sense is putting forward two different principles. The one presented at the beginning of this chapter prescribed that research on *plainly* human beings should be absolutely prohibited whereas the one described above claims that research on human beings should be absolutely prohibited. The reason is, I think, that Warnock by the first principle wants to formulate a principle which will have a very strong intuitive appeal to very many people, and which therefore will support that part of the Inquiry's recommendation which concerns the *absoluteness* of a prohibition against research on human embryos.

[7] I believe that normally when we use the expression plainly or fully human we use it to denote a very large collection of properties which someone would have to have in order to qualify. Peter Smith mentions one such property when he claims that "a humourless creature would not count as a full human person in the sense we have introduced, although it could be (so to speak) next door to being human" (1990: 78). Indeed Smith discusses criteria for human *personhood*, but my point is merely that I believe it hard to formulate any precise criteria of being plainly human whether or not we think of human persons or human individuals generally, and therefore we will have to discuss these questions without demanding precision.

8.6 Warnock's Second Claim

Many questions hide behind the seemingly simple proposal that the moral status of a newly fertilized egg is lower than the moral status of a plainly human being, for instance an embryo which is capable of experiencing pain. If we talk of intuitions we might ask whether or not the difference comes gradually so that an embryo which is a couple of weeks old will be regarded as more valuable than the newly fertilized egg but less valuable than a plainly human embryo. I will simplify the question by comparing merely the status of the newly fertilized egg (particularly what Warnock calls a "pre-embryo") and a plainly human being, for instance a several-month-old human embryo.[8]

No doubt, very many people would sense a moral difference here and I do not believe it necessary to construct examples in order to show this. I believe it safe to conclude that judging from our intuitions a newly fertilized egg will have a lower moral status than a plainly human being.

Instead I briefly want to address the question *why* this is so; why does a fertilized human egg have a comparably low moral status? We have already considered one kind of theoretical reason: up to the fourteenth day the embryo can divide and become two individuals and therefore it is difficult to classify the pre-embryo as a human being. Another consideration has to do with something which was discussed in the previous chapter, namely that it might be difficult to *see* a newly fertilized egg as a human organism; a microscopic collection of cells will only with some difficulties be regarded as human.

Warnock has got a similar idea. She writes:

> how do we decide whether an embryo or a fertilised egg is *sufficiently* human to warrant protection? The alternative to thinking of it as human, as I have suggested above, is to think of it as "just a collection of cells" [...] there is, I believe some justification for so considering the newly fertilised egg, and *not* so considering an adult human creature (1983: 242–3).

Even if we like to think that an organism has intrinsic importance based on its membership of the human species, we will have some difficulties in regarding the newly fertilized egg as such a member.

However, there are certain differences between my proposal and Warnock's. I am not sure whether or not they are significant or interesting, but they should be noted.

My proposal is that we will find it difficult to see the early embryo as a human being, although we may not be able to account for this difficulty. And this is once again a phenomenon which lies somewhere between the deception sense and the "as-if" sense of "seeing as"[9]—in a purely intellectual sense we are prepared to accept that a newly fertilized egg is human, but we

---

[8] Sometimes one defines an embryo as "a foetus before the eighth week of gestation" (M. G. Hansson, 1991: 27). However, since it is controversial whether the capacity of feeling pain is present before the eighth week of gestation, I will not agree with any precise definition of "embryo".

[9] Recall Hermerén (1969: 34–6).

have a spontaneous tendency not to regard it as human, we so to speak only "half-believe" that it is human. The reason why this is not to be seen as the same distinction as the one between a human organism and a human being above is that I figure we would have the same kind of difficulty in seeing a three- or four-week-old embryo as a human being.

Now compare this with Warnock's statement. She seems to believe that it is a question of *deciding* how to regard the early embryo, whether as human or merely a collection of cells. This is not exactly what I propose, since I was thinking of a psychological fact which is not within reach of a decision in this way. On the other hand, Warnock does not seem to have in mind the "as-if" sense of "seeing as" either, i.e. the sense which, as you may recall, is described by Hermerén in the following way: "When a person is looking at clouds on a sunny summer day and sees a cloud as a big animal, say a bear, he does not mistakenly believe that he is seeing a bear; and he is not disposed to act as if a bear was present [...] he simply sees a cloud as a bear" (1969: 36). Warnock is not talking about seeing something as something else, either knowingly or unknowingly; she is talking about deciding how to regard an object in the first place.

The choice she considers is between regarding the early embryo as human or just a collection of cells, which seems to be a question of all or nothing—to be merely a collection of cells does not suggest any protection at all—whereas the intuitive difference I had in mind was not that categorical.

8.7 The Moral Status of Newly Fertilized Eggs

There are two questions that ought to be considered. First, what kind of evidence is there that we tend to endow an early embryo, for instance a newly fertilized human egg, with *any* moral significance? Second, what kind of importance, if any, are we prepared to recognise in these organisms?

Concerning the first question we have to invent some examples to show that we make intuitive discriminations between embryos from different species. One attempt in that direction would be the following one. Suppose that at an exhibition an artist has made the following arrangement. In room A there is a big reservoir containing several million newly fertilized eggs from pigs in some kind of liquid which will allow them to survive the exhibition. When the exhibition is finished the early pig embryos will be destroyed. Now in the next room, B, we find another exactly similar reservoir. The only difference is that this one contains newly fertilized human eggs. These too will be destroyed when the exhibition is finished. Of course, the artist's thought behind this arrangement is to show that there is a moral difference between being and not being human. Will she be successful?

My instinctive reaction is that she would succeed in making at least me sense a difference between the content in the different reservoirs. I would find the idea of collecting a large amount of living pig embryos and keeping them in a big reservoir for a while and then killing them as somewhat repugnant. But I would find the idea of treating human embryos in this way as even more repugnant. And what is more, I would find it repugnant in a different way; I would ask myself whether the arrangement in room B was morally acceptable.

What reason do I have to suppose that people *would* sense a moral difference here? Honestly, I only have indirect evidence.[10] There is indeed a discussion about what to do with the so-called "spare" embryos fertilized *in vitro*, a discussion of which Warnock's articles are good examples, where it is asked whether they may be destroyed, used for research or stored for future implantation. Whatever position we take in this debate I believe we at least find it meaningful. It is not like discussing whether we may destroy or use for research the leaves on the trees outside the window. What is more important, however, is that there are very many people who do not think that we may treat these spare embryos in whatever way we like, and that suggests that they sense that the embryo has a value resembling the one I sense in the face of the example described above.

To turn to our second question, what kind of importance is it that we recognise in the early embryos? This is a difficult question, since the rationale behind our attitude towards the organisms might be very different from person to person, and it is not certain that our attention will be drawn to this as long as the reactions look the same. For instance, I guess that some of us are prepared to endow the fertilized embryo with a value which is due to the fact that the embryo has a potential for developing into a plainly human being, and that is a reason to react differently to what is in room B. Killing all these embryos means destroying an enormous amount of potentials!

This might be true, and I think that very many people might be attracted to some kind of potentiality argument. However, the crucial question will concern whether this is the only explanation to our reaction to the reservoir. To find this out we will have to add to the original example just as we did in our comparison between (C1) and (C2) above:

Suppose that there is a third room C in which there is a reservoir full of newly fertilized human embryos which will be destroyed when the exhibition is finished. The arrangement in C is exactly similar compared to that in B. The only difference is that in C only such eggs are collected which will not be able to develop into plainly human beings anyway. The question is whether we would have the same reactions to C as we have to A?

I am still prepared to claim that there is an intuitive difference between A

---

[10] The best kind of direct evidence would of course be to present the example to people and then ask them what their reactions are. The normal state of affairs is that a philosopher knows more about other philosophers' reactions. A philosopher's reported intuitive reactions, however, are not always reliable, since they tend to be influenced by the theory she defends. And, of course, the same will be true of my own reactions.

and C, which means that the potentiality consideration is not the only explanation of a difference between A and B. Therefore, we still have a reason to believe that SA might be applied also to newly fertilized human eggs.

But we have not yet answered the second question. Supposing that SA really is the explanation to our reactions to this example, what exactly is it that we react against? *Why* do we find the exhibition morally problematic?

Part of the reason, I think, is that the embryos are killed after the exhibition. Recall what Dworkin said about inviolability of humans in Chapter 6: "It is not important that there be more people. But once a human life has begun, it is very important that it flourish and not be wasted" (1993: 74). This would explain in a direct way our reactions against B, but it would also in a more indirect way explain our reactions against C. Even if there is no possibility for these embryos to develop and flourish if the artist refrains from destroying them after the exhibition, she is responsible for the fact that they will never develop and flourish anyway, since she could have refrained from collecting the eggs in the first place.

But I still believe that this is only part of the reason, since I think we might add to the example and get an even more complicated picture. Suppose that in yet another room, D, there is another reservoir full of early human embryos. The arrangement is exactly like that in B and C, the difference is only that here the artist has collected embryos which are already dead.

Now it might be complicated to compare the different strengths of one's reactions towards the content in the different rooms, but I do not think that this is the important objective. Instead it is to ask oneself whether one senses a moral difference between A and D, that is, will one regard the keeping of an enormous amount of dead human embryos in this way as morally more suspect than the keeping of the same amount of pig embryos (whether they are alive or dead)?

Again I will have to generalize from a single instance (myself), aware of the risks that are associated with such a procedure. I sense a difference here, even if it is fairly small and vague. But I also confess that it is difficult to distinguish between what might be a moral reaction and a merely aesthetic one, so to speak. That is to say, it might in certain circumstances be hard to distinguish between what is repugnant on moral grounds and what is repugnant on other grounds, for instance because it is distasteful. And I think that this situation is an example of this difficulty.

One of the reasons why I believe there is a dominant moral factor in one's reactions here, is that it is fairly easy to find analogous cases which definitely concern what might (morally) be done to a human embryo when it is dead. For instance, there is a moral discussion whether or not aborted foetuses might be used to supply bone marrow for medical purposes. It is true that some of these foetuses might be considered as plainly human beings and it is also true that one of the questions considered has been whether or not one has to procure the woman's consent before one takes the bone marrow or whatever it might be, but I do not think that these considerations provide the full explanation of the moral problem. Part of the problem seems to concern how to treat human organisms after they are dead too, and I believe that for many of us this question also applies to early embryos, although I am prepared to admit that the question is less pressing when we talk of very early embryos.

Therefore, I do not think the list of elements in the phenomenology of SA discussed in Chapter 6 was really complete (and that was not the intention either), since we also seem to want a human organism to be shown some kind of reverence even after its death. I am not going to insist that this is an independent element which cannot be derived from the ones already mentioned—for instance, the fourth one about using a human being as a means—since this is not the important issue here. What this reasoning shows, however, is that there is a (small) case for claiming that SA may also include dead human organisms. But once again, this claim rests on very shaky grounds, and the more important conclusion will instead concern the intuitive difference between living human and non-human organisms even at an early stage of development. Therefore, let us stick with the assumption that SA is an attitude according to which there is an intrinsic value in the complex property of being a human *and* being alive.

8.8 Summary So Far Plus Some More Examples

Let us try to collect the threads before we continue.

In the previous chapter I considered Tooley's attempts to establish the falsity of SA by means of examples. He wanted to show that there is no intrinsic moral difference between a human and a non-human being, a conclusion he arrived at after having considered some examples where species membership was the only difference between two beings and where we fail to see any moral difference. I claimed that Tooley was partly successful in these attempts. He managed to show that the species distinction between two persons which would have all their psychological and physiological properties in common, except that one was genetically a human whereas the other was not, did not place them in separate moral categories, which would be expected if SA were true.

In the present chapter I have considered the very opposite attempt, namely Warnock's attempt to confirm SA, or at least an attitude very similar to SA, by means of an example. Her example is about human embryos "kept alive *in vitro* for so long that they became plainly human". What she wanted to show is that it would be out of the question to use these embryos for experimental purposes. So this is a case where there would be a total moral difference between treatment of humans and treatment of other animals.

In my interpretation she makes two claims. First, that these plainly human beings should have a very strong moral protection compared to non-human beings. Second, that there is a difference in the moral protection which should be granted to the plainly human beings compared to the early human embryos (whatever the size of this difference).

Concerning the first claim, I concluded that Warnock is probably wrong when she claims that these prohibitions should be absolute, since it is easy to show that every kind of absolute rule will appear counter-intuitive when its consequences are spelled out. However, that does not exclude the possibility that most people would believe that there is a difference, if not absolute, between using human beings solely as a means in this way, and using non-human ones the same way. To prove that, I used Warnock's example as an inspiration when constructing another slightly altered example, which in my view better than Warnock's example could provide an intuitive support for SA. The example concerned human embryos bred *in vitro* solely for research purposes, human embryos which have been manipulated at the egg stage so that they will not develop into something that will look human. Instead they will have the same morphology as a rabbit embryo. I concluded that there is an intuitive difference between breeding such human embryos and breeding proper rabbit embryos.

Warnock's second claim seemed to be obviously true, at least judging from common sense. However, I tried to show that even if there is an intuitive moral difference between being and not being plainly human, that does not mean that being human but plainly so has no significance at all when one is compared to a non-human being or organism, and I finished by concluding that this is probably applicable also to very early embryos, perhaps even to what Warnock calls "pre-embryos".

Is it possible to give further support for SA? Since the results of this discussion depend upon whether or not I manage to interpret our normal intuitions and since this interpretation requires examples against which to test our intuitions, I believe there is value in trying to give some more examples. Unfortunately I am not sure that I am able to construct examples which have a realistic appearance. Therefore we have to trust not only our intuitions but also our imagination when judging these examples. Here is a small collection.

Suppose that one morning you read in the newspaper that outside your local slaughterhouse someone has left three sucking-pigs to die in a skip. The reason seems to be a congenital deformity which has made the pigs useless for the production of meat.

Suppose that the next day you read about a very similar story, but this time someone has found three seriously deformed eight-month-old human foetuses left to die in a skip outside the general hospital in your city. The reason this time, it has been found, is that it was necessary to abort these embryos in order to save the mother from dying. Although the doctors might have tried to save the foetuses too, they chose not to do so because of the grave deformities.

These two cases are similar enough to be compared. We might suppose that the pigs and the foetuses had a comparable capacity to feel pain and furthermore that because of the deformity and what follows from it the foetus might never develop any psychological capacity that would exceed the mental capacities of the kind of pig that the sucking-pigs might have developed into. We might also suppose that these poor beings were suffering from comparable deformities. Both kinds of beings had a comparable appearance. Although this is constructed, it is not totally unrealistic; these things could happen.

Now suppose one asked oneself honestly which news would provoke the strongest (moral) feelings in oneself. I am pretty sure that very many would react much stronger to the second day's news. And the best explanation for this, although I am aware that there could be alternative ones, is in my view that we intuitively sense a moral difference between the cases, a difference which is founded on the fact that in the one case a human being is mistreated whereas in the other a non-human being is.

Here is another example. Suppose that the director of an animal factory suddenly realizes that the arguments delivered by the organizations fighting against cruelty to animals are correct and therefore expends all his energies on developing an organism, by means of genetic manipulation, which has no mental capacities at all and the life of which is more like that of a vegetable than an animal. He succeeds in his ambitions and the result is an animal which genetically is a rabbit but of a kind which neither looks like nor behaves like any other known (healthy) rabbit. The resulting organism is rather to be compared to some kind of a pumpkin. If the fighting organizations still object to the breeding (although the director prefers to call it "growing") of these organisms, they will have to find new arguments.

Suppose now that by chance another director has also become impressed by the moral arguments of these fighting organizations and decides to create by means of gene manipulation a non-suffering meat producer. However, his strategy is to proceed from human genes and place them in animal embryos (since he does not believe that one is allowed to conduct experiments on normal human embryos which have the potential to become plainly human beings). He is successful and the resulting organism is an organism the meat of which tastes wonderful; genetically it is human although by chance this organism too looks like and has the same mental life as a pumpkin (=nil). Morally satisfied with himself, the second director starts to breed these organisms insisting that what he is doing ought to be morally compared to the growing of vegetables.

Once again, are these two situations really morally comparable, that is, do not the actions of the second director offend your moral feelings more than those of the first director? Just as above, I would be surprised to hear that these two situations were on an equal moral footing.

Let us be content with these examples, which are constructed more or less from to the same recipe. Where will this leave us?

I claimed above that at least one of Tooley's examples was problematic in that it seemed to support the falsity of SA. Part of the solution was to construct arguments which supported the truth of it. This is what we have done now. The initial paradox and problem remains, however, since even if I succeeded in showing that it is easier to find examples to support SA compared with examples with the opposite effect, that does not eliminate the problem. The problem is that we seem to have intuitive support both for the truth and for the falsity of SA.

Let us compare the two kinds of examples which speak for and against the truth of SA respectively and see whether we can find some feature which might explain why we judge them differently. Tooley asked whether we would sense any moral difference between a normal human being and a non-human Martian having the same morphology (overall biological structure) and mental capacities as the normal human being.

The examples supporting SA were different. They concerned for instance whether one would sense any moral difference between hearing that sucking-pigs on the one hand and human foetuses one the other had been left to die in a skip. I added that both kinds of beings suffered from severe deformation. Another example asked whether there would be any moral difference between breeding human and non-human "vegetables" for food.

One obvious difference is that in Tooley's example we were dealing with *persons*, whereas the beings figuring in the other examples were all non-persons. (I have once again assumed an everyday conception of personhood.) So it seems that we could try the following generalization: *SA is applicable only to cases where we deal with non-persons*, and that might be the reason why Tooley failed to see that there *is* some truth in SA after all.

8.9 "The Compromise View"

Is it possible to claim that SA can be applied to some cases but not to others? One fairly uncontroversial demand is that the principles which can be extracted from our intuitions should not yield inconsistent judgements. The question is whether or not our generalization will have that effect.

Judging from some philosophers, that is the case. For instance, writing about the distinction between killing and letting die, Rachels considers an idea very similar to my generalization, namely that the distinction might be important in some cases but not in others.

Rachels writes:

Some philosophers concede that, in the case of Smith and Jones,[11] there is no moral difference between killing and letting die; but they continue to maintain that in the euthanasia cases the distinction *is* morally important. Thus, it is suggested that the Bare Difference Argument commits an elementary fallacy—the fallacy of hasty generalization. It leaps from one example, in which the distinction appears to be unimportant, to the general conclusion that the distinction is *never important* (1986: 123).

Now an alternative to Rachels' position (supporting "the Bare Difference Argument", which says that "the bare difference between killing and letting die does not itself make any difference to the morality of actions concerning life and death" (1986: 113), is formulated in the following way (by Rachels):

Perhaps the truth is simply that the difference between killing and letting die is sometimes morally important, and sometimes not, depending on the particular case you choose to think about (1986: 123, his italics).

This is described by Rachels as "the compromise view" and it seems to be directly applicable to our discussion about Tooley. If Tooley concludes that SA lacks importance because he has found one example in which it does so, then we may accuse him of committing the fallacy which Rachels describes above. And the conclusion we have reached is very similar to "the compromise view". What I have suggested, to paraphrase Rachels, is that *the difference between being and not being human is sometimes morally important, and sometimes not, depending on the particular case you choose to think about.* However, Rachels thinks that this position is inconsistent, since it violates a formal principle of logic "that everyone must accept regardless of the content of his or her particular moral code" (1986: 125):

Principle I. If the fact that *A* has *P* is a morally good reason in support of the judgement that *A* ought (or ought not) to be done, and *B* also has *P*, then that is also a reason, of equal weight, for the judgement that *B* ought (or ought not) to be done (1986: 125).

As a general principle about reasons this principle, as it seems, is false, at least if we leave it unqualified. It might well be the case that the fact that one action has a certain property is a reason for performing it in one kind of context but not in another. For instance, suppose that action A is taking a cake (A has the property, P, of being the eating of something sweet). After having had my dinner I may well say that the fact that B has P is a reason for performing it whereas before having had my dinner I may say that the fact that A has P is a reason for *not* performing it. Whether or not P is a reason for an action depends therefore on the situation. It might also depend on the person performing the action. If I am a slim person then the fact that A has P might be a reason for me to perform it after I have had my dinner, whereas if I am a fat person then the fact that B has P is a reason for me not

[11] Smith and Jones figure in a thought experiment where Smith actively kills his younger cousin in order to get his inheritance, whereas Jones "sees the child slip, hit his head, and fall face-down in the water. Jones is delighted; he stands by, ready to push the child's head back under if necessary, but it is not necessary. With only a little thrashing about, the child drowns all by himself, 'accidentally', as Jones watches and does nothing" (1986: 112).

to perform it (neither after nor before the dinner). It might also, of course, depend on our set of values—if I like sweets, then the fact that A has P is a reason for performing it whether or not I am fat, whereas if I do not value sweets, then this fact will not be a reason for performing A. So it seems that Principle I is false in a literal interpretation. (I return to the question whether Rachels has failed to realize this.)

Therefore, if we suppose that moral reasons behave like reasons generally, then Rachels has not succeeded, as it seems, in showing what is wrong with the compromise view and therefore what he says cannot be used against our generalization either. It does not seem inconsistent to claim that the distinction between killing and letting die is important in some cases but not in others and also that the same is true of the distinction between being a human and not being one. It would have been inconsistent if we had claimed that the distinctions both are and are not important *in the same type of situation*. But that is not what we are doing; that would be an infringement of the universalizability of moral judgement. On the contrary, the reason why we specify the kind of case where the distinctions do and where they do not make any moral difference is precisely to avoid being inconsistent in our moral judgements.

What is it that goes wrong in Rachels' reasoning? According to Shelly Kagan the problem lies in the kind of argument used to establish the falsity of the distinctions in question. Kagan does not discuss Rachels in particular but instead the kind of argument which Rachels (and several other philosophers) employs, namely what Kagan calls "the contrast argument":

A very common form of argument proceeds by offering a pair of cases that differ only in terms of the factor in question. If we judge the two cases to be morally different, it is argued, this difference must arise from the different values of the given factor (everything else being held constant), and so the factor is shown to be morally relevant. If we judge the cases to be similar, on the other hand, despite the variation in the given factor, this shows that the factor is not actually morally relevant after all (1988: 5).

Clearly this is exactly the way Tooley proceeds when offering his example of the Martians and also the way Rachels proceeds in offering his example about Smith and Jones. However, Kagan claims that this way of reasoning rests on a thesis which he believes to be false:

the contrast strategy must be assuming that if variation in a given factor makes a difference *anywhere*, it makes a differences *everywhere*. Let us call this the *ubiquity thesis* (1988: 12).

I fail to see why the contrast strategy will *have to* presuppose the ubiquity thesis. As this thesis is formulated I would reject it but still insist on the usefulness of the contrast argument, since I can think of no other method of deciding whether a given factor is important (in a given type of situation) than comparing two cases which are similar in all respects except that the factor is present in one of them but not in the other. This method might then be used not only to argue that the factor is *always* important, but also to show that it is important in precisely the kind of case discussed; that is to say, we have to employ the contrast argument if we want to establish that a factor merely sometimes plays an important moral role.

But the important thing now is to consider what will happen *if* we believe that the contrast strategy can be used in combination with the ubiquity thesis.

Proceeding from our normal intuitive responses, that would actually enable us to derive inconsistent moral judgements, since we may easily show that some distinctions both are and are not morally important. This is true of the importance of being human, and Kagan has also shown that it is true of the distinction between killing and letting die or at least doing and allowing harm:[12]

First, let us use the following two cases (described by Kagan) in a contrast argument:

a) Gertrude pushes Bertrand into a deep pit, hoping that the fall will kill him so that she will inherit the family fortune; b) Seeing that Bertrand is about to fall into a deep pit, Gertrude deliberately refrains from warning him, hoping that the fall will kill him so that she will inherit the family fortune (1988: 7).

This example is very similar to Rachels' example about Smith and Jones, and if one believes that Jones's inaction was just as bad as Smith's action, then one will probably feel that b) is just as bad as a) in Kagan's example. If that is the way one reacts, one would have to conclude that there is no moral difference between doing and allowing harm, provided that the ubiquity thesis is accepted.

But then consider another pair of cases:

c) Ludwig sees Sylvia drowning, but since the rocks beneath the water would do extensive damage to his boat, he decides not to rescue her; d) Ludwig sees that his boat is about to hit Sylvia, but since avoiding her would mean steering into the rocks, which would do extensive damage to his boat, he decides not to change course (1988: 7).

I believe, just like Kagan, that many of us are inclined to judge these two cases differently. Very few would consider Ludwig's inaction in c) to be morally acceptable, and therefore the difference is not between what can and what cannot be accepted—the difference concerns that the action in d) is even *worse* than the inaction in c). If that is the way we are inclined to respond and if we proceed from these cases to construct a contrast argument, then we will also have to conclude that there is a difference between killing and letting die or doing and allowing harm.

This is inconsistent. With the help of the contrast argument and the ubiquity thesis we reach conclusions which seem to be hard to reconcile with the

---

[12] Steven Sverdlik argues that it is true also of motives for action: "I do not claim that motives always determine the rightness or wrongness of an action. I say only that they sometimes do this" (1996: 343).

ubiquity thesis. What is more, we reach conclusions which seem to clash with very simple principles of reasoning, namely that one and the same distinction cannot at the same time be both important and unimportant in all those cases where it figures. Therefore, it seems that Rachels in accepting the ubiquity thesis will be exposed to the criticism which he directs to all those who deny the ubiquity thesis—it is the one who accepts the thesis who is inconsistent and not the one who denies it.

I am not sure as to whether what Rachels intends to say really is incompatible with what Kagan says. In my view, what has gone wrong in Rachels' reasoning is not necessarily the ubiquity thesis but instead that he has forgotten one single but in this context very important word when stating his principles.

What Rachels wants to claim is, I believe, that if a factor makes an *intrinsic* difference anywhere, it makes an *intrinsic* difference everywhere. For instance, consider the following passage:

Suppose, again, that someone wants to be allowed to die but does not want to be killed. In those "particular circumstances", one may allow him to die; but, as she [Philippa Foot] says, "it does not *follow* that one may also kill him". The Equivalence Thesis does not imply otherwise. The Equivalence Thesis only says that the reason one course, but not the other, is permissible, isn't simply the intrinsic "moral importance" of the difference between killing and letting die. In this case that difference is *correlated* with another difference (between permission and objection) and this other difference is, indeed, morally important (1986: 128).

What Rachels claims here is only that the distinction in question *in itself and independently of its relation to other factors* makes no moral difference and that the contrast argument can be used to show this. Therefore, our next question will be to consider whether or not this thesis is true: is there any evidence that contradicts the idea that the distinction between killing and letting dies lacks *intrinsic* importance and that this is established by Rachels' example about Smith and Jones?

I can think of two possibilities. Suppose one believes that there *is* a difference between Smith's action and Jones's inaction. That would at least *support* the idea of an intrinsic importance of the distinction in question. The other possibility is if we could show that Rachels' thought experiment for some reason is badly constructed. Except for these possibilities I fail to see what might contradict Rachels' theses.

Let us take a closer look at the difference between cases c) and d) above. For instance, when assessing a contrast argument we have to make clear what factor or factors we allow to vary in the different cases. Kagan is, of course, fully aware of this. Considering the things that can go wrong with this kind of example, the first thing he mentions is precisely this: "Since contrast arguments are based on the idea that the effect (or lack of effect) of a given factor will be exposed when all other factors are held constant, a pair of contrast cases is useful only if all other things really *are* held constant" (1988: 9). The reason is obvious. If more than one factor varies and if we

sense a difference between the two cases, then we cannot know which factor
is responsible for the difference. On the other hand, if we fail to sense a
moral difference between the two cases, then if we let more than one factor
vary we cannot know whether both lack importance or whether one of the
factors neutralizes the other factor in a particular case.

I believe that Kagan fails to hold all other factors than the difference between
allowing and doing harm constant in this particular argument. The factors
which vary together with this difference concerns what will be the immediate
cause of Sylvia's death in the two cases. In c) Sylvia drowns, but in d) she is
killed by being hit by Ludwig's boat.[13] I am fully aware of the difficulties
surrounding this talk of what causes the death in each of these cases, but I
nevertheless believe that the distinction I indicate makes common sense.

The next question to consider is if this difference has moral importance.
What difference does it make that in the one case Sylvia dies (*by drowning*)
as a result of my not using my boat, whereas in the other case she dies (*by
being hit by my boat*) as a result of my using my boat? We have indeed a
variation here besides allowing and doing, namely what is described in the
parentheses, and the question is whether this is what makes us judge the
cases differently (if that is what we do). I believe it is.

The reason is that I think that being responsible for the fact that one's
boat (or car, or bicycle, or lawn mower, etc.) is the direct cause of someone
being harmed is a special kind of responsibility, which tends to be stronger
than the responsibility for the fact that another object is the direct cause of
someone being harmed. And I believe this is true of both positive and negative
responsibility. Therefore, if we let the factor which concerns whether the
object belongs to this category vary, then we may get a difference between
cases which describe doing and cases which describe allowing, whereas if we
keep it constant, then that difference will probably disappear. In other words,
I believe that there is a *relative* difference between the responsibility of someone
being and not being harmed by these kinds of objects: allowing someone to
be harmed by these objects is worse than allowing someone to be harmed by
some other kind of object; and doing something that directly will cause
someone to be harmed by these objects is worse than doing something which
causes someone to be harmed by some other object.

The only way of justifying this belief is to construct other contrast
arguments. Consider first the following pair of cases:

1)   Suppose that A has dug a lake on his grounds, knowing that there
        will be a certain probability P that someone might fall into it and
        drown. One day A sees that B is about to fall into the lake. A delib-
        erately refrains from warning her, hoping that she will drown (just to
        be able to watch someone die).

---

[13] We have no such difference between a) and b)—the immediate cause of Bertrand's death in
both cases is the fact that he hits the bottom of the deep pit.

2) Suppose that A has taken his automatic boat to a pond. He has started it, knowing that there will be a certain probability P that someone might get killed by it, and now he watches its movements (unable to influence them) from the shore. Seeing that his boat is about to hit B, A deliberately refrains from warning her, hoping that the boat will kill her (just to be able to watch someone die).

In my view what A allows to happen in 2) is worse than what he allows to happen in 1), and the only explanation I can give for this judgement is that the fact that one starts a boat (or car, or automatic lawn mower, or the like) will make one more responsible for what this object may cause to another being compared to the fact that one for instance digs a pond or lake. Therefore, it is morally worse just to watch someone being killed by one's boat than just watching when someone drowns in one's lake. And this is true not only of responsibility for states of affairs which are negatively valued but also for those that are positively valued. Suppose for instance that the lake dug by A in 1) will save B's life (for instance, by making it possible for B to jump into it to escape a swarm of extremely dangerous bees). Suppose also that the automatic boat started by A in 2) will save B's life (for instance, B is drowning when she suddenly can reach the passing boat). I figure that A in the second situation would be considered to be a greater (minor) moral hero than he would be in the first.

However, the conclusion that it is worse to allow harm caused by certain kinds of objects will not explain the fact that we react differently to Kagan's example about c) and d) compared to a) and b), since it is a reaction to the effect that a case of *doing* (d) is considered worse than a case of allowing. Therefore, to complete our argument we need to show also that it is worse to do harm that is caused by certain kinds of objects compared to do harm that is caused by other objects.

Compare the following two cases:

3) A pushes B into the deep water hoping that he will drown (just to be able to see him die).

4) A pushes B into the deep water just in front of his automatic boat hoping that the boat will hit him and kill him (just to be able to see him die).

Although the difference between these cases is perhaps small, I believe it is there nevertheless, and the best way of explaining it is, it seems, to relate it to the different direct causes of B's death in the two cases.

What is the difference between drowning and being killed by a boat? One obvious difference is that one's death in the second case is more *violent*, at least in the sense that there will be more blood involved. Steering one's boat at a person is a much more "fleshy" way of killing her. And that might be what lies behind the difference between 3) and 4).

One possibility is that there is a rationale for judging 1) and 2) differently but no such rationale for judging 3) and 4) differently. The reason why we tend to do so nevertheless may be that we are exposed to some kind of psychological spillover mechanism.

There are reasons for ascribing some kind of general negative responsibility for the harm that might be caused by certain objects which are such that there is a comparatively greater probability that these objects will cause harm compared to many other objects. Therefore, being a possessor of such an object is somehow being an owner of a certain kind of responsibility as well. For practical reasons this responsibility is considered to be general, which means that it is not and should not be very sensitive to the conditions that prevail in every particular situation. In other words, even if in a particular situation I have no reason to believe that my automatic boat will be more likely to cause harm to other people than the lake that I have dug, I nevertheless have a greater negative responsibility for what happens to the boat compared to what happens to the lake, because of what is stated above. So already here we have some kind of a spillover, although it is something that can be defended; there is a reason for a general intuition concerning the negative responsibility *vis-à-vis* a certain category of objects (cars, boats, chain saws, lawn mowers, and so on.)

Now, due to certain psychological facts we will have some difficulties in distinguishing these cases of negative responsibility from cases of positive responsibility. We tend to think that what is true concerning these objects of negative responsibility is also true of positive responsibility, or at least a trace of the feelings concerning the one kind of responsibility can also be found in connection with the other. The reason is that they share certain conspicuous features—they concern a certain class of normally dangerous objects. Similar things happen every day. For instance, consider one of Rachels' examples above: even if one believes that one can only defend a prohibition against killing in cases where the one killed would object to being killed, it is hard to escape a feeling of doing something wrong also in a case where one is explicitly requested by a person to end her life, for instance by giving her a lethal injection. This can explain why we judge 3) and 4) differently, and also why this difference is less obvious than the difference between 1) and 2). And this is exactly what could be expected from the presence of a spillover.

That will not however affect the main point: Kagan fails to keep all the factors between c) and d) constant. In d) one is affected by the effect whereas in c) one is not, and that might be what lies behind the intuitive difference and not that the one case is a case of allowing harm whereas the other is a case of doing harm. Therefore, the criticism of Kagan's contrast argument remains.

8.10 "The Additive Assumption"

This is part of my criticism of Kagan's objection against the contrast strategy and the ubiquity thesis. Another part concentrates on Kagan's analysis of what is wrong with the contrast argument, namely that it rests on what he calls "the additive assumption", which states that "the function that determines the overall status of the act given the values of the particular factors is an *additive* one" (1988: 14), which means that the value of every morally relevant factor adds to the overall value of the situation. This assumption, according to Kagan, is not true, since the contribution of one factor might be a function of the presence of another factor. The example he chooses to illustrate his point concerns self-defence:

Most of us believe that in some situations killing someone in self-defense can be morally permissible. Imagine such a situation, and compare these two cases: e) In order to defend myself against the aggressor, I push him into a pit, expecting the fall to kill him; f) In order to defend myself against the aggressor, I refrain from warning him about the pit into which he is about to fall, and I expect the fall to kill him. Most of us will certainly want to claim that the moral status of these two cases is the same, even though, obviously enough, in the first case I do harm, while in the second I merely allow it (1988: 18).

Now Kagan claims that this conclusion might be reached also by the person who advocates the distinction between doing and allowing. The distinction makes no moral difference in legitimate cases of self-defence. Therefore, what this advocate will have to claim is that typically there is a moral difference between doing harm and allowing it to happen, but in cases of self-defence there is no such difference. And, as Kagan says, this is not only a coherent view, it is the view which most people believe is the true one:

Yet if the additive assumption is correct, then the view I have just described *must* be false, since it violates the ubiquity thesis to claim that although the do/allow distinction normally makes a difference, in cases of self-defense it does not (1988: 19).

Therefore, what Kagan's example shows is that most of us do not in the end accept the implications of the additive assumption. The additive assumption makes the mistake of counting each factor as though it makes an *independent* contribution to the value of the situation or the moral status of the act, and a contribution which is simply "added to that made by other factors" (1988: 19). What Kagan suggests instead is that, at least in the case of self-defence, this factor acts as a "zero multiplier", a term which is explained in the following way:

Recall the earlier mathematical example where $S = x \cdot y + z$, and suppose for simplicity that x can equal only zero or one. When x is equal to one, the differences in y will make a difference to S; but when x is equal to zero, differences in y will not matter at all. The self-defense/non-self-defense factor seems to act somewhat like x in this example: normally, with a value of one, it allows the do/allow distinction to make a difference; but in cases of self-defense, it takes on the value of zero, and so differences between doing and allowing harm do not affect the moral status of the act at all (1988: 19).

I interpret this in the following way. It makes a moral difference whether an action is an example of doing harm or an example of allowing harm provided that the person who performs the action/inaction wants to harm someone for other motives than self-defence, i.e. she has aggressive motives for what she does/allows. But this is the same as saying that the distinction between doing and allowing harm is important in combination with another factor, i.e. the factor which is the possession of aggressive motives. The self-defence factor acts like a zero multiplier in the sense that its presence will mean the absence of that factor the presence of which is necessary for the distinction between doing and allowing harm to play any moral role.

But as far as I can see this analysis in no way contradicts the ubiquity thesis on the condition that it is stated in terms of the *intrinsic* moral importance of a factor, and this, as I claimed above, is a reasonable interpretation of Rachels in view of what he says about a case where someone wants to be allowed to die but does not want to be killed. Recall that the Equivalence Thesis defended by Rachels does not deny that there is a difference between killing and letting die in such a case. This thesis is only about "the intrinsic 'moral importance'" of this distinction: "In this case the difference is *correlated* with another difference (between permission and objection) and this other difference is, indeed, morally important" (1986: 128).

I am not sure that Rachels would accept what I am going to say now but what he says here could be rewritten in a way that is consistent with Kagan's analysis of the self-defence factor. What Rachels claims is that the absence of an objection against killing in particular (or allowing to die in particular) acts as a zero multiplier in so far as it will render the distinction morally uninteresting, whereas the presence of the factor about an objection will indeed make the distinction relevant. So in order for the distinction to be morally important it would have to be combined with the objection factor.

But is not this exactly what Kagan says of the aggression factor, and if so, how can his analysis be an objection against a defence of the ubiquity thesis? The point of Kagan's criticism is that it is a mistake to try to "identify the separate and independent contributions of individual factors". The best we can do is instead to "attempt to identify *clusters* of features which together always combine to generate a reason of a particular strength for or against performing an act" (1988: 28). But this does not contradict the ubiquity thesis, since it only denies that we can find a factor which has intrinsic importance for the value of a situation or the status of an act. What the ubiquity thesis states is that *if* we find a factor which is intrinsically important anywhere, it will be important everywhere, which means that if we can show that a certain factor in one case has importance not for the results to which it may lead nor the sake of the things with which it is normally associated nor for it being combined with another factor,[14] then we may safely conclude

---

[14] Observe that "intrinsic value" is used here in contrast also to being valuable as a factor in combination with another one.

that the factor in question has this kind of importance in every other case as well.

Where does this leave us? Is Rachels right and Kagan wrong? I am inclined to think that there are some aspects of what they claim that seem correct but there are also aspects of what they both claim that seem incorrect or at least that could be expressed somewhat differently.

As far as Rachels is concerned there are two question marks that ought to be considered.

(1) If we state the ubiquity thesis (which in Rachels' words says that logic "requires that the distinction be always, or never, important" (1986: 124) in terms of intrinsic importance, then we may avoid the criticism that Kagan directs against it. The question is if such a thesis is capable, as it was intended, of showing that the compromise view is wrong. It seems to me that in that case the ubiquity thesis will be compatible with the compromise view, which, as we said above, only claims that the distinction "between killing and letting die is sometimes morally important, and sometimes not, depending on the particular case you choose to think about" (1986: 123).

This—what is stated in the quotation—can easily be interpreted as exactly the same view as Kagan's. A distinction might be important in some cases but not in others, due to the fact that in some cases the distinction acts together with some other factor or factors whereas the absence of these other factors will act as a kind of zero multiplier in some other cases. And once again, this is a perfectly consistent view. The distinction is important in every case of a certain type (where the other factors are present) and unimportant in every case of a certain other type (where the other factors are absent). It is true that Rachels when stating the compromise view talks about the importance of what *particular* case one chooses to think of, but I do not think that is inconsistent with claiming that the importance of the distinction in the particular case will depend on what type of case it is, where "type" refers to these combinations or clusters discussed earlier.

(2) The next question is perhaps more serious. So far I have not questioned the ubiquity thesis. I have only questioned whether it is able to do the work that Rachels wants it to do. Now I also want to call the ubiquity thesis into question.

Recall the two cases that gave rise to this discussion. On the one hand we claimed that Tooley was able to show that the distinction between being and not being human had no relevance in a case where the moral status of two persons was compared, whereas I claimed that by reformulating one of War- nock's examples we could show that the distinction had importance in a case where we compared the moral status of two non-persons. I suggested that may- be being human has intrinsic importance in all cases where only non-persons are involved but lacks such importance in all cases where persons are involved.

One might think that these two cases are consistent with Kagan's analysis of the distinction between killing and letting die in cases of self-defence, since we might describe the presence of personhood as a kind of zero multiplier just as Kagan described the factor of self-defence. But in my view there is a difference, since all cases which cannot be described as self-defence and where Kagan admits that the distinction between doing and allowing might have some relevance, all these cases have one positive factor in common—they contain an aggressive motive. And it does not sound too far-fetched to claim that doing in combination with an aggression factor is morally more serious than allowing in combination with the aggression factor. At least there is some logic in this.

On the other hand, if we look at the two cases where being human plays a different moral role, we will not easily find a *positive* factor that might explain why this is so. I have claimed that the distinction seems to be important in all other cases except in cases that concern persons. The distinction will have importance in the *absence* of a positive factor. And therefore Kagan's analysis will not be directly applicable to our cases.

There is also a difference in the analysis of the phenomenon between Kagan and Rachels. Rachels is willing to admit that the distinction between killing and letting die sometimes might be morally relevant. But, Rachels says: "All the Equivalence Thesis requires is that, in such a case, it is some *other* feature of the case that makes the difference" (1986: 127). Therefore one might state the general difference between Rachels', Kagan's and the view proposed here in the following way. We are all prepared to admit that a distinction might be important in some cases but not in others, *but*:

The explanation for Rachels is that we have such a situation when there is some other factor responsible for this difference. This other factor is the morally important one and not the distinction, which makes a difference only *in the light of* this factor.

The explanation for Kagan is, as we have seen, that the distinction might be important *together with* some other factor. The distinction is not important in itself but in a cluster of other factors.

In my view there is no need to look for certain combinations of factors in this sense to explain the variation in moral importance.[15] It is enough to point out that cases differ in this regard—some of them provide the necessary *background* for a certain distinction to stand out and some of them do not.[16]

[15] Indeed I assume that it is *not* the property of being a living human being together with being a non-person that lies behind the goodness of being a living human, since then being human would not be intrinsically good. I thus assume, in Thomas Hurka's words that "a state's good-making properties, the ones that make it intrinsically good, must themselves be intrinsic properties" (1996: 566–7). Cf. also Christine M. Korsgaard (1983) and Noah M. Lemos (1994).

[16] The difference between my position and Kagan's is indeed fairly small, and in a recent correspondence Kagan seems to think that there is no difference at all: "even if a factor lacks intrinsic difference in this sense, it might still possess 'extrinsic' significance—that is, *genuinely* make a difference, but only in the right kind of context. I remain confident that this last point is enough to challenge many of the uses of contrast arguments (both positive and negative) in

Am I claiming that the distinction has intrinsic importance only in some cases, and would that make sense if we understand intrinsicality in terms of independence, which in this context would mean a value or importance of a thing or property or characteristic irrespective of its relation to other things? Yes, maybe what I want to say is that being human has intrinsic importance after all, importance in all possible worlds and circumstances. However, combined with the value of being a person, that value so to speak outweighs or shouts louder than the value of being human, although the latter value is there nevertheless.

I do not feel obliged to develop the details of my position, as long as it is clear that it is not, in my view, the combination of the property of being human and some other factor that is important in our thought experiments.

8.11 Summary, Conclusion and Further Reflections

In this chapter I have tried to present a counterweight to Tooley's examples which in his view undermine SA. I claimed that Warnock has constructed an example which might give us a skeleton to a type of example which instead *supports* SA.

The arguments considered were all so-called contrast arguments, where the ambition is to hold all other factors constant except the distinction that is investigated. Now the problems come if we believe that a distinction is always or never important, since then we can find conclusive arguments both for the truth and the falsity of SA. Therefore, in the second part of this chapter I tried to make sense of the idea that a distinction might be important sometimes, and sometimes not, depending on the type of case one considers. I claimed that both the proponents of the idea that the moral importance of a certain distinction may vary and the proponents of the opposite idea tend to be careless when stating the object for their attack.

For instance, Rachels is a proponent of the ubiquity thesis which claims that a distinction has intrinsic moral importance either always or never. However, this thesis does not hit the view he wants to argue against, i.e. the compromise view, which claims that a distinction *may* have importance only sometimes, since this view is not, as it seems, about *intrinsic* importance.

Kagan makes a similar mistake when he tries to defend the compromise view. His strategy is partly to show that the ubiquity thesis is untenable, but he tends to ignore the fact that the ubiquity thesis should be formulated in terms of intrinsic importance. In other words, many of the very ingenious examples that Kagan constructs fail to hit the ubiquity thesis.

---

the literature. (Indeed, using this vocabulary, we might say that one of the main points of the additive fallacy paper was that many larger arguments that appeal to contrast arguments conflate the difference between intrinsic and extrinsic significance.)"

However, I claim, although with some hesitancy, that those examples which were built of Tooley's and Warnock's original examples *might* support the idea that the distinction between being and not being human has intrinsic moral importance only sometimes, an idea that *will* contradict the ubiquity thesis, formulated the way Rachels intended it to be formulated.

What is the conclusion to draw from this? Well, if we believe that the idea of human dignity can be defended by pointing to people's adherence to SA, and if we want to have a clear picture of the scope of this dignity, then we also have to know to what kind of human beings special worth is ascribable, according to SA.

If there is some substance in the ideas discussed above, SA is applicable only to human beings which are not also persons. This will of course circumscribe the scope of SA and one may wonder if this is what those who formulated SA in the first place really had in mind, for instance Roger Wertheimer. I do not think so, but this is less important. The important thing to consider is whether this kind of SA might be of any use. I think that the principal part of the force of SA will remain even after we have stated that it applies only to non-persons, since I dare to say that most of the cases where SA turns out to be relevant are cases in which the life and wellbeing of non-persons are at stake. This is the case when we discuss experiments on foetuses, abortion, euthanasia on people in irreversible coma, and so on. Therefore, the question of human dignity will be as morally relevant as ever even if we restrict the scope of SA in the way suggested here.

There is a somewhat more serious problem, namely that the restriction suggested is not only incompatible with the scope of the original SA but also seems to be incompatible with its *content*. For instance, recall the way Wertheimer defined SA: "a human being has human status in virtue of being a human being (and thus each human being has moral status)" (1974: 107–8). Now, as it seems, it turns out that only some of the human beings have human dignity—the non-persons.

I do not think we have a contradiction here. Surely, what I have tried to show in the last two chapters is not that persons are *less* valuable than non-persons, since that would be absurd. What I have tried to show is instead that the special value which comes from being a human in itself, i.e. having human genes, pertains to non-persons only (or at least can be perceived only in those beings). Again, human persons have a direct value on their own (since people generally think they have a special value) which compensates for the lack of value which is genetically grounded, but then they will share this value with all other persons, human as well as non-human.

The value of persons will also be discussed in Part III, but these values will not concern values which emanate from the fact that people normally find persons more valuable than non-persons by the mere virtue of being persons.

8.11.1 SA AND AGENT-RELATIVITY

I will soon consider an objection to my analysis of SA raised by Ingmar Persson. I am not sure that I am able to meet it but in order to be able to provide something like an answer I think we may profit from a more detailed discussion of one possible element in SA.

My thesis is that it is the fact that a being is a human one *per se* that lies behind our evaluative attitude towards this being. I have in other words supposed that SA is a *basic* attitude; it is an attitude that is in one sense belief-independent. We have been considering two kinds of *derived* attitudes in particular: First, an attitude according to which a property has value in virtue of its causal connection with other things (which are valued for what they are in themselves). Second, an attitude according to which a property has value in virtue of what normally comes with this property.

Now I will consider whether SA is a derived principle in another sense (which was mentioned in Chapter 7), namely in the sense that it rests on a belief concerning what species one belongs to. Is it really the fact that other human beings are human *per se* that makes us believe that they are more valuable than non-humans; is it not rather that we are fellow members of the *same species*?

One of the reasons why we have to take this suggestion seriously is the way we have argued for the existence of SA. We said that it is reasonable from an evolutionary perspective to expect a built-in sensitivity to species membership. But if so, would not the most reasonable mechanism work with agent-relative similarities, so that one can expect a sensitivity to belonging to *the same species* as one does oneself? There is no obvious biological reason why I should protect another human being unless it is the case that I am myself a human being.

It might well be the case that we can *explain* the fact that most people embrace SA by pointing to the biological value of such an attitude.[17] But there is no automatic correspondence between the explanation of an attitude and its phenomenology. The reason why we embrace SA might be that we are humans ourselves, but this does not mean that it is this *relation* to other humans beings that we value, since the biological value of having an attitude with this particular phenomenology is more doubtful.

The only way to settle this question is to make some more thought experiments, I believe.

Suppose you participate in the HUGO project and are one of the persons whose genes are to be thoroughly analysed. The result is astonishing, since it turns out that due to a radical genetic change your genetic make-up is more similar to the genetic make-up of a baboon than to that of a human. Therefore,

---

[17] I will in this discussion ignore the difficulty of explaining from an evolutionary perspective what is asserted in the previous part of this chapter, i.e. that SA is applicable only to some human beings, namely non-persons.

given the genetic species concept, you are to be classified as a member of the species *Papio sphinx* (for instance) rather than as a member of the species *Homo sapiens*.

What would your reactions to this be? Of course, we have to speculate. Is it reasonable to believe that you would suddenly regard other human beings as being a little less valuable than you did before you had this knowledge? That is doubtful, and spontaneously I would say that the opposite reaction would be the more natural one—you would *regret* the fact that you were not a member of the human species.

This is problematic, however, since we cannot without being inconsistent use this as an argument for the intrinsicality of SA. The reason is, of course, that we have claimed that SA makes an evaluative difference between non-persons that are and non-persons that are not humans. Therefore, claiming that you would consider yourself to be less valuable (which I believe would be the natural interpretation of the fact that you felt regret) would so to speak prove too much. It would not only prove that SA is about the intrinsic value of belonging to the human species and therefore lacks agent-relativity; it would also prove that SA makes a difference as to whether a person belongs to the human species or not. The latter question was discussed in Chapter 7 and will not be resumed.

So let us modify our example. Suppose that there is a risk that the genetic change you have undergone is hereditary. You have two newborn daughters who are twins and it turns out that one of them has been the object of the same kind of genetic change as you have, a change, it should be added, that has no overt, behavioural or functional effects whatsoever. What would be your reactions to this piece of information? Would you regret that your daughter had undergone the genetic change or would you consider it to be a good thing from her perspective (which would be the natural thing to expect if SA were agent-relative)? Would the genetic change mean an increase of value in relation to her sister? I do not think so. If I try to imagine what it would be like to be placed in this situation, I would rather regret the fact that one of my daughters had undergone the change, and that seems to suggest that the change in question will not mean an increase of value in my eyes.

Another thought experiment might be to try to imagine what it would be like first to get information about this change in your personal genetic identity and then to undergo the kind of thought experiments considered in this chapter. For instance, suppose that one morning you read in the newspaper that outside the zoological garden in your city someone has left three young baboons to die in a skip. The reason seems to have been a congenital deformation. Then suppose that the next day you read about a very similar history, but this time someone has found three strongly deformed eight-month-old human foetuses left to die in a skip outside the general hospital in your city. Also this time the reason seems to be the fact that the foetuses had grave deformities.

Would one really consider the first case to be worse than the second case after one has received information about one's genetic identity? I doubt so; I believe the second case would still provoke the strongest moral feelings in oneself.

And there is a natural explanation for this. I believe that there is no obvious biological reason why we should understand SA in an agent-relative way. As long as these thought experiments have nothing to do with reality we have no use for a qualified SA, which exhorts one to assign a special value to human beings *only on condition that one is a human being*. In *this* world it is enough to exhort one another to assign a special value to the humans *period*, since in this world no other beings than human ones are capable of having an intellectual grasp of an attitude like SA. It is particularly the simple norms that get internalized and that manifest themselves in, among other things, SA.

8.11.2 OBJECTIONS

Now I will consider some objections raised by Ingmar Persson.[18] Persson seems to admit the existence of SA, but he does not think that it is in the end about the *intrinsic* value of being a living biological human, but instead rests on certain metaphysical assumptions which we may be forced to give up.

Recall that I claimed that even if SA is applicable only to non-persons it will be relevant in many morally pressing situations, for instance in situations where we consider whether or not it might be right to perform euthanasia on a patient. And I claimed that part of the problem here seems to be that we regard the body as a living human organism and that that in itself means that we feel morally unfree in our treatment of it—it is not as morally unproblematic as it would have been if the body instead belonged to a non-human animal.

Now Persson asks us to consider the following thought experiment. Suppose that we have a human being, A, in chronic coma. Suppose furthermore that we know that A would welcome death in these circumstances. Persson is willing to admit that there might be a tendency in many people nevertheless to regard as morally problematic the killing of A—most of us would not be able to kill her with a light heart; we would not be able to free ourselves of a feeling that killing A would be a morally serious action.

Then consider another scenario. Suppose that we were able to transplant those structures in A's brain that underlie A's consciousness and personality to another human body. The result of the operation would be A's personality residing in a new living human body. We might also add that the body had belonged to A's twin sister who unfortunately had been killed in a car accident

---

[18] Since these came up in conversations I can only hope that I am able to reproduce his position correctly.

which left the body in a vegetative state while those parts of her brain that were responsible for her consciousness were destroyed for ever.

It is plausible to assume that this new information about a successful transplantation will change our attitude towards the possibility of killing the body that the brain structures underlying A's consciousness were collected from. We would probably find it *less* morally problematic to kill this body now. But how to explain this if my analysis of SA is true, according to which there is something morally special *per se* about a living human organism? The body in question is still a living human, nevertheless we seem to have changed our attitudes towards it when informed about the transplantation.

Persson suggests that we analyse this in the following way. We have an attitude towards other human beings—both those who are conscious and those who are not, and that attitude rests on two assumptions. The first assumption is that a human organism—for instance a human being in chronic coma—is one of us. So one element in SA, according to Persson, is that we value other beings in so far as we believe that they belong to our community. The second assumption is a metaphysical assumption about identity. According to this assumption we are identical with animals or organisms of the species *Homo sapiens*.

Let us begin with the second assumption. Persson believes it to be false. We are not essentially individuals of the species *Homo sapiens*, since we would not consider it essential for the identity of A that she remains the same human animal during all the phases of her existence. We would regard A as continuing to exist as numerically the same individual also after the transplantation.

In this example A continues to exist in another human body, but this is not essential for our diachronic identity. We will get the same result if we imagine that the brain structure was transplanted into a body of an intergalactic being that definitely would not qualify as a member of the human species. I believe Persson is correct here, and that was also the point of the discussion about Gregor Samsa in Chapter 2. This was also a tacit assumption in the former section.

So Persson believes that we ultimately value persons and not human beings as biological organisms and that the reason why we are inclined to value a human being also in a state of unconsciousness—as for instance A in chronic coma—is that we make the mistaken metaphysic assumption that A is identical with the human body that is left in a vegetative state. We *think* of the body as A—if the patient is our grandmother we have a tendency to think of our grandmother as still existing in the bed in front of us when we visit "her" at the hospital and take part in a decision as to whether or not to let her die. This tendency will vanish in Persson's thought experiment, or at least we feel much less confident about it—under pressure our tendency towards animalism diminishes—and we tend to cease to think of the body as our grandmother and cease also to think of it as dictating moral concerns, which proves that the foundation of our human dignity may well lie not in our existence as members of the human species but instead in our existence as *persons*.

We tend to regard not only the killing of bodies of persons in coma as morally problematic but also the killing of human foetuses which evidently are not yet persons and perhaps even not merely conscious beings. I think Persson would explain this case in a similar way. Since the baby when born no doubt is one of us—which according to Persson is one important element in SA—and there is a natural tendency to regard the baby as the same individual as the foetus before it is born, then it follows fairly naturally that we regard the foetus also as one of us and therefore also regard it as valuable, even when it lacks a capacity for conscious thought and experiences.

But I am not so convinced that this analysis fits in also when we discuss the kinds of cases we have considered in this chapter. For instance, in what sense is a fertilized egg without any possibility to develop into a normal adult human being one of us? Yet we seem to react against using it in the way described in the example about the reservoir in the exhibition. And the same is true about the example of the director of an animal factory. In what sense is this meat-producing organism with human genes one of us? Yet we seem to regard it as morally repugnant to actually use it as a meat producer.

So I believe that it is not at all clear that there exists an indispensable element in SA according to which we value other human beings and organisms in virtue of a belief that they belong to our community, and that was also one of the points in the previous sub-section where the example from the HUGO project was discussed. SA does not seem to be agent-relative.

So I am not convinced that Persson's analysis of SA is to be preferred to the one I have suggested. It might be that there is an important aspect of SA that is correctly analysed by Persson, but I also think that there is a case for analysing another aspect of SA in the way I have suggested. One reason for claiming this is the following fact. In order to show that what we value is personhood and not membership of the human species it is not enough to show that our attitudes towards, for instance, our grandmother's previous body will change as a result of the transplantation, since that will follow also from my analysis of SA. I also believe that personhood dictates a special moral concern—and it might be that after the transplantation we realize that we need no longer hope that our grandmother will wake up in her previous body. So we cease to have an attitude towards the body which is dictated by the belief that there might be a small chance that our grandmother will wake up again (in this body).

What we need to show in order to reject my analysis is that after the transplantation there is *no value at all* left in the living body from which the brain structure was taken, or at least that the body is no more valuable or morally important than a similar body from an animal. This can be doubted or at least it has to be shown. Is it reasonable to believe that we would be capable of killing the body with as light a heart as if it had been the body of an animal?

To be sure, Persson might explain this judgement, given that it exists, by referring to half-believing and similar phenomena, but then his analysis will also be more complicated. What I claim is that there is still a case for my analysis and that it is very difficult to decide conclusively which of the aspects is the most central one in SA—the one about personhood, which Persson suggests, or the one about membership of the species *Homo sapiens*, which is what I suggest.

Now I will consider another objection from Ingmar Persson. In order to settle what SA is about, Persson exhorts us to consider the following thought experiment.[19]

Imagine that there are three possible ways of going out of existence in a nuclear explosion. For instance, we might imagine that there are three kinds of nuclear bombs the use of which will have different effects for us humans. Let us imagine a nuclear explosion

(1)   which instantly turns us to dust.

(2)   which makes us irreversibly comatose at once but lets us linger in a vegetative existence for a short time and then preserves our bodies for a longer time.

(3)   which instantly removes life and consciousness but preserves our organisms intact for a longer time.

Persson comments: If human *life* has intrinsic value, (2) is best. If the existence of a human *organism* has intrinsic value, then (3) is as good as (2). If human *consciousness* has a special intrinsic value—concern—(1), (2) and (3) are of equal value.

Since I have claimed that SA holds particularly that human life has intrinsic value it seems that I would have to claim that most people would regard (2) as the best alternative. However, this is probably not so, since I believe that most people would not consider (2) to be better than (1). Quite the contrary, they would consider (1) to be better than (2)—it is better for us humans to go out of existence instantly than to linger in a vegetative state for a short time and then having our (living?) bodies preserved for a longer time.

I believe that this can be met in different ways.

Suppose that SA really is about simply valuing the existence of human life. This does not mean that we value also the tragic existences described in (2) and the reason is simply that these bodies once did belong to persons that probably would prefer to go out of existence instantly rather than linger on in a vegetative state like that. We tend to think—rightly or wrongly—that a person's body belongs to the person, and we tend furthermore to think, I believe, that this is the case also after the person has died. What we have in (2), therefore, is the remnants of persons who probably would not be interested in this kind of hopeless bodily existence and that is, I figure, the reason why we tend not to think that (2) is better than (1).

---

[19] Also this is based particularly on verbal discussions with Persson.

I also believe that a similar point can be made without bringing in the attitudes of those persons who died as a result of the explosion. The existence of an enormous amount of bodies in a vegetative state is tragic in virtue of the fact that we know that these bodies before the explosion did belong to living human persons. We do not judge the value of the existence of these bodies by considering these living bodies for what they are in themselves, but instead we consider them in the context of the tragic explosion.

Finally, in view of the elements of SA discussed in Chapter 6, we are allowed to claim that SA is about an intrinsic value of the existence of human life in the sense that we would consider the existence of human life better than the non-existence of it *per se*. Remember that one element in SA was inviolability—SA assigns an inviolable value to their objects, which means that it regards an object as valuable only once it already exists. We do not necessarily want more of an inviolably valuable object and that includes also, I believe, that we will not necessarily regard the future existence of an inviolably valuable object as valuable. And that might be the reason why we do not consider (2) to be better than (1). On the other hand, what SA claims is that once we already have situation (2), that is, once we already have a world in which human existences linger on in a vegetative state, then it might well be the case, according to SA, that certain moral concerns are appropriate in relation to that situation that would not have been appropriate in relation to (1). And that is not, it seems to me, a point of view that it is unreasonable to ascribe to common moral sense.

CHAPTER 9

CRITIQUE OF ARGUMENTS FOR SA

> Almost (but not quite) everyone who considers the matter comes
> quickly to the belief that human beings should assign higher
> moral priority to the interests of other humans than to the
> comparable interests of other animals. But a convincing
> justification for this belief has not been easy to find.
>
> Harlan B. Miller & William H. Williams
> *Ethics and Animals*

In the previous two chapters we have considered arguments for and against SA. These have been so-called contrast arguments, a type of argument which shows whether a certain distinction either has or lacks moral importance, by comparing two cases that differ merely with regard to this distinction. Of course, the contrast argument thereby appeals to our intuition. If we feel no moral difference between the cases, then we conclude that the distinction is morally unimportant (at least in this type of case). And the opposite conclusion is reached if we sense a moral difference. This argument would be a non-starter if moral intuitions were not allowed to play some role in our moral thinking.

In the present chapter I want to consider some arguments which do not appeal to our intuitions, at least not as arbiters in contrast arguments. The choice of arguments is more or less random. But I believe that the kind of *criticism* expressed will affect most of those arguments that actually have been used to show why human beings have a certain kind of worth.

The main difference between the two previous chapters and the present one can also be expressed in the following way: we have so far tried to show that we sense a moral difference in the distinction between being and not being human. In this chapter I will consider some attempts to show why we are justified in sensing such a difference. In previous chapters we demonstrated a moral difference whereas the present chapter discusses attempts to give it some rational foundation.

There are some other important differences.

(1) We have discussed arguments for and against the intrinsic or direct importance of being human also in previous chapters. The problem has been that the philosophers discussed seem to be sliding between this thesis and another thesis about the indirect importance of belonging to our species. Therefore, one reservation concerned whether these philosophers actually were arguing about SA or about another thesis.

In the present chapter I would like to sharpen this reservation. The arguments considered are not obviously arguments for SA, even if some of the philosophers seem to think so. Therefore, the present chapter will somehow end up between the arguments for SA and the arguments for another thesis which will be considered in the next chapter, namely that being human is important not for what it is in itself, but for what normally comes with being human.

(2) I do not believe that there exist any convincing arguments for SA besides the contrast argument. The only way to show that there is an intrinsic moral difference between a human and non-human being is to appeal to our intuitions. The various attempts to justify SA in other ways have failed, or so I shall claim.

However, this too has to be qualified. In one sense the present study can be seen as some kind of justification for SA, since what I claim is that given subjectivism concerning what makes things valuable and given that people normally consider being human as something that justifies treating human beings differently from non-human ones, then we actually have a reason for regarding human beings as morally special. But observe that this is a kind of second-order justification for the idea of a human dignity, not a first-order one, which I believe that most of the attempts to argue for SA are.

The difference is the following one. In my view one cannot possibly argue for a special worth of humans unless one supposes that being human either already is or in the future will be valuable for a significant number of subjects who have the capacity for valuing this property (for what it is in itself). Therefore, I have no argument to convince someone to adopt a special attitude to being human if it should turn out that my ideas concerning the frequency of such an attitude like SA were false. My ambition is not to make people believe that humans are morally special unless a significant part of them already think so. This is a second-order justification since it will pre suppose an already existing evaluation. Furthermore, it is not exactly an attempt to justify SA if this is interpreted as an attitude according to which a human being has human status *only* in virtue of being human. What the idea of a human dignity defended here says instead is that being human is intrinsically important in a qualified sense, that is, humans have their status in virtue of the property of being human and *given* an already existing tendency to value this property. And this is precisely what the idea of a human dignity defended here says: human beings are valuable since we believe they are; the idea of a human dignity is made up of the existence of SA. I want therefore to distinguish between arguments for human dignity and arguments for SA.

The arguments for SA or at least for the idea that human beings are very special considered in this chapter do not make these kinds of presuppositions. They do not try to justify the idea of a special worth by pointing to an existing evaluation (although Blumenfeld and Nozick come very close to doing so). As I interpret them they are attempts at first-order justifications of a special attitude to humans, since they would probably regret a change in our attitudes to other humans in the direction that, for instance, the animal rights movement strives for. The philosophers try not merely to draw conclusions from an attitude that happens to exist; they want, I believe, these attitudes to exist in the first place as well.

It is hard to avoid overlapping aspects of both the arguments for SA and the critique of them considered in the previous chapters and the present one. But I believe it wise to make a collection of positions which in different ways argue for the direct importance of being human before leaving this question. One of the reasons is that much of the discussion about, for instance, animal rights has been concentrating on the possibility and impossibility of such arguments.

9.1 Gaylin's List

The reason for choosing Willard Gaylin is that I believe he represents a common type of proponent of SA, and therefore he is also subject to a type of critique with an extensive area of application.

He writes:

I have selected five unique and inter-related attributes of our species that make us special: Conceptual thought; the capacity for technology; the range of human emotions; a "Lamarckian" genetics; and the last, if not autonomy, is very close to it, and that is freedom from instinctual fixation (1984: 60).

One obvious problem with this reasoning is that if you want to show that one kind of being is more valuable than other kinds, then it is not enough to point at certain characteristics that make up the difference between the being in question and other beings. Gaylin makes a classic mistake which also has been attributed to Aristotle, namely the mistake of searching for demarcation criteria when the question concerns what reasons there are for treating beings demarcated in a certain way differently from other beings.

To believe that there is no need for such a reason is to break what has been referred to as Hume's law which roughly states that no normative conclusion can be derived from empirical premises alone.[1] The step from establishing the fact that a certain species is special (for instance, in the sense that Gaylin believes it to be special) to concluding that this species is "particularly worth saving" (Gaylin, 1984: 69) is illegitimate.

On the other hand this step is legitimate if one presupposes a normative premise to the effect that beings with these kinds of special properties ought to be given a special moral protection. But then the crucial question will be to make sense of this premise.

In my view Gaylin fails to do so. And I believe that one reason why is that he most of the time insists on the *intrinsic* importance of the capacities listed;

---

[1] The passages which usually are believed to express this thought can be found in Book III, Part I, Section I in Hume's *Treatise* (1896: 496). It is not necessary here to start a discussion as to whether Hume really would accept Hume's law as we have formulated it above.

he lists all kinds of manifestations of these capacities but he does not account for their importance. Let me take some examples.

9.1.1 CONCEPTUAL THOUGHT

Concerning the first characteristic, he writes:

> Conceptual thought is an exclusively human capacity and is a function of that extraordinary thing called the human brain. I list only four specific manifestations—language, symbolism, anticipation, and imagination. [...] The use of symbolism allows us to do all sorts of extended things. The world of mathematics rests on our capacity to abstract and symbolize. Poetry and arts are testaments to its power (1984: 60, 62).

What is lacking here is an explanation why a being capable of doing mathematics and writing poetry is particularly worth saving. Of course, one can always try to appeal to intuitions. But suppose we construct a contrast argument in which the task would be to assess the worth of two individuals on a desert island. They have all properties in common except that one of them is capable of doing mathematics. Is the one with the mathematical capacity more intrinsically valuable than the other one? Most of us would not think so, I believe.

Gaylin also mentions the capacity of anticipation, which, according to him, "represents a great advance in the struggle for survival [...] If you have an appropriate sense of fear then you can anticipate the pain at the mere sight of the predator, and run like hell" (1984: 62). Once again, what is it in this that makes the being which has this capacity especially worth saving? Intuitively it seems that we have *less* reason to save a kind of being that is capable of saving itself in this way.

It is much easier to account for the indirect importance of these capacities. If a being has a mathematical capacity, then it is easy to imagine various kinds of consequences of this. For instance, many people find pleasure in the execution of this capacity and furthermore the capacity can have a significant instrumental value. And in view of the various good effects that may come from a certain capacity it is easy see a value in the preservation of a being that has the capacity in question.

Almost the same is true of anticipation. Pointing to the role that this capacity plays for the survival of the human species is not a convincing argument, which can easily be seen if we look at an analogous case. For instance, suppose I want to show that a cheetah has a special kind of worth and argue in the following way. "Running extremely fast is a unique feature of cheetahs. The significance of this capacity is shown in its great value in the struggle for survival." This is no argument. A certain being does not become valuable because of some property which can be useful in its struggle for survival. Every kind of being has such properties.

It is true that there is a difference here. All species probably have some conspicuous features which can explain why they have been successful in the history of evolution. But many of these features are shared by more than one species. For instance, being camouflage marked is something that is typical of more than one species, and the same is true of being a skilled flyer, and so on. What is special about the attributes Gaylin considers is that they—at least according to him—can be assigned to human beings only.[2] What is so special about the capacity of anticipation, for instance, is that human beings are alone in taking evolutionary advantage of it.

But this is no good argument, since even if it were true that only human beings may profit from having the capacity for anticipation and therefore are unique in this respect, human beings are not the only kind of being that possesses some property which is advantageous for it but not for other kinds of beings. Being unique in the way human beings are is not unique—having a unique feature which one has profited from in the struggle for survival is not something unique. Consider once again the cheetah. Being able to run faster than every other quadruped is unique for cheetahs and it is no doubt something that has promoted this species' chances. But this is not the same as claiming that there is a special value in preserving this species. This conclusion is a *non sequitur*.

There is a possibility of making sense of the moral importance of the capacity for anticipation. For instance, killing a being who can anticipate the fact that she is going to be killed is probably worse than killing someone who lacks this capacity for the simple reason that foreseeing that one is going to be killed is under normal conditions something painful. And this is of course not only true of killing; to anticipate every kind of negative experience is under normal conditions something that is negative in itself. Therefore the suffering of a being which has this capacity is often double. There might be a primary source of suffering and in addition to that there is the anticipation of what will happen. And most people would say that these facts are morally relevant.

This is far from the intrinsic importance that Gaylin intended to assign to the features he mentions. If what makes anticipation important is that it may play a role in a being's suffering, then suffering is the primary thing. And this capacity is not unique for human beings. At most Gaylin might show that human beings are unique insofar as their capacity to suffer is more developed, but this is probably not what Gaylin wanted to say in the first

---

[2] This is controversial, and once again, Gaylin does not present any convincing evidence for the contention that only humans have this capacity. He quotes Julian Huxley (1944), but that is not enough. Several present-day scientists interpret even classic experiments in terms of anticipation. For instance, Stephen Walker writes: "it makes sense to say at least some of the time that Pavlov's dogs salivated because they believed that a buzzer should be followed by food, Thorndike's cats released latches because they remembered that this would allow them to get out of confinement, and Skinner's rats pressed levers because they expected, on the basis of previous experience, that this would enable them to eat food pellets" (1983: 112). See also Rosemary Rodd (1990: 131).

place. He believes that human beings are unique in a much stronger sense. Therefore, my point still remains: he does not show why conceptual thinking plays the kind of moral role he wants it to do.

9.1.2 CAPACITY FOR TECHNOLOGY

Then consider the second attribute:

The ultimate value of real knowledge is, for the most part, in its (often unanticipated) applications. The theoretical is the plaything of the creators until applicability lends it nobility through service to humankind. Science is the servant of technology, not the other way around. Technology and application lend glory to science (1984: 64).

First of all, this is problematic since not all human societies have a technology, if by this term we mean applied science. Primitive societies have a technology only in a primitive sense.

Gaylin may point to the fact that he refers to the *capacity* for technology and not the actual use of it. But I figure that that will not help, since primitive societies do not even have the capacity for technology if by this term we understand what they can do if they get the opportunity. Primitive societies have the capacity for a technology only in a much more primitive sense than the one Gaylin seems to have in mind, and therefore it seems reasonable to assign less value to them if Gaylin's attributes are taken to be necessary for having a full-fledged value.

Perhaps "capacity" instead should be understood as "potentiality". (I believe there is such a use of the term as well. For instance, I might believe that I have the capacity to get a result below seven hours in the Vasa ski race on the condition that I go into training for it. I believe that I have the capacity *now*; it lies in my capacity to be able to do such a thing in the future if I go into training.) Then we may very well ascribe the capacity for technology also to primitive societies, since there is nothing in their constitution that will prevent them from developing this capacity if they want to and if they get the opportunity. So Gaylin can avoid our objection by resorting to a weak interpretation of "capacity". And until further notice I will assume that this is also what he does.

Second, what Gaylin says is problematic in another respect. Consider what he says in the quotation. First he makes a comparison between the value of knowledge and the value of technology. What he suggests is that knowledge has no worth except as a possibility to be applied. That is why technology is valuable—technology *is* applied knowledge. However, if we then look at his reason for valuing applicability we see that he refers to the service to mankind. So Gaylin seems to reason in the following way. Knowledge is valuable in virtue of its applicability, or in virtue of developing into a technology. Technology in turn has its value in virtue of the services it might do to humankind.

In my view this argument is open to serious criticism. It has the same kind of circularity that we found in connection with the first point. We cannot explain the value of humankind by referring to the fact that humans have access to knowledge that when applied might be useful for humankind! We cannot explain the special value of a being by citing the fact that it has a capacity that might be valuable for this being. For one thing it is a *non sequitur* and for another very many species have such capacities.

And notice that the problem is not only that the value of an attribute in this reasoning seems to be indirect—Gaylin is willing to admit that—the big problem is that Gaylin would need an independent argument to establish the value of mankind, otherwise he would not be able to make sense of the value of applied knowledge as a means. A means will have positive value only as long as the same is true of its end.

Therefore I maintain that Gaylin fails to show why the capacity for technology might be a foundation for human dignity.

9.1.3 THE RANGE OF HUMAN EMOTIONS

The third capacity that Gaylin points to is the range of our emotions: "While lower animals share with us rage and fear, they share none of the ennobling emotions" (1984: 64). The only ennobling emotion Gaylin mentions is the emotion of guilt, but what he seems to drive at is moral emotions generally.

He also notes that we are prepared to ascribe some of these moral emotions to animals in some situations and he replies:

My wife is convinced that when our dog does some outrageous canine feat he is terribly guilty and he should not be punished. That dog is never guilty. What she is seeing is fear, albeit a "guilty fear". He is terrified that he is going to be caught (1984: 64).

In my view Gaylin handles this question somewhat light-heartedly. First of all he seems to reject one common-sense opinion (his wife's) in favour of another one (his own). The only argument he gives is that "true guilt", as he puts is, "implies that we have internalized a set of noble standards by which we judge ourselves and that if we have done wrong we punish ourselves" (1984: 65). Of course, described in this way it does not seem unrealistic to suppose that this is a uniquely human emotion, but Gaylin's talk of *true* guilt indicates that his definition is persuasive, and furthermore his requirement of the internalization of *noble* standards means that Gaylin very easily can dismiss every suggestion to the effect that animals seem to be able to have the emotion in question by refusing to regard the internalized standard as noble. This idea of *noble* standards is not the kind of independent foundation of human dignity that Gaylin would need, since the crucial question will remain: what is a *noble* standard of conduct?

Second, even if we accept Gaylin's definition of guilt, he has not shown that non-human animals are incapable of having *any* moral emotion. For instance, if we count compassion among the moral emotions there is ample scientific evidence that at least some of the primates are capable of having that emotion. Experiments have been made where rhesus monkeys at the price of severe suffering refuse to watch another animal suffer from an electric shock; "a majority of rhesus monkeys will consistently suffer hunger rather than secure food at the expense of electroshock of a conspecific" (Masserman *et al.* 1964: 585). Such scientific evidence is not at all considered by Gaylin.[3]

Third, there is in my opinion some tension between the characteristics discussed in 9.1.1 and this section. The reason why the capacity for concept formation was morally important, according to Gaylin, had to do with certain of its manifestations, for instance, anticipation and imagination. However, if Gaylin believes that non-human animals really have the capacity for fear, he must believe that they also have an anticipatory capacity. And this is exactly what he does—we humans share these stress emotions with many lower animals, Gaylin says (1984: 62). But why then are only some of the beings with the anticipatory capacity uniquely valuable? Furthermore, if anticipation is a manifestation of conceptual thought and if animals are capable of anticipation, does this not show that they probably are capable of conceptual thought as well?

Fourth, we have not yet considered Gaylin's whole list of attributes, but we can already see that many innocent, so to speak, humans will fail to fulfil the necessary conditions on it. For instance, many severely mentally handicapped people do not have the capacity for guilt, and neither does a one-month-old child or a human being in irreversible coma. Have they no human dignity? It would be very surprising if Gaylin said so and claimed that human dignity is reserved for normal adult human beings and can be lost, for instance, during the last demented phase of life.

This is simply not the way people normally treat the concept of human dignity, and therefore Gaylin's view is susceptible to the so-called "argument from marginal cases", described by Regan in the following way:

(1) Given certain criteria of the possession of rights, some marginal humans and not just all animals will be excluded from the class of right-holders. (2) However, humans, including those who are marginal, do have rights and so belong in the class of right-holders. (3) Therefore, each and every one of the criteria of which (1) is true must be rejected as setting a requirement for the possession of rights (1979: 193).

---

[3] S. F. Sapontzis claims that compassionate, courageous, etc. actions are not restricted to the primates and he also denies that such actions can be accounted for by instinct or conditioning. Thus he writes: "The cases of porpoises helping drowning sailors must be spontaneous acts of kindness. There is no reason to believe porpoises have developed an instinct for saving humans, and they certainly have not been conditioned to perform such acts through training or repetition" (1980: 47). Sapontzis denies that this capacity will make animals into moral agents and he also claims that when he is talking of kindness, honesty etc. this is primarily referring to a pattern of behaviour and not to the agent's relation to it. Nevertheless, in my view Sapontzis defends a thesis which Gaylin probably would deny, since Sapontzis is not interpreting these behaviour patterns the way Gaylin does.

Regan refers to this description as "the critical phase of the argument from marginal cases" among other things because it appeals to the assumption that marginal humans *have* rights.

In fact all the attributes considered so far are vulnerable to this argument. Many marginal cases lack the capacity for conceptual thoughts; they do not even have a potential for developing a capacity for technology and as we said they lack the range of human emotions Gaylin describes. Either he will have to deny them human dignity or reconsider his criteria for the possession of it. Since he cannot reasonably do the first thing, he will have to do the second one.

What I have said here also applies to the last two attributes that Gaylin mentions. Let me just make some comments on them as well.

9.1.4 LAMARCKIAN GENETICS

Gaylin describes human beings as "Lamarckian animals", referring by this to our capacity for culture:

In the human species alone acquired characteristics are transmitted, not by protoplasmic design, but by the power of a transmitted culture. The power of being able to transmit knowledge to avoid rediscovery is of enormous adaptive value (1984: 66).

Apart from being susceptible to the critical phase of the argument from marginal cases, I wonder whether this is not also susceptible to what Regan refers to as "the constructive phase". The crucial question then is not whether *all* human beings have the capacity on Gaylin's list, but instead whether *only* human beings have them. Is Gaylin really pointing to capacities which are *uniquely* human?

This question has been incidentally considered in connection with the other attributes. But I think it should be evident by now that Gaylin is listing attributes which hardly can be denied to animals altogether, at least not without argument. This is true of conceptual thought, moral emotions and also of cultural power (animals may learn what kind of beings to watch out for and what to eat by being in close contact with their parents during an early phase of their life).[4]

If this is true and if one has a solution to the critical phase of the argument from marginal cases, then the following argument is applicable instead:

(4) Humans, including those who are marginal, have rights and therefore belong in the class of right-holders. (5) However, given the most reasonable criterion of the possession of rights, one that enables us to include marginal humans in the class of right-holders, this same criterion will require us to include some (but not all) animals in this class. (6) Therefore, if we include these marginal humans in the class of right-holders, we must also include some animals in this class (1979: 196)[5]

[4] See also C. Boesch (1991). For an anthropological perspective on this question, see Barbara Noske (1993: 264–7).
[5] Notice that the argument from marginal cases might be stated in terms of *legal* protection as

The contention of what we have said in 9.1.3 and this section is that someone who wants to defend human dignity by means of criteria which resemble those on Gaylin's list is trapped in a dilemma. One can only solve one but not both of the following problems: (a) The problem of selecting criteria that apply to *all* human beings to whom one wants to assign the moral privilege in question. (b) The problem of selecting criteria that apply *only* to these humans and not to any animals. The only criterion considered so far which manages to avoid this dilemma is the purely biological one: all and only those beings with human genes have dignity.

This is not the only problem. Once again Gaylin's main reason for putting the attribute in question on his list seems to be the fact that it has played an important role in evolution. Gaylin is pointing to the power of culture as an adaptive mechanism: "Since we do not have to rediscover the wheel anew in each generation, we are free to build on that knowledge to develop the cart and then the car and then the spaceship—and then?" (1984: 66). This is no argument for assigning special privileges to human beings, unless one has presupposed a more basic principle according to which having evolutionary advantages over other species means having a higher worth as well.

In one sense the factual premise behind this kind of argument might be correct: human beings are special in evolutionary terms, since they control their environment in a way that other species do not. On the other hand, this reasoning is also risky, since it implies that we will have to assign dignity to whatever kind of species will turn out to be evolutionarily superior. Therefore, the day we humans lose the fight against the rats and the rats start to multiply at the expense of the human species, then we would have to deny dignity to the humans and assign it instead to the rats.

Furthermore, if evolutionary advantage turns out to be a basis for comparing the values of different species, why not also for comparing the values of different individuals within one and the same species? That would mean that healthy, good-looking, muscular and intelligent persons probably would have a higher value than persons who lack these attributes. Both conclusions are undesired.

9.1.5 AUTONOMY

The final point is

freedom from instinctual fixation. I would make the point that if we are not truly autonomous agents, freedom from instinctual fixation is as close to autonomy as is necessary to insure our dignity (1984: 66–7).

It seems that there is some kind of correspondence between the attributes in 9.1.2 and in this section, since they both concern moral capacity. However,

---

well. See Gary L. Francione (1993).

in the end Gaylin will disappoint one, since he does not argue for the connection between having the capacity for being moral and having a particular worth. Perhaps he does not believe there is any need for arguments:

The capacity to do evil, while a risk of freedom, is a component in defining the good. [...] But I also know that freedom is intrinsic to what makes our species worthwhile. If we sacrifice that freedom, if we sacrifice that special inquiry, that capacity to look to the stars, to reach out for something new, we cease to be a species particularly worth saving. The human species is the glory of creation. I have very little sympathy for people who talk of "rights" of animals (1984: 68–9).

Without commenting on the other statements in the quotation, I suggest that Gaylin would at least need to make clear what is valuable in the moral capacity. Is it the capacity as such or is it the capacity for doing morally good things? In view of some other passages I think it is the latter, but in that case human dignity seems to be something that can be forfeited, unless the *mere* capacity to do good things, and not its actual manifestation, lays the foundation of human dignity.

9.2 Blumenfeld's Moral Collectivism

Jean Beer Blumenfeld expends some effort trying to answer (the critical phase of) the argument from marginal cases, that is, the problem of what kind of criteria to choose in order to include all human beings in the class of right-holders (which Gaylin fails to solve). She formulates the problem as follows:

Certainly what is interesting about humans is that they are thinking, or rational, animals. Nevertheless there can be and are human beings who do not possess sufficient abilities to qualify as thinking beings: infants, idiots, lobotomized persons, persons in coma, and so on. This shows, I believe, that the ability to think, speak, or form concepts is not a necessary condition for being a human being, or a person. Furthermore, it seems unlikely that any other criterion which makes use of psychological properties will be more successful than this one (1977: 262).

This needs to be commented upon. In the quotation she addresses the conceptual question of when to call an organism a human being or person (she does not distinguish between these concepts, as it seems). Her positive answer is that an organism is a human being if it at least possesses a human brain (1977: 263). This will avoid the problems that pertain to various psychological criteria.

However, given that one believes that being a human being or person *means* being entitled to certain moral privileges, Blumenfeld's quotation might very easily be *read* as a formulation of (the critical phase of) the argument from marginal cases.

One crucial thing is that Blumenfeld admits that it is the mental capacities that are *interesting* about humans even if they could not possibly figure in the criteria for human dignity (or a right to life) unless one is prepared to exclude the marginal cases from the class of humans who have it. And Blumenfeld is not prepared to do that, since she believes that moral intuitions assume "that all human beings do possess the right to life" (1977: 266). This suggests that the mental capacities of an organism are what lies behind the fact that we are prepared to ascribe the right to life to the being in question, although denying the right to life to every being which lacks these capacities would have counter-intuitive consequences.

The solution of this problem is, according to Blumenfeld, to make a distinction between the capacities one has as an individual organism and the capacities one has as a member of a class of beings with certain typical features. Blumenfeld's solution thus is to deny what has been referred to as moral individualism, which Rachels describes in the following way:

The basic idea is that how an individual may be treated is to be determined, not by considering his group memberships, but by considering his own particular characteristics. If A is to be treated differently from B, the justification must be in terms of A's individual characteristics and B's individual characteristics (1991: 173–4).

Notice that (the critical phase of) the argument from marginal cases will presuppose moral individualism. In order to believe that some marginal cases and not just all animals are excluded if certain criteria for the possession of a right are accepted, is to assume that these criteria should be applied to the individual—the individual has to possess the necessary properties and therefore every criterion which is about properties that *some* of the marginal cases do not possess has to be rejected—*all* human beings have to fulfil the criteria *individually*.

Blumenfeld denies that "each individual creature, regardless of its species, stands or falls on its own with respect to the right to life" (1977: 266) and formulates the following principle instead:

It is morally wrong to intentionally kill an innocent individual belonging to a species whose members typically are rational beings, unless at least one of the following conditions obtains:... (1977: 266).[6]

This is a way for Blumenfeld to escape an objection to the effect that the principle she takes as one of her points of departure—"Intentionally killing an innocent human being is morally wrong, unless [...]"—is "speciesistic" in that it directly favours a certain species. Blumenfeld's principle is in her own words a non-species-specific principle, and she even considers the possibility that it may turn out that innocent members of the cetacean family have a right to life in this sense (and therefore she has not refuted the constructive phase of the argument from marginal cases; she has instead utilized it).

Even if Blumenfeld's principle does not expose a preference for one particular species, one might well argue that it is speciesistic in another more

---

[6] Blumenfeld is discussing the moral problem of abortion and one of the exceptions she has in mind is when killing is necessary to save the mother's life.

literal sense in that it seems to lay stress on one particular *class* before all others, namely the species class. Normally speciesism is understood as the favouring of *Homo sapiens* before other species, but here Blumenfeld is instead proposing the favouring of a member in virtue of its belonging to a *species* (rather than other classes) the members of which have certain typical properties. Every individual organism on earth is a member of various biological collectives or classes, and why choose the *species* as the morally fundamental collective when deciding what moral status to grant an individual?

9.2.1 SPECIES VERSUS OTHER BIOLOGICAL CLASSES

Let us first consider how Blumenfeld's principle works in relation to other biological classes. For instance, what plausibility would a principle have that claimed it morally wrong to kill an innocent individual belonging to the class of white-skinned primates whose members typically are rational beings, unless...? May the biological class of white-skinned primates play the same role in a moral principle as the biological class of a species?

This question can be interpreted in different directions. It can be seen as a general question concerning whether Blumenfeld's principle is a basic one or merely a derived one. Tooley discusses this question and his argument seems to have the following form. Suppose Blumenfeld's principle is an instance of a general principle, namely the following one:

It is morally wrong to intentionally kill an innocent individual belonging to any *class* whose members typically are rational beings, unless [...] (1983: 70).[7]

If we can show that there are instances of this general principle that have to be rejected, then we have to reject the general principle as well, which of course means that Blumenfeld's principle lacks justification. One instance of this principle is the one I proposed above which states a moral collectivism in terms of white-skinned primates. Is it plausible?

No, I do not think so. I have to speculate, but suppose that the hominids are in majority amongst the class of white-skinned primates, which probably means that the typical member of this class is a fairly rational being. Furthermore, suppose that, as it happens, one day a lemur is born white-skinned in contrast to (as I assume) all other lemurs. Would that mean that it could be ascribed the right to life? Would it be reasonable to do so? I do not believe so. At least it would be hard to imagine that the *white skin* of the mutant lemur would be a good reason for ascribing the right. If it has the right, it will probably have it on other grounds.

Therefore, one line of reasoning concentrates on the implications of the general principle, rejects it and consequently also the foundation of Blumenfeld's principle. This reasoning assumes that Blumenfeld's principle is a derived one.

[7] A similar principle is discussed by Rosalind Hursthouse (1987: 103–7).

Another line of reasoning does not make this assumption, but instead it asks the following question. If Blumenfeld's principle is basic and if we can construct other basic principles with exactly the same logical form and if we can also show that these other basic principles are implausible, would that not cast a gloom over Blumenfeld's principle as well? Or is there any morally important difference between the class of species and other biological classes, for instance the class of white-skinned primates?

There is indeed one difference, namely that one can easily imagine what it would be like for an individual to be born as a member of the latter class by parents who *fail* to be members of that class. It is easier, so to speak, to pass from a class that lacks a right to life to a class that has such a right given that we formulate the right in relation to the class of white-skinned primates, whereas a situation of species migration is much harder to imagine.

But it is difficult to see what relevance this could have for the present issue. Why ascribe the right to life only to individuals of whom the parents could be ascribed the same right? Why *restrict* the right to life in this way? On the contrary, it seems to be much more *fair* to state the criteria for a right to life in such a way that the children of certain biological classes are not automatically excluded from the class of right-holders.

Furthermore, even if there did exist a difference like this between the class of species and, for instance, the class of white-skinned primates, and even if we had a satisfactory reply to the objection concerning the fairness of the criteria, the same kind of reasoning would apply to other biological classes and then why not instead refer to them in a principle concerning a right to life? For instance, if it is difficult to migrate between different species, it will be equally difficult to migrate, in the way described above, between classes of animals such as birds and mammals. These collectives seem to have the same standing as far as migration from one collective to another is concerned, and if migration has this kind of relevance, then the criteria for a right to life could be related to this collective just as well.

However, consider the following principle: "It is morally wrong to intentionally kill an innocent individual belonging to a class of animals (such as mammals, birds, reptiles, etc.) whose members typically are rational beings, unless..." From the human perspective this would not, I imagine, be an acceptable principle, at least not if it implied that an individual lacked a right to life if it did not belong to such a class of species. The reason is of course that human beings do *not* belong to a class of animals whose typical members are rational beings. Given such a principle there would not be *any* holder of the right to life, since there exists no class of animals whose typical members are rational beings. Mammals can display some degree of rationality, but when Blumenfeld refers to rationality in her principle, she has probably in mind a fairly high-level capacity, since otherwise she would not be able to deny it to those marginal cases that she mentions, that is, infants, idiots, lobotomized persons, and so on. If mammals typically display some degree of rationality I doubt that it exceeds the capacity of these marginal cases. On the other hand, *if* we choose to talk of rationality in the sense that is typical of all mammals, then our problem will be that the principle stated will be too inclusive, since then also rats and sheep and every individual mammal would have a right to life. It might be that they have, but Blumenfeld does not think so, and that is enough for our purposes.

Therefore, Blumenfeld has failed to explain what is so special about the class of species that makes it possible to figure in a collectivistic moral principle whereas other classes, even biological ones, cannot figure there without offending moral feelings. She has failed to show that the species has the special kind of moral relevance that she believes it has and therefore I have assumed that we may point to the results that would follow if we formulate collectivistic moral principles in terms of other classes than species and use this as an argument.

This strategy could be questioned. For one thing, it seems contradictory to assume that Blumenfeld's principle is basic and at the same time compare it with other principles which are constructed out of the same general logical form as Blumenfeld's principle. In order to make an impression on Blumenfeld that kind of reasoning will presuppose that she actually accepts the general principle from which both her principle and the principle with which we compare it are derived.

If I accept a certain principle as basic, may I as a consequence of this reject every principle that deviates in the slightest way from my basic one? In principle, yes. But I believe that if we can show that very counter-intuitive results follow from principles that have a similar logical form compared to the principle under investigation, then that will at least increase the burden of proof of the proponent of this principle to show that this counter-intuitiveness is not common to all principles displaying this logical form.

This means that our strategy or argument from comparison can be used if we bear in mind that one has to be careful when drawing conclusions from it.

9.2.2 A COUNTERPART OF BLUMENFELD'S PRINCIPLE

What does a principle like Blumenfeld's suggest? What does it mean to say that it is morally wrong to intentionally kill someone who has got a certain property if it does not mean that it is *not* wrong to kill someone who lacks this property? For obvious reasons, you cannot infer the latter from the former, but it seems nevertheless plausible to understand Blumenfeld's principle as a *criterion* for having a right to life.

Therefore, we may test Blumenfeld's principle against the following counterpart of it:

It is not morally wrong to intentionally kill an innocent individual belonging to a species whose members typically are not rational beings, unless at least one of the following conditions obtains:...

This is not a plausible principle if one considers for example the following situation. Suppose that one day we are visited by a being from outer space who has the same physical appearance as a human being, although there is no genetic correspondence. Furthermore, its emotional and intellectual capacities are comparable to the capacities of any human being. Surely, you would be inclined to ascribe a right to life to this being.

Now, suppose that it is not the case that the individual has the intellectual capacities which are typical of beings of its sort. Suppose instead that one characteristic of the members of its species is that most of them lack mental capacities that could be compared to what is normal in the human case. Suppose furthermore that even if the proportion between the rational members of this species and the irrational ones is one to two, there are twice as many rational beings of this species as there are human beings on earth. But since the non-rational ones are in the majority they will determine what is typical of the species.

After having received this piece of statistical information, would you be prepared to reconsider the spontaneous judgement that our visitors are entitled to a right to life, i.e. that it would be wrong to kill them? I doubt you would, and that will be the argument against Blumenfeld. To take into consideration the above mentioned statistical facts when pondering whether or not it would be wrong to kill someone would indeed be absurd.

9.2.3 POSITIVE AND NEGATIVE MORAL COLLECTIVISM

One possibility for Blumenfeld is to argue for an asymmetry between, so to speak, positive and negative moral collectivism. She might claim that only the positive form is reasonable, i.e., the form which says that you may be accorded the moral privileges that ultimately are reflections of the properties that the majority of your biological class are in possession of whereas you must not be *denied* a moral privilege with reference to the fact that the majority of your biological class does not deserve them. This is an instance of a general principle according to which you are allowed to benefit by belonging to a certain biological class whereas you are not allowed to do the opposite—the properties of the typical member of your biological class may never be held *against* you.

I believe this general principle has intuitive appeal. Imagine the following cases.

A is the child of one of the world's most well-known altruists, B, who has twice received the Nobel peace prize for her outstanding charitable deeds. Surely there is a tendency in people to have a positive attitude towards A in virtue of the fact that she is the daughter of B. C, on the other hand, is the son of one of the world's most evil men, D, who has tortured and killed innocent children in thousands. Surely there might be a tendency in people to have a negative attitude to C in virtue of the fact that he is the son of D. However, I also believe that there exists another parallel inclination, namely to be indulgent towards the first kind of tendency and not to make allowance for the second one. The most reasonable interpretation of this is that we accept that A *gains* because of the fact that she belongs to a biological class (B's family) whereas we do not normally accept that C *loses* because of his belonging to a certain biological class (D's family).

And if there is an intuitive foundation of a principle like this, then Blumenfeld may well claim that moral *individualism* is applicable in a case where we have a rational member of a species the typical member of which is non-rational whereas moral *collectivism* is applicable in a case where we have a non-rational member of a species the typical member of which is rational and that that explains why the marginal human cases might be accorded the right to life, according to Blumenfeld's principle, whereas the visitor from outer space must not be denied a right to life.

What is the rationale behind this asymmetry? Can we explain these intuitions (as being derived from some more basic one)? Yes, I think we can. We tend to believe that no individual is harmed by this general principle but that some individuals will gain from it; i.e., we believe that we give to some individuals without taking something away from others. We think that our principle is an exclusively generous one; it has only positive effects.

However, if we consider the case carefully we will see that this could be questioned. Surely, one way of describing what you do when you confer a privilege upon some individuals in a certain group of beings (for instance, the class of non-rational animals) is that you make some individuals better off than they would have been if the privilege was not conferred on them. But at the same time, this very action could also be described as a harm, at least in some sense of this term, done to the individuals upon which the privilege is not conferred, since evidently they are worse off than they would have been if the privilege instead was conferred on them. This is one way of describing an injustice—Blumenfeld's principle does have negative effects for those non-rational individuals which do not belong to a class of beings whose typical member is rational, since they will suffer from an injustice. And you cannot, I believe, deny this without begging the question at issue.

So, it is not the case that positive collectivism will have no negative effects for any individuals and therefore Blumenfeld will not be able to justify a division between positive and negative moral collectivism by appeal to intuitions about generous moral principles.

9.2.4 AN ARGUMENT FROM GENETIC CHANGES

Tooley has discussed Blumenfeld's principle and proceeded from the assumption that it is basic. Now proceeding implicitly also from the assumption that Blumenfeld is formulating a criterion, that is to say, a necessary condition of a right to life, he makes the following thought experiment, which I want to quote at length:

Suppose that there is some species, typical members of which are rational beings, and that this species is divided into two groups that, as a matter of fact, never interbreed, though they are certainly capable of doing so. Let John be an individual belonging to the smaller of the two groups. If the situation is as stated, and if Blumenfeld's principle is correct, it will be wrong to kill John even if John is not a rational being. Now imagine the world changed in the following way. A long time before John is born, a disease strikes the other group, causing a genetic change which destroys the rationality of all members of that group, and of all their descendants. Such a change is compatible with the two groups still being capable of interbreeding. If this had happened, it would no longer be true that the majority of individuals belonging to the species were rational beings, since the individuals belonging to the larger group would no longer be rational. Consequently, Blumenfeld's principle would not apply, and there would no longer be any reason to refrain from killing John (1983: 71).

This is in my view a fairly convincing argument against Blumenfeld's principle. But I think by paraphrasing it we may make it even stronger.

Suppose we use Tooley's example as a description of the human species. Then let us assume that some thousands of years ago a small highly civilized group of human beings discovered a way of travelling to other solar systems. Let us say that they went to an earth-like planet in the solar system of Alpha Centauri and managed to establish a colony which since then has had no contact with earth. Eventually the inhabitants of this planet, let us call them Alphas, became twice as may as the inhabitants on earth. However, a short time after the colony was established a disease struck the Alphas, which caused a genetic change that for ever destroyed their rational capacity (which is also part of the explanation for why they lost contact with earth). However, they are still members of the human species.

Now suppose furthermore that the truth of these emigrants and their fate has been unknown to us human beings on earth until very recently. We suddenly realize that we do not belong to a species the typical member of which is rational. Would that knowledge affect our moral concerns for human beings on earth? If this story were true, would Blumenfeld be prepared to claim that it was a mistake to confer a right to life even on a rational human being on earth? Would she really reconsider the conviction that a normal adult human being possesses a right to life? I doubt she would, and therefore her principle has to be rejected, once again on the assumption that it states a criterion for a right to life.

My reason for these doubts has of course to do with the enormous moral change that would follow from a piece of information that I believe many of us humans would consider to be extremely surprising and stimulating to the imagination but that very few, if any, would consider to be relevant for how we humans on earth ought to treat each other. For Blumenfeld's part the difference between the existence and non-existence of the colony would not only be a difference in the moral status of non-rational human beings, but also a difference in the status of the *rational* ones!

If our analysis of Blumenfeld's principle is correct and if our arguments against it have the force I believe they have, we have to reject the kind of moral collectivism that Blumenfeld's principle suggests.

We have to keep in mind, however, that arguing successfully against Blumenfeld's moral collectivism is one thing and doing so against moral collectivism in general is another.

Blumenfeld's principle assigned importance to what is *normal* for a species. This was interpreted simply as what is true of *most* of the members. The term "typical" which figures in Blumenfeld's principle was given a mathematical or statistical interpretation. And it was mainly this feature that made it untenable, which we tried to show in some examples.

We also made the assumption that Blumenfeld's thesis was basic, which meant that there was no explicit justification to consider. In what follows I want to discuss an idea which at first glance seems to be an instance of collectivism and that does *not* build on statistics. Furthermore, we will not assume that the principle to be discussed is a basic one.

9.3 Nozick's Defence of Speciesism

In a critical review—which has attracted quite a lot of attention—of Regan's book *The Case for Animal Rights*, Nozick hints at an idea that he believes underlies partiality to conspecifics. Like Blumenfeld he realizes that the argument from marginal cases presents a problem and just like her he seems to believe that the solution lies in the rejection of moral individualism. He writes:

it is not easy to explain why membership does and should have moral weight with us. Shouldn't only an organism's own individual characteristics matter? Normal human beings have various capacities that we think form the basis of the respectful treatment these people are owed. How can someone's merely being a member of the same species be a reason to treat him in certain ways when he so patently lacks those very capacities? This does present a puzzle, hence an occasion to formulate a deeper view. We then would understand the inadequacy of a "moral individualism" that looks only at a particular organism's characteristics and deems irrelevant something as fundamental and essential as species membership (1983: 11).

Here Nozick seems puzzled over how being a member of the human species can be morally important whether or not she has certain capacities, although the moral importance of being human is founded on these capacities. The puzzle concerns, in my view, a conflict between whether the privileges conferred on humans should be justified in terms of species membership or certain mental capacities, i.e. whether the importance of being human is direct or indirect.

Rachels remarks: "To say this is a 'puzzle' is to *assume* that species membership *is* important, as though that were something we know to be true, and to take it merely as outstanding business to figure out why" (1986: 74).

Here Rachels criticizes mainly what Nozick proceeds from, namely that we somehow know that being human is morally important. If this is false, then it follows fairly naturally that we do not have to explain and justify why this is so. However, in my view, Nozick's problem is the very opposite. I believe he is correct when he claims that membership of the human species does have moral weight with us, in view of SA, but I am not so sure that we have to explain why species membership has this significance, let alone that we have to justify that it *ought* to have it.

9.3.1 NOZICK'S FIRST SUGGESTION

Nozick's attempt at formulating a deeper view has two independent parts. The first suggestion is the following one:

The traits of normal human beings (rationality, autonomy, a rich internal psychological life, etc.) have to be respected by all, including any denizens of Alpha Centauri. But perhaps it will turn out that the bare species characteristic of simply being human as the most severely retarded people are, will command special respect only from other humans — this as an instance of the general principle that the members of any species may legitimately give their fellows more weight than they give members of other species (or at least more weight than a neutral view would grant them). Lions too, if they were moral agents, could not then be criticized for putting the interests of other lions first (1983: 29).

I am not sure how to interpret this. Recall the question Nozick wanted to answer: "How can someone's merely being a member of the same species be a reason to treat him in certain ways when he so patently lacks those very capacities [which are the basis of the respectful treatment]?" (1983: 11). Here it looks as if Nozick wants to defend some kind of moral collectivism in order not to be vulnerable to (the critical phase of) the argument from marginal cases. Moral individualism is explicitly regarded by Nozick as an inadequate doctrine.

The problem is that this first suggestion does *not* present an alternative to moral individualism, since if the reason why human dignity should be ascribed also to a marginal case is that she after all belongs to our species, then that is of course a characteristic that *she* has—and therefore it is an instance of moral individualism. In fact, there is a tension between claiming that a marginal case should be respected in virtue of the capacities of some of the members of her class and claiming that a marginal case should be respected by members of the same species in virtue of being a member of their species. There is no reference whatsoever to any mental capacities in the second claim. On the contrary, the marginal cases should, by this suggestion, be respected for what they are in themselves—members of a certain species.

This tension is caused partly by the fact that Nozick formulates the general principle in terms of what is true of the members of *any* species, which suggests that the basis of discrimination is the common species membership *alone* and not common membership of a species which normally, typically or sometimes display certain properties, such as rationality, autonomy, and so on. Therefore, suppose I am the only member of a species who actually had these capacities; suppose I am unique in this respect compared to all my conspecifics. Nozick's principle suggests that I ought (or at least legitimately may) give my fellows more weight than members of other species, which, once again, proves that there is no reference to the capacity for rationality or autonomy, etc. in the basis of discrimination.[8]

The tension is also caused by the fact that Nozick's principle is agent-relative whereas I take moral collectivism (at least if it has the same structure as Blumenfeld's) to be agent-neutral. Whether it is right to show special respect to some individual does, according to Nozick, depend on the properties of the agent, i.e. on whether or not she belongs to the same species as the individual in question. Blumenfeld's principle, on the other hand, prescribes special treatment of all the members of a species (whose members typically are…) by any agent, irrespective of whether or not she belongs to the species.

There is another question that has to be decided, namely whether Nozick's principle not only allows the members of *any* species to give their fellows more weight but also allows them to give *any* fellow more weight than they give members of other species.

There are actually two questions involved here. First, we may ask whether Nozick subscribes to an idea discussed in the previous chapters, namely that species membership has intrinsic importance when non-persons are compared but not when persons are. There are certain passages in the quotation from Nozick that might suggest such a view (for instance that he only discusses how to treat those beings who lacks the capacities that he believes are the basis of respectful treatment by all beings). In this view all persons are equal whereas non-persons are unequal depending on whether or not they belong to one's own species. Nevertheless, I shall decide not to make this interpretation of him.

Second, if one claims that any conspecific may legitimately be given more weight than any member of another species, that means in one interpretation that we may even give an individual who lacks the traits of normal human beings (rationality, autonomy, etc.) more weight than an individual who has these traits—human non-persons might be placed before non-human persons.

---

[8] Unless, of course, I justify the special respect by the fact that they belong to the same species that has one rational individual, namely me. But this is not even prima facie plausible as a foundation of some kind of moral collectivism.

This is, however, very counter-intuitive, especially against the background of Tooley's thought experiments in Chapter 7.

Actually, I am not going to make a decision as to how Nozick should be interpreted. He may subscribe to the radical thesis above. He may also intend to say that a human person might have more weight than a non-human person whereas a human non-person might not have more weight than a non-human person (and therefore reject the equality thesis). We have to leave this second question open.

We have enough material nevertheless to criticize Nozick's principle. For instance, consider the following thought experiment (which, if you want, can be seen as a worldly variant of Tooley's argument about the Martians). The human species consists of various races, even if the concept of a race is problematic. Suppose that one day it turns out that one human race is incapable of interbreeding with the other races. What we believed to be a racial difference turns out to be a species difference, and the reason why this has not been discovered before could probably be ascribed to the fact that the members of the "race" in question had always stood up for old traditions which prescribed marriage within the "race". Now these members want to break this cultural isolation and want also to mingle with other human races (and this, incidentally, is how the inability to get fertile children with "other" races has been discovered). We may add that their mental capacities are indistinguishable from those of "other" races.

Is there any reason to treat these beings differently after the discovery? I would say no but Nozick would say yes. If membership of the human species does and should have moral weight with us, then we should not regard these beings as equals (unless, of course, we abandon the kind of species concept that lies behind the judgement that they belong to a different species).

Another problem with Nozick's principle is that it seems to invite a kind of objection which was considered briefly in an earlier chapter, namely, if it is legitimate to discriminate against some kinds of beings with reference to their species membership, why could it not also be legitimate to discriminate against some beings on racial grounds for instance? If one believes that species differences ought to have moral importance, how to argue against someone who believes that racial differences have moral importance without getting hit by one's own argument? The problem is of course to find a difference between these biological classes which may justify that we use the one class but not the other as a basis of discrimination.

The only possibility seems to be to interpret Nozick as being a moral anti-individualist and to argue that whereas there normally is a difference in those capacities that Nozick believes form the basis of respectful treatment, such as rationality, autonomy, etc. between different species and particularly between the human species and all other species, we discern no such difference between the different races within the human species.

However, this line of reasoning is problematic for two reasons.

First, it is not entirely clear that there are no such differences between the human races, at least not if we by rationality mean high IQ. In a much debated book by Herrnstein and Murray it is argued that intelligence levels differ among ethnic groups (1994). Now, several scientists reject these findings, but suppose, for the sake of argument, that these critics are wrong. How is Nozick then to argue against someone who claims that these differences justify that we discriminate against those races with the lowest IQ?

Second, Nozick would of course expose himself to all the arguments considered in connection with Blumenfeld's moral collectivism.

9.3.2 NOZICK'S SECOND SUGGESTION

The other element in the deeper view concerning what is so special about a human being even if she is a marginal case, is the following one:

> We see humans, even defective ones, as part of the multifarious texture of human history and civilizations, human achievements and human family relations. Animals, even year-old mammals, we see against a different background and texture. The differences are enormous and endless. It will be asked, "But what precise aspects of these endless differences legitimately make the moral difference?" This question assumes that something much simpler than the total differences between two rich tapestries (one richer than the other) will, by itself, constitute the morally relevant difference. Yet this need not be so. For the two particular organisms, human and other mammal, we can state a difference. One is part of one tapestry, one of another (1983: 29).

This suggestion is also problematic for various reasons. Let me mention just two.

(1) Nozick seems to propose that the total difference in the tapestries containing the history, civilization, achievements and family relations that two different beings are part of should be the basis of a moral difference between them. But as a general principle this will have serious consequences, since members of different ethnic groups, for instance, are parts of different tapestries. There is no doubt a very big difference between the tapestries that a Swedish farmer and a Swedish gypsy (who does not farm) are parts of but to claim that this difference is morally relevant in the sense that they ought to be treated differently is once again an attempt to justify racism or at least something very similar to it.

And this point can be expanded to a comparison not only between different ethnic groups but also different cultures and civilizations. Thus James Rachels points to the fact that there has not been very much interaction between the West and Oriental history and civilizations. With this and the passage above from Nozick's article in mind, he says: "We could then rewrite this entire passage (substituting 'Westerner' for 'human' and 'Oriental' for 'mammal') as a justification for treating Westerners better. (The same trick might be tried for 'Europeans' and 'Africans'.)" (1986: 76).

(2) Another argument that Rachels mentions is that it is not at all clear what it means to say that the marginal cases are parts of this kind of tapestry. Nozick's proposal ignores "the fact that the defective human in question *has had nothing at all to do with* the history and civilizations being cited" (1986: 76). Rachels is here proceeding from the assumption that the marginal case is a severely retarded human.

According to Rachels the problem is that Nozick ignores the fact that these human beings are totally outside the rich human tapestry, whereas I believe the problem is instead that their part of this tapestry is comparable to that which very many non-human animals share. No doubt the severely retarded human beings play some part in human history and culture—for instance, in some cultures they are taken care of and in others they are not— and it is no doubt possible to have (social) family relations with a severely retarded human. The problem is that the extent to which this happens is comparable to the extent to which similar things happen to many animals, particularly to pets. The dog and the horse have played an important part in human history and every normal dog owner knows that a dog may be regarded as a family member. Therefore, Nozick has *not* escaped the argument from marginal cases. On the contrary his second suggestion is directly hit by the constructive phase of this argument.

And this problem is also accentuated by one of the conclusions that Nozick reaches, namely that a "human civilization will find the time to formulate and establish a balanced treatment of animals. A human civilization will want this as part of its own texture" (1983: 30). I find it hard to see how to succeed in this without as a logical consequence also regarding the animals as part of the human tapestry. And therefore, I also find it hard to see in what sense Nozick's proposal would be a solution to the problems considered in this chapter.

9.4 A Short Summary of the Chapter

To summarize, I have considered three different attempts to defend the idea that being human is something morally special. The main conclusion is that these various attempts at justifying SA or a supposed SA have failed for several reasons. For instance, Gaylin's list of attributes does not explain why being human is morally superior to being something else. Nor does Gaylin succeed in picking out attributes that all humans have and that are exclusively human. This means that he is exposed to the argument from marginal cases.

Blumenfeld tries to avoid the argument from marginal cases by rejecting one of its fundamental assumptions, namely moral individualism, which in short claims that the treatment of an individual is to be determined by considering his own particular characteristics. Blumenfeld suggests instead that an individual's group membership might be morally relevant and that is what makes every human being so morally special—they belong to a species whose members typically are rational beings. Among other things we argued that this is a principle which yields counter-intuitive results. For instance, we would have to reconsider the human right to life if it turned out that there was a colony of non-rational humans somewhere on another planet in another solar system.

Also Nozick claims that moral individualism is inadequate and wants to provide an answer to the argument from marginal cases, i.e. he wants to show that human beings can be morally special although they lack the properties that provide the ultimate basis for a special treatment of humans. He makes two suggestions; first, that any species may legitimately give their fellows moral privileges. This is problematic in virtue of the fact that it can either be used as a defence also of racism, sexism and things like that, or it will be hit by the same counter-arguments as those discussed in connection with Blumenfeld. The second suggestion is that humans are valuable for humans in virtue of being "parts of the multifarious texture of human history and civilizations, human achievements and human family relations". Also this idea will be hit by the two phases of the argument from marginal cases.

Therefore, we seem to have SA, but not yet any sound reasons for embracing it.[9]

---

[9] Cf. Mary Midgley (1984: 104).

PART III
INDIRECT IMPORTANCE

One central distinction in this study has been that between a property being valuable in a direct and in an indirect fashion. I have claimed that also in a theory which denies what we have called "objective" values or what Kant would have called "absolute" values and affirms only so-called "subjective" ones—or "relative" ones in Kant's terminology—also in such a theory there will be room for talking about the intrinsic value of being human, referring then to the value that the property has in itself and not in virtue of what it comes together with or brings.

In the previous chapters we have been concentrating on this direct aspect of the importance of being human, but now I will discuss two attempts to show that being human is instead important in an indirect way, particularly because of some other property which under normal circumstances goes hand in hand with the property of being human.

In both the attempts considered the attendant property is the property of being a person. And since this is not something that we will find in every member of the species *Homo sapiens*, being such a member will at most have a secondary or indirect importance.

Another distinction is the one between basic and derived moral principles, where basic moral principles are those moral principles the acceptability of which does not rest on any non-moral facts. I have tried to show that the property of being human might figure in basic moral principles and now we will discuss attempts to show that it figures in derived ones: we can derive moral principles about how to treat human beings from moral principles about how to treat such beings together with propositions expressing non-moral facts about some empirical connection, either statistical or causal, between the property of being a human and the property of being a person.

The philosophers discussed in this part will, as far as I can see, acknowledge particularly this indirect or derived importance of the property of being human. However, one of them, Peter Singer, might very well agree that human beings also have the kind of direct value that I have proposed they have in a subjectivistic value theory. As far as I can see he does *not* acknowledge such a value in humans, but if I am right in my assumptions concerning our actual reactions in the face of different thought experiments, considered in Chapter 8, this is a mistake. One explanation why he commits it is, I believe, that he confuses two possible senses of "intrinsic" value: (1) being intrinsically valuable in the sense of being objectively or absolutely so in contrast to

having a relative value, i.e. value *for* someone, and (2) being valuable in itself
and not instrumentally so or in virtue of what comes with it.[1]

So we might say that the philosophers discussed in Part III for various
reasons fail to see that being human has the kind of direct subjectivistic
importance that we have analysed in this study. Instead they are prepared to
acknowledge the indirect importance of being human in virtue of its empirical
connection with personhood. In a sense I am of the very opposite opinion. I
am prepared to acknowledge the direct value of the property of being human,
and of course, I am also prepared to acknowledge an indirect moral importance
of it, but I am sceptical of making as much of the property of being a person
as these philosophers do. Therefore, I believe they underestimate the moral
importance of being a biological human whereas they overestimate the moral
implications of being a person.

Now let me also explain the selection that I have made. The philosophers
discussed are important names in the discussion of the value of being human.
Furthermore, they also represent important and classical theories in this
discussion.

Carruthers (who develops a kind of contractualism) can be described as
defending an indirect duty view concerning our moral relationship to non-
humans. That is to say, he believes that our treatment of non-humans should
be morally regulated, but not primarily for the sake of the non-humans but
instead for the sake of us humans (the term "indirect duty view" comes from
Regan, 1984). So we get a rather complicated picture where Carruthers'
theory will be classified as indirect both as far as the property of being

---

[1] Consider, for instance, the following passage from Peter Singer's book *Practical Ethics* (second
edition): "The drowning of the ancient forests, the possible loss of an entire species, the destruction
of several complex ecosystems, the blockage of the wild river itself, and the loss of those gorges
are factors to be taken into account only in so far as they adversely affect sentient creatures. Is
a more radical break with the traditional position possible? Can some or all of these aspects of
the flooding of the valley be shown to have intrinsic value, so that they must be taken into
account independently of their effects on human beings or non-human animals?" (1993: 276–7).
Eventually Singer rejects the idea of an intrinsic value to be ascribed to the valley. Now,
compare this with another passage in the same book: "Something is of intrinsic value if it is
good or desirable *in itself*; the contrast is with 'instrumental value', that is, value as a means to
some other end or purpose" (1993: 274). Even though Singer talks of what is desir*able* in itself
and not what is desir*ed* in itself, I believe that the contrast here concerns the general distinction
between value as an end and value as a means. (Let us call this distinction 1.) However, in the
first passage this is not a natural reading of intrinsic value. A more natural interpretation is that
he wants to contrast an object having value independently of the object's effects on sentient
beings and an object having value exclusively *in virtue of* the effects of the object on sentient
beings (distinction 2), that is, a distinction that recalls our distinction between objective and
subjective value (though as I understand subjectivism, an object can be valuable for a subject
even when it does not have any direct *experiential* effects on the subject; but let us ignore this
difference). Therefore, proceeding from distinction 1 we may argue that the aspects of the valley
have intrinsic value, but nevertheless deny that they have intrinsic value considering distinction
2. And in view of his subjectivistic point of departure Singer may well agree with this. Furthermore,
this is probably an example of the confusion Korsgaard describes in her 1983 work.

human and the property of being non-human are concerned—human beings are important in so far as they are persons and non-humans are important in so far as our treatment of them will affect the way we treat those human beings who are persons.

Carruthers' theory can be directed *against* the animal rights movement, whereas Singer has been very influential *in* this movement. Singer is a proponent of utilitarianism and has, in my opinion, brought forward forceful arguments for the moral necessity of regarding the well-being of non-humans not only as important in an indirect way—like Carruthers—but also in a direct way.

To summarize, we may say that Carruthers to some extent is vulnerable to the very critique presented as directed against the Western tradition in the introductory chapter of this study, to the effect that he pays too much respect to humans and too little to non-humans. Of course, Carruthers would accuse Singer of committing the very opposite mistake.

CHAPTER 10

PETER CARRUTHERS' CONTRACTUALISM

> In fact, I regard the present popular concern with animal rights
> in our culture as a reflection of moral decadence. Just as Nero
> fiddled while Rome burned, many in the West agonise over
> the fate of seal pups and cormorants while human beings
> elsewhere starve or are enslaved.
>
> Peter Carruthers *The Animals Issue*

In *The Animals Issue* Peter Carruthers argues against the philosophical
foundation of the so-called animal rights movement from the perspective of
contractualism. I will here let Carruthers represent this influential moral
theory. The main reason is that he is, to my knowledge, the only contractualist
who has devoted more than marginal attention to the topic under discussion,
i.e. what kind of importance to attach to the property of being a human and
the comparative status of humans and non-humans.

The main thought behind contractualism is in a way Kantian, in that both
Kant and contractualism regard morality as a result of rational construction.
For Kant the moral principles to follow are those a rational individual would
want to see universally observed.[1] This is not in itself contractualism, but
according to Carruthers, Kant might nevertheless be regarded as a contractualist, since "the distinctive feature of Kantian moral construction is that
agents should be seeking rules that all can rationally agree to" (1992: 36).[2]

Carruthers' strategy is to show that contractualism is a more reasonable
basis for our dealings with non-humans than particularly Peter Singer's version
of utilitarianism. I intend to show that Carruthers fails in his attempts to
convince that contractualism is a more reasonable theory than is utilitarianism
as far as our dealings with non-humans are concerned, and furthermore I
want to show that contractualism is even worse off than utilitarianism in
those aspects that Carruthers regards as most problematic for utilitarianism.

---

[1] See for instance Kant (1964).
[2] Onora O'Neill would agree here that both Kant and, for instance, Rawls share a "conception
of ethical principle as determined by constraints on principles chosen by rational agents" (1993:
184). The big difference, according to O'Neill, lies in the fact that Kant emphasizes what
rational agents regardless of their ends *could* consistently choose, whereas Rawls emphasizes the
principles that *would* be chosen by instrumentally rational agents (1993: 184). For a discussion
of Kant and contractualism, see also Will Kymlicka (1993: 191–5).

10.1 Two Demands

Carruthers formulates two demands on an acceptable theory of morality:

First, an ethical theory should contain a *governing conception* of the nature of morality. This will provide a distinctive picture of the source of moral notions and moral knowledge, and of the basis of moral motivation. Second, and distinct from, though perhaps derived from the first, an ethical theory should contain some *basic normative principle* or principles that are to guide our judgements of right and wrong (1992: 23).

First a few words concerning the second demand. As I interpret him, what Carruthers wants to put forward is a demand for intuitive acceptability, based on an idea of reflective equilibrium. A theory has to have principles that explain and unify considered common-sense beliefs and must not contain principles that are in conflict with such beliefs, unless the theoretical disadvantage of giving them up is greater than the disadvantage of disregarding the beliefs. Therefore, as I understand the second demand, it is not only a demand for the existence of a basic normative principle (principles) but also for the intuitive plausibility of it (them).

Carruthers believes that the idea of reflective equilibrium is more than an idea about a balance between normative principles and considered beliefs; he also wants to see the *first* demand as a consequence of his adherence to reflective equilibrium. What one ought to strive for is not only principles with theoretical merits but a unified theory with as many theoretical advantages as possible. A theory of morality has to provide an account of the nature of morality which explains why we should care about it and why it should have a central place in our life; for it is plain, as Carruthers says, that morality is not just another special interest, like for instance stamp-collection, which we might or might not have (1992: 23). Furthermore, people generally claim to know that certain acts are morally wrong, like child-abuse, and, therefore, what a theory of morality has to contain is somehow an idea of what this kind of putative moral knowledge is knowledge *of*; what is it that we claim to know when we claim to know that something is morally right or wrong? (Intuitionism fails to comply with this demand, according to Carruthers.)

Turning to utilitarianism, Carruthers claims that its greatest attraction lies in the governing conception. Carruthers regards this governing conception as an imaginary construction, like the governing conception of contractualism, but with the following content: morality is to be regarded as "the set of decisions that would be made by an impartial benevolent observer—an observer who is aware of all the conflicting interests in a given situation, and of the consequences that different policies would have for those interests, and who is equally sympathetic towards all of the parties involved" (1992: 25).

Now if this kind of God-like being were to decide what strategy to adopt in a given situation it is plausible to assume that he would choose the maximizing strategy; he would try to maximize utility, since as an impartial observer he would be insensitive to the identity of the being who has the utility and furthermore, since he is also benevolent, he would try to do as much good as he ever can.[3]

This governing conception is attractive, according to Carruthers, because it may not only give us an idea of the origin of moral notion, it will also give a satisfying explanation of the source of moral motivation.

Carruthers seems to proceed from the assumption that we (all?) have an innate impulse to feel sympathy for the feelings of other human beings. I suppose that this impulse is approximately the same one that Hume builds his theory of morality around, which means that the capacity for sympathy will mean an impulse to share the feelings of other human beings. This impulse is most powerful when we are directly confronted with the beings who have these feelings and it will, according to Carruthers, concern particularly "the unhappiness, frustrated desires, or sufferings of other people" (1992: 26).[4]

The next step, according to Carruthers, is to rationalize this natural impulse towards benevolence. We then realize that there is no rational difference between the feelings of a person to whom we come into close contact and the feelings of other people—socially and geographically distanced from us. This also includes an understanding of the fact that the feelings of people we care for are not more important from a moral perspective than the feelings of people we do not know and spontaneously care for. The rational conclusion is that we ought to respond equally to all feelings of a similar kind wherever we find them.

So, morality, according to Carruthers' picture of utilitarianism, "arises in the first place when the natural impulse towards benevolence is universalised through the impact of reason" (1992: 27). Furthermore, morality is motivating in so far as we cannot resist the sympathetic impulse—it lies in our very nature. Neither can we resist its universalization, if we are rational, and this capacity too is something that lies in our nature.

10.2 Utilitarianism and Intuitions

The problems with utilitarianism concern the second demand. The weakness of utilitarianism lies in its basic normative principle which exhorts us to maximize utility. The consequences of this principle are counter-intuitive.

---

[3] This idea has certain similarities to Will Kymlicka's description of one argument for utilitarianism: "The requirement that we maximize utility is entirely derived from the prior requirement to treat people with equal consideration" (1990: 31).

[4] The quotation suggests that Carruthers uses "sympathy" somewhat differently from Hume. As far as I can see, Hume does not only intend to claim that we have a propensity to feel pity about the fact that people suffer from various negative feelings, i.e., it is not only the negative feelings of other people that we tend to share with them, but also the positive ones. This is not sufficiently clear in the quotation, but it is important to note, and the main reason is that otherwise we would be led only to negative utilitarianism, to minimization rather than maximization.

This is not in any way an original approach to utilitarianism: one is willing to acknowledge its theoretical advantages whereas one finds its normative conclusions repugnant. And there are many aspects of the counter-intuitiveness of utilitarianism. These concern utilitarian conclusions in the question of distributive justice, punishment of the innocent, the demands of morality, and so on.

Carruthers' judgement is based on the following example (which is a development of an example about a kennel owner, Kenneth, whom Carruthers has presented in an earlier chapter):

You arrive at a fire in his dogs' home to find Kenneth unconscious on the floor, while the dogs are still locked in their cages. You judge that you have just enough time either to drag Kenneth to safety or to unlock the cages, but not both. Suppose you also know that Kenneth is quite old, and is something of a recluse who lives entirely for his work, without anyone to care for him. In these circumstances a utilitarian is clearly committed to the view that you should opt to rescue the dogs. For this is obviously the way to ensure the greatest future pleasure, and/or the greatest future desire satisfaction (1992: 95–6).[5]

According to Carruthers, the utilitarian conclusion is morally outrageous. This is also true, he says, of its further conclusions—for instance that regular slaughter of animals, farming and some forms of experiments on animals will fall into the same moral category as the Nazi holocaust, which means that even violent opposition, such as planting bombs and poisoning baby-foods, will be justified in utilitarianism. This, Carruthers claims, is morally abhorrent and he is convinced that according to common sense, it would be wrong to place the lives of many dogs in the example about Kenneth over the life of a single human being.

I believe that Carruthers is making too much of his conclusion.

First of all, even if the correct utilitarian action to perform in this situation would be to rescue the dogs, that does not also mean that the correct attitude towards farming and experiments on animals will be the militant one described by Carruthers. The terrorist actions described are illegal and one might well claim that they are counter-productive from a utilitarian point of view. People in general will not be more sympathetic to the animal cause when animal rights activists put poison in their babies' food. Quite the contrary, I assume.

Secondly, it is not at all sure that it *would* be a utilitarian ideal to save the dogs in the situation described by Carruthers. In principle and judged in isolation it would be the right thing to do, according to utilitarianism, and

---

[5] It has to be added that this conclusion will follow only on condition that there are the same direct reasons against killing humans (or persons) and non-humans (or non-persons) in utilitarianism. Some utilitarians have denied this, notably Peter Singer, but Carruthers tries to argue that there is no coherent way for a utilitarian to assign a special kind of value to the life of a human or person as compared to the life of a non-human or non-person. Since I believe that Carruthers is right in this, which I shall try to show in the following chapter, I am also prepared to accept Carruthers' conclusion about what a utilitarian in principle should do in a situation like this one. However, this is not automatically to say that a utilitarian actually would save the dogs in a real-life situation, which I will try to show below.

that is perhaps enough for Carruthers to judge the theory the way he does. But as he has noted, the most plausible form of utilitarianism would *not* consider the situation as isolated from the rest of the world. A quality-of-character utilitarian would ask herself what kind of action would be performed by a person the character of whom would most likely promote the total utility in an optimal way. Proceeding from that question, the correct answer might well be that she would save the human being. This would probably be the right answer on condition that the life of a human being *normally* is more valuable than the life of an animal. And this is what I believe that a utilitarian would say—the total amount of utility in a human life is normally greater than the total amount of utility in a non-human life (which will be a result of a number of factors of which expectation of life is one). Therefore, it might be a good thing that we inculcate a spontaneous inclination to save a human being before a non-human one (or even several non-human beings) in a situation where there is no time for making utilitarian calculations. In Carruthers' example we have precisely this kind of situation and consequently we may expect the utilitarian to rescue Kenneth.

Let us for the sake of argument assume that we are wrong in this—let us assume that from a utilitarian perspective the correct action to perform in this situation would be to rescue the dogs. Let us also assume that this will be in conflict with our common-sense beliefs; let us suppose even that it would be a *serious* counter-intuitive consequence. This means that the theoretical advantages of utilitarianism which Carruthers is prepared to acknowledge would have to be weighed against the intuitive disadvantages concerning its normative consequences.

Then our task will be to find out whether or not Carruthers' suggestion will be more attractive after we have summed up its advantages and disadvantages. Once again, Carruthers thinks so, but I shall try to show that this belief is false.

10.3 Contractualism

Carruthers' theory is a fairly general form of contractualism which does not take a definite position as to what version of contractualist construction to accept.

He describes the governing conception of contractualism in the following way:

A contractualist moral theory, as I shall understand it, is an attempt to justify a system of moral principles by showing that they *would* be agreed upon by rational agents in certain ideal circumstances. It is an attempt to exhibit the rationality of moral rules, not an attempt to legitimate those rules by appeal to past agreement or present self-interest (1992: 35–6).

This, according to Carruthers, has certain theoretical advantages. The model avoids the problem with intuitionism which concerns how to understand the proposal that values are objective in the sense that they exist in the world independently of us, and which we have discussed in previous chapters. It will also avoid the problems of a subjectivistic view of morality in which there might indeed be room for reason and argument in the moral discourse but in which there might also be room for radical or irreconcilable moral disagreement.

Contractualism is, according to Carruthers, a weakly objective moral theory in the sense that morality can be regarded as something that is rationally imposed upon us, which means that in so far as we are rational, we cannot but choose the contractualist system of moral concepts.

Furthermore, as I interpret Carruthers, he roughly accepts Rawls's picture of the conditions under which this imaginary agreement is to be made; he accepts the idea of a veil of ignorance behind which we imagine that those rational agents who are going to make the agreement are placed—which means that they have general knowledge of the human condition but are ignorant of their own particular characteristics—and furthermore he accepts the idea that their choices should be our moral guide.

There is a difference between Rawls and Carruthers, however, and it concerns the scope of this guidance. Rawls's main interest is political philosophy and therefore he wants to determine primarily the basic institutions and structure of a *just society*. Carruthers, on the other hand, wants to use Rawls's model to construct a general theory of morality (1992: 37), that is, one that can determine not only just and unjust basic structures in society but which can determine all kinds of moral questions, also questions concerning our treatment of non-human animals.

Now, as we have seen, Carruthers puts certain specific demands on the governing conception of an acceptable moral theory. It should give a plausible account of the source of moral notions and furthermore of the basis of moral motivation. Does contractualism fulfil those demands?

It does seem that contractualism can give a plausible picture of how morality came up: "moral notions are presented as human constructions that arise in order to facilitate human co-operation and the life of community" (1992: 43–4). It will give an idealized picture of this process, since it "presents us with a way of seeing what our morality should be, if the only constraints on its content are rational ones" (1992: 44). In the real world morality is shaped by various other factors. But the general contractualist picture of the origin of morality may be true nevertheless.

The second demand concerns moral motivation. One might wonder why we as non-rational beings should shape our lives in accordance with principles that not we but instead fully rational beings would choose in Rawls's original position behind the veil of ignorance. Why should *I* feel constrained by an agreement that individuals under other conditions than those in which I live would be motivated to make? Carruthers expresses this question in the following way: "Why would this be something worth dying for, in the way that many have laid down their lives in the service of justice" (1992: 44)?

Carruthers' simple answer is based upon a picture of human nature that is inspired by T. M. Scanlon's postulate (1982) that, in Carruthers' words, "human beings have a basic need to justify their actions to one another in terms that others may freely and rationally accept" (1992: 45). According to Carruthers, even scoundrels characteristically attempt to justify their actions in this way. Scanlon wants to look upon this need as something that is produced and sustained by moral education, whereas Carruthers looks upon it as something "innate (inborn), in such a way as to emerge gradually at a given stage in maturational development" (1992: 45). The most powerful argument for the existence of such an innate need is that Carruthers sees a survival value in it in view of the fact "that we depend crucially for our survival upon co-operative modes of living" (1992: 45).

But I can also see a problem in this suggestion. Does it really answer what I take to be the fundamental question, namely why I should feel motivated by knowledge of what would have been the case in a purely *hypothetical* situation? In one sense I believe that knowledge of what is purely hypothetical might indeed have a motivational impact on me, namely when I ask myself what I would have done in a certain actual situation given that I were fully rational and had complete knowledge of the relevant facts about that actual situation. I think that a desire to be rational can be almost universally found among beings that have the capacity to be rational to a certain extent, for instance, corresponding to the degree of rationality of a normal human adult.

And in my view it seems very natural to give an evolutionary explanation of this; it is reasonable to expect that my chances to spread my genes will increase if I somehow show preparedness to do what I have reason to suspect that I would do if I were fully rational and informed about the various features of the actual situation. Actually, this is what I believe that a being with a limited capacity for rationality should do (from an evolutionary perspective)—asking herself what she would have done if she were even more rational and thereby stretching her rational capacity by displaying some kind of cognizance of her own rational limitations.

In order to reach the conclusion Carruthers wants us to draw, however, we would have to presuppose something quite different, namely that there is an evolutionary value not only in a preparedness to ask what I would have done in an *actual* situation provided I were fully rational and informed, but also that there is such a value in asking what I would have done if I were rational in a purely *hypothetical* situation, i.e., a situation one knows will never be actual. To be sure, there might also be such a value in this, but to me it seems less obvious than the value of figuring out what my rational self would do (or advise me to do)[6] in situations that are or might be actual.

---

[6] See Michael Smith (1995).

10.4 Practical Implications

Next, we have to consider the practical implications of contractualism.

Generally, contractualism is intuitively more plausible than utilitarianism, Carruthers asserts, since it will, for instance, not allow us to interfere with individuals' lives and interests merely in order to promote the overall utility. It will also provide us with the kind of non-moral space discussed above, since there will always remain behaviours the regulation of which other rational beings will not take any interest in. Contractualism is primarily interested in *interactions* between people, not in ways of living which will only have consequences for the individual herself.

Now recall Kenneth and the dogs. Contractualism will of course say that we ought to save Kenneth, since according to contractualism morality is a human construction, as long as we do not believe that non-human animals have the kind of capacity for rationality that is required to enter an agreement with other rational beings. Describing Rawls's version of contractualism, Carruthers writes: "Morality is viewed as constructed *by* human beings, in order to facilitate interactions *between* human beings, and to make possible a life of co-operative community. This is, indeed, an essential part of the governing conception of contractualism" (1992: 102).

However, to claim that animals lack moral standing in contractualism does not mean that one is allowed to do whatever one wishes to the animals. Carruthers denies that animals have direct moral significance, but claims instead that they have *indirect* moral significance. Once again, this is a position which Kant also holds; the concern we ought to show the animals is to be explained primarily as stemming from the duties we have to human beings. And the thing is that this might account for the intuition that ascribes moral standing to animals.

Carruthers claims that there are two obvious ways in which his theory may confer indirect moral significance on animals.

First, we can let the rules which deal with private property apply to the animals as well. This means that at least some animals will be protected by property rights: you must not kill your neighbour's dog, since that would be to destroy his property. This account has certain shortcomings, which Carruthers also notes: it will not apply to the wild animals and it will not prohibit the *owner* of an animal from killing his animal, and consequently it will explain only a small amount of cases where we normally consider that animals should be protected from arbitrary killing.

Secondly, another and in Carruthers' eyes more plausible way to account for our normal intuitions is to point to the fact that many people care very deeply about animals, which might make the manner in which we treat "animals a matter of legitimate public interest" (1992: 106). The idea is that contractualism, as noted above, will only (almost, at least) regulate that behaviour of an individual which will affect the interest of other individuals.

And given that people are distressed by seeing an animal's suffering, then an individual's freedom to cause suffering even to his own dog will be curtailed.

Is this speciesism? Normally speciesism is considered to be wrong because it discriminates, one claims, on the basis of a property—species membership or some species-typical property—that is not morally relevant. From this perspective, discussing the question of whether it is right to breed and slaughter animals in factory-like conditions, the relevant question to put concerns whether they suffer under these conditions.

Contractualists take no direct interest in this capacity to suffer when pondering normative questions, since you cannot do something directly wrong to a non-rational being if morality is an affair between rational individuals. Suffering will not make you qualified as a member of the moral sphere; only a fairly high degree of rationality will. The argument against contractualism is this: suppose we can show that a being might suffer even if it does not have the degree of rationality required for participating in morality, then it seems that rationality is morally irrelevant as far as the question of animal breeding is concerned. So contractualism is speciesistic in so far as it discriminates on the basis of a morally irrelevant property typical of humans.

But here Carruthers replies, correctly I think, that this in a sense begs the question, since a property is morally relevant only in relation to a moral theory or at least in relation to a conception of morality. For instance, suffering is relevant in relation to the governing conception of morality that we described in connection with utilitarianism above, but not in relation to the governing conception of contractualism. The only way of comparing these concepts, according to Carruthers, is to consider their theoretical advantages and to assess their practical implications.

This means that if we cannot claim that utilitarianism on the whole is more appropriate than contractualism for reaching a reflective equilibrium, then neither can we accuse contractualism of being speciesistic in the sense of laying stress on a morally irrelevant property; to do so will in the absence of independent arguments only be to assume what is to be proved—that utilitarianism is better than contractualism.

Now we have to discuss whether contractualism really *does* reach a reflective equilibrium. Does contractualism accord with our intuitions better than does utilitarianism? Once again, I would say no.

Carruthers admits that there are two hard cases which cannot be solved by his account of why a being might have indirect moral significance even though it has no direct significance; there are, Carruthers says, two elements in common-sense morality that his account cannot accommodate. Let us consider them in turn.

(1) It might be that animals are protected from public mistreatment in virtue of the fact that there are animal lovers who will protest, but this will not apply to cases of secret mistreatment, which most of us believe just as

wrong as public mistreatment. Carruthers constructs the following imaginative thought experiment:

Recall that Astrid has left earth on a space-rocket, on an irreversible trajectory that will take her out of the solar system and forever out of contact with her fellow human beings. Now in her rocket she carries with her a cat, and a famous work of art of which she is the legitimate owner (the *Mona Lisa*, say). As the years pass she becomes bored with her books and tapes, and seeks alternative entertainment. Then contrast two cases: in the first case she removes the glass cover from the *Mona Lisa* and uses the painting as a dart-board; in the second case she ties the cat to the wall and uses *it* as a dart-board. I think we should feel intuitively that there is a great difference, morally speaking, between these two cases (1992: 108–9).

Carruthers believes that Astrid would do nothing wrong by throwing darts at the painting, since no one is ever gong to see it again. On the other hand she *would* do something wrong if starting to throw darts at the cat out of amusement. This seems to be a problem for contractualism, which is prepared to acknowledge merely the indirect moral significance both of artworks and non-rational animals.

But I think this is too hasty a conclusion. This case is troublesome for Carruthers only because he chooses to look upon the concept of harm and frustration as something subjective, where a being is harmed and her desire is frustrated only on condition that she believes herself to be so. This has been discussed above, but the point is that with an objective understanding of harm and frustration, according to which these phenomena might be present whether or not they are mentally registered, animal lovers might well be said to be harmed by the very fact that Astrid throws darts at the cat.

As a matter of fact, I would say that Carruthers' example functions as a good illustration of the implausibility of the subjective conception of harm and frustration. Carruthers says that it "is surely no part of benevolence to do something that satisfies someone's desire in circumstances in which the person will never know what has happened" (1992: 83). But surely, it is not absurd to think that benevolence *has* to do with this, since I would not consider a person to be benevolent *vis-à-vis* my person if he did what I wanted him to do only on those occasions where I could test whether or not he did so, although I had begged him to do so also in those situations where I could not possibly test him. Would an unreliable person who just did the good things he thought would be recognized really qualify as a benevolent person? I doubt that.

(2) The second problem for contractualism is the problem of the marginal cases. If animals are placed outside the moral sphere in virtue of the fact that they lack the necessary mental equipment, then will not also those human beings—such as young babies, very senile old people, and people with severe mental retardation—who lack these capacities suffer the same fate?

It is true that the case of young babies is special in so far as there does exist a more direct contractualist reason why they should not be harmed, namely that this might have effects on the rational agents they one day will become. Damaging a baby's arm will have effects for the possibility of using this arm by a rational individual in the future. This reasoning does not pre-suppose a potentiality argument to the effect that we ought to treat a poten-tiality as if it were an actuality; it only presupposes that an action might be wrong because it has certain consequences for actual people in the future.

But the other categories discussed—senile old people and severely mentally retarded people—will not be protected by this reasoning. Damaging the arm of a senile human being will not directly curtail the rational use of this arm.

Carruthers illustrates the problem by modifying the thought experiment about Astrid:

Suppose that Astrid has taken her grandfather with her, who becomes increasingly senile as the journey progresses. Would it not be very wrong of her to start using *him* as a dart-board to relieve her tedium, or to kill him because the sight of his dribbling offends her? Yet on what grounds can such actions be wrong, if only rational agents have moral standing? For no other person will ever be worried or upset at the suffering or death of her grandfather (1992: 111).

The problem with this example is of course that Astrid, if she starts to throw darts at her grandfather, will do something that will offend (most) people's feelings to an even greater extent than she would do if she started to throw darts at her cat, and therefore that the present example will function as an even stronger argument against contractualism. A theory which is unable to provide direct protection for non-rational human beings is in deep trouble: "For example, no one is going to accept the testing of detergents on the senile, or the hunting of mental defectives for sport" (1992: 111).

After having dismissed some imperfect replies to this argument, he presents what he considers to be a solution to the problem. This solution has two parts.

10.4.1 A SLIPPERY-SLOPE ARGUMENT

Carruthers believes that there is a way in which direct moral rights can be secured to the marginal human without also securing such rights to the non-human animals:

The strategy depends upon the fact that there are no sharp boundaries between a baby and an adult, between a not-very-intelligent adult and a severe mental defective, or between a normal old person and someone who is severely senile. The argument is then that the attempt to accord direct moral rights only to rational agents (normal adults) would be inherently dangerous and open to abuse (1992: 114).

This argument presupposes the risk of misuse of certain moral principles, but I am inclined to think that the main problem with the argument is precisely that it is so easy to abuse *this* very argument! No doubt there exist situations where it can be correctly applied; some moral principles run the risk of being abused, but this is far from true of all kinds of moral principles.

The slippery-slope argument often stresses the risk of using a moral principle in a way that will serve the user's own purposes, but exactly the same risk is, in my view, attached to the slippery-slope argument—it is so easy to use when it serves one's own moral purposes, and the reason is of course that it is built on empirical guesses which might or might not be true and which are extremely difficult to test.

If we compare Kant and Carruthers I also think we have a good illustration of this problem. Carruthers uses the argument to prove the existence of a moral protection for all human beings but thinks that it does not apply to the animals: "there is not the same practical threat to the welfare of rational agents in the suggestion that all animals should be excluded from the domain of direct moral concern" (1992: 115). Of course, neither would Kant say that we have *direct* duties to the animals, but he is prepared to acknowledge the impact of the manner in which we treat animals on the way we treat humans. According to Kant animals have indirect standing precisely because of the slippery slope, whereas Carruthers thinks that there is a sharp boundary between human beings and all other animals, which means that there is no risk of a slippery slope.

What is more, if we look at the thought experiment about Astrid and her grandfather in the spaceship, I am unable to see how there might possibly be any slippery slope to watch out for. Suppose that Astrid is able to reflect intelligently on moral matters and that she asks herself whether or not it would be morally right for her to throw darts at her grandfather in order to dispel her boredom. She realizes that on earth she would take certain risks if she allowed herself to make a distinction between those human beings who have and those who have not got moral rights (not to be used as a dart-board, for instance). But the reason why this would be a risk on earth is that whatever the boundary we choose between people who do and people who do not have such moral rights, there will always be some people on the boundary and very close to it on either side, and they will so to speak function as some kind of a bridge on our way down the slippery slope. Their existence will explain why we without noticing it can slide all the way down the slope.

But as the example is designed these people are not present on the spaceship, which means that Astrid does not have to worry about a slippery slope for this reason. This would, as far as I can see, be true also if the spaceship did carry other passengers, as long as they could not be placed on or near the boundary intellectually speaking. So a slippery slope presupposes the borderline cases and in the absence of such cases Astrid will realize that throwing darts at her grandparent is without any risk and therefore morally all right.

It is still true that in *this* world Carruthers might have a point; there might be a risk connected with pronouncing the moral rights of marginal cases, but if so, then the risk will have a contingent foundation and it is not far-fetched to imagine circumstances under which the risk would be eliminated.

Suppose the following is true. One day a psychologist presents research which argues that much of the aggression in society could be countered if only we humans could exercise our aggression under controlled forms. This is indeed in line with every-day psychology, but what is new here is that the psychologist argues that the best results probably will be achieved when aggression is practised on real human beings. Therefore she wants to test her ideas under realistic conditions and use people with severe mental defects and senile old people as objects in a bigger study. Her plan will of course be to study what happens to those humans who get an opportunity to exercise violence and aggression on human subjects.

What would Carruthers say? Well he could once again point to the risks involved in the project—if it proves to be a failure, then the people who carry out the experiment will run the risk of losing their sensitivity for human suffering. But this risk must also be weighed against the possible benefits if the project succeeds. All rational beings will benefit if they have an effective means of controlling their aggression, and the possible discovery of such a means by the project cannot be rationally ignored. Therefore, Carruthers would have to approve of the project (in view of the arguments hitherto considered).

And note the logic behind the example: there would be no reason to fear the kind of slippery slope that Carruthers describes if practising aggression on the marginal cases really were an effective means to control our aggression, since then the motive for sliding down the slope would have vanished. What Carruthers fears is that—if we deny moral rights to the marginal human beings on the ground that their intellectual capacities are insufficient—we "shall be launched on a slippery slope which may lead to all kinds of barbarisms against those who *are* rational agents" (1992: 114). You need not fear barbarism from a non-aggressive being.

Would not this conclusion follow from utilitarianism as well? If we could invent a means towards less aggressiveness between rational beings then that might well be advantageous in utilitarian terms as well. However, there is in my view one decisive difference. Utilitarianism would in its calculus count the suffering of the objects of our aggression also when these objects do not reach beyond a certain intellectual level (as long as they are conscious); in order to show that the project is profitable from a utilitarian perspective we have to make certain that the suffering of the marginal cases somehow is *outweighed* by the benefits for other people. It is not clear that this kind of reasoning is morally acceptable, but at least it involves the equal consideration of the feelings in the marginal class and feelings in the class of rational human beings. And I would like to think that this difference is important— it may be objectionable to let the feelings of the marginal cases be overridden by the feelings of rational beings, provided that the quantity is sufficient, which will be the case in utilitarianism, but it is, in my view, even more objectionable to let the feelings of the marginal cases be overridden by *any* amount of advantages for the class of rational beings, however small it is and however trivial the benefits. So contractualism seems *extra* problematic in how it deals with our example compared to utilitarianism.

10.4.2 SOCIAL STABILITY

Carruthers' second argument for including the marginal human cases in the moral sphere concentrates on social stability, which every rational contractor will value. Carruthers claims that

human beings are apt to care as intensely about their offspring as they care about anything, irrespective of age and intelligence. A rule withholding moral standing from those who are very young, very old, or mentally defective is thus likely to produce social instability, in that many people would find themselves psychologically incapable of living in compliance with it (1992: 117).

The idea is that we have to take into account known psychological facts when constructing the principles and rules in the contract. One such fact is that we care very much about our close relatives independently of whether or not they qualify as rational. Therefore, a system of rules that is incapable of giving the marginal cases moral protection would be psychologically impossible in the sense that people could not possibly accept it.

I find this statement problematic as well.

First of all, I cannot see why this reasoning necessarily leads to the conclusion that we should assign moral rights *to the marginal cases*. Why would it not be enough to *derive* moral protection of the marginal cases from the moral rights of rational beings? If it is psychologically impossible for me to accept that those people whom I love get harmed, then other people would have an *indirect* reason not to harm those people, out of respect for my feelings.

Carruthers is aware of this objection, and his reply is that this kind of protection will not be enough, since it will only place the marginal cases in the same category as items of property. The reason why I am not allowed to kill your baby would be identical with the reason why I am not allowed to destroy your Mercedes. And the main problem is that obligations built on this foundation will be possible to override in a way that we do not want obligations towards those marginal cases that are object of our love to be.

Carruthers says:

Suppose, for example, that your Mercedes blocks the entrance to a mineshaft in which I have become imprisoned. You have become accustomed to use the entrance as a garage during the week, and I should face a five-day wait to get out. Then I may surely destroy the car if this is my only means of escape, no matter how much you may care about it, and even though my life may be in no danger (1992: 118).

On the other hand, Carruthers claims, it would be absurd to claim that I had a right to kill your child in a similar situation, and that shows that we cannot place the marginal cases in the same category as property.

But Carruthers fails, in my view, to distinguish between the status of a moral protection and the strength of it. It is true that my property rights in some circumstances, like for instance those described by Carruthers, might legitimately be overridden by some more fundamental rights. But the reason for this is, I figure, that people normally are more deeply attached to the things covered by these fundamental rights than to the things covered by the property rights. Furthermore, property, for instance a car, is under normal circumstances replaceable. This means that being imprisoned for five days will probably do more harm to me than having your car destroyed (and probably replaced) will do for you. And I believe that these background assumptions explain why we are prepared to agree that it would be morally acceptable to destroy the car in these circumstances.

This means that there is a way of explaining why we believe that I may destroy your car but not kill your child in these circumstances which does not presuppose that we assign direct rights to the child (and to human marginal cases), namely to say that normally you value your child much more than you value a piece of property (especially if the piece of property is replaceable). Property rights are overrideable by rights to things that we normally value more than property. You need not claim that the protection of the child is to be placed in another category compared to the protection of property such as cars in order to cope with the reactions to Carruthers' example; it just has to be strong enough to outweigh the protection of things that we normally value less than we value the protection of our nearest and dearest even when they do not qualify as rational.

So I claim that Carruthers will fail in his attempts to include the marginal cases in the sphere of direct moral right holders, as long as he insists that rationality is the fundamental property, since there is a way to argue for a strong protection of the marginal cases that is consistent with this claim and that will confer merely *indirect* rights on the marginal cases. Carruthers' fails to explain why a contractualist would have to grant direct moral rights to the marginal cases in order to preserve social stability. Strong indirect ones seem to be enough.

Furthermore, suppose my argument is faulty. Then we may question whether this kind of reasoning concentrating on known facts about what is psychologically possible for people to accept could not be used as an argument for conferring direct rights on animals. Once again, what Carruthers says is that withholding moral rights from the marginal cases would probably produce social instability "in that many people would find themselves psychologically incapable of living in compliance with it" (1992: 117). But why not use the same reasoning in connection with the animals?

Probably, many animal lovers will find it very hard to accept that animals are not strongly morally protected. Some of these are very militant and there might be a risk of social instability when vegans use violence to protest against slaughterhouses and transports of animals. Likewise, many pet owners will find it hard to accept that their pets are not strongly protected—a pet owner may well find it unacceptable that her pet is killed under the circumstances described by Carruthers in the example above. And if this is so, then why would not Carruthers claim that we have reason to assign direct moral rights to animals as well?

The upshot of this is that I believe Carruthers will fail in his attempts to assign direct moral rights to the marginal human cases, rights that do not apply to animals.

10.5 Contractualism and Character

Suppose, for the sake of argument, that Carruthers' reasoning holds; suppose he can show that marginal humans have direct rights but that non-human cases have not. That will solve Carruthers' second problem (2), discussed in 10.4, but not the first one (1), if he sticks to the subjective conception of harm and frustration. Carruthers wants a strong protection of marginal human cases but he does not want to deny the animals moral protection altogether, since he does *not* want to say that there is no moral difference if Astrid out of boredom in her space-rocket starts to throw darts at her cat compared to if she does so at a famous painting.

How does Carruthers' cope with this problem? Once again, he modifies the example from Astrid to make his point:

Suppose, as before, that she has set her craft irreversibly to carry her out of the solar system, and that she is travelling with her cat and her grandfather. Now, at a certain point in the journey the grandfather dies. Out of boredom, Astrid idly cuts his corpse into bite-size pieces and feeds him to the cat. Is her action not morally wrong? It seems to me intuitively obvious that it is (1992: 146–7).

The problem is to explain why, since no one is harmed, nor need any rights be violated since, as Carruthers says, *if* dead persons after all have rights, then Astrid would be doing something wrong even if her grandfather before he died had waived all relevant rights.

No, what "Astrid does is wrong because of what it shows about *her*. Her action is bad because it manifests and expresses a bad quality of character [...]" (1992: 147). So Carruthers utilizes an idea which is very similar to the quality-of-character utilitarianism which claims that we should primarily assess neither actions nor rules but instead qualities of character. What this kind of utilitarianism will do is to judge a person's actions in terms of whether they are expressions of a character that is suitable for the achievement of a maximal amount of overall utility. What Carruthers will do is to assess a person's actions as expression of a character suitable for living in accordance with the agreement made up by rational persons beyond a veil of ignorance.

Carruthers is eager to stress, however, that the contractualist treatment of the value of developing the right kind of character is different from the utilitarian approach in one significant respect, which is revealed by his example of Astrid in the space-rocket. According to contractualism

the criticism is that she has failed to do her fair share, in the moral sphere—like anyone else, she was obliged to try to create in herself the sort of moral character that would (in the right circumstances) contribute to the form of society that all would wish for. Utilitarians, in contrast, must deny that Astrid does anything wrong, since no harm of any sort will result (1992: 153).

I fail to see where the difference lies, and consequently I fail to see why Astrid would do something unacceptable according to contractualism but not according to utilitarianism. Suppose utilitarianism makes a distinction between right and wrong action and good and bad character. The first distinction is defined in terms of the actual consequences of an action, i.e., in terms of whether or not the action will be the one that contributes to the greatest overall utility more than any other available alternative. The second distinction, on the other hand, will employ a criterion of moral standing of character according to which a good character is the one which most likely in normal circumstances would contribute to the greatest overall utility. Now suppose furthermore that Astrid's actions can be described as "disrespectful" and "inhuman" and that such character traits under normal circumstances have a negative utilitarian value, then certainly what Astrid does may be condemned on the grounds that it reveals a bad character although it will have no bad consequences—she does not perform any wrong action.

But exactly the same line of reasoning would, as far as I can see, be used by the contractualist. Being disrespectful and inhuman will not be compatible with being the kind of person that under normal circumstances would act in accordance with rules agreed upon by the rational beings behind the veil of ignorance. Therefore Astrid's character will be condemned on contractualist grounds. But I cannot see why her actions have to be condemned on these grounds as well, since actually she does not seem to break any contractualist moral rule. Indeed we have seen that Carruthers believes that there do exist contractualist principles assigning rights also to beings which are not persons, as for instance in the marginal human cases. But as far as I can see, he will not include dead persons in this class of marginal human cases; he is not, as far as I can see, prepared to assign rights to dead persons. Therefore, I cannot see any reason why Astrid's action would be wrong in contractualist terms, if wrong is defined in a fashion parallel to the way it is defined in utilitarianism, namely as an action which actually breaks a moral rule that would be agreed upon by rational contractors behind a veil of ignorance when there exists an alternative action which does not break any such rule.

Neither will the difference be that the contractualist can *derive* a case of wrong-doing from the example whereas the utilitarian cannot. It is true that a contractualist would say that Astrid's behaviour proves that she has failed to work on her moral character, and in so far as acts and omissions are morally equivalent, then she might well be said to have done something wrong. But the utilitarian may reason in exactly the same way—from a utilitarian perspective Astrid's behaviour proves that she has not worked hard enough on creating the kind of moral character that under normal circumstances would contribute to the utilitarian goal. She has done something wrong, if "doing" includes also "allowing to happen". So, wrong-doing might be derived from Astrid's case whether you are a contractualist or a utilitarian, and consequently I conclude that Carruthers has failed to show in what sense a contractualist would approach Astrid's case in a different manner than a utilitarian would.

What is the relevance of this for our attitudes towards animals? Carruthers believes that treating animals badly will reveal a bad character-trait in almost the same way as treating the corpse of your grandfather the way Astrid did. Therefore, Carruthers will have an answer to the problem he considered in an early version of the example. We can now explain, he says, why from a contractualist perspective

it may be wrong of Astrid to use her cat as a dart-board, even though no other person will ever know or be distressed. Such actions are wrong because they are cruel. They betray an indifference to suffering that may manifest itself (or, in Astrid's case, that *might have* manifested itself) in that person's dealings with other rational agents. So although the action may not infringe any rights (cats will still lack direct rights under contractualism), it remains wrong independently of its effect upon any animal lover. Animals thus get accorded indirect moral significance, by virtue of the qualities of character that they may, or may not, evoke in us (1992: 153–4).

Carruthers tries to give an account of why it would be correct to say that Astrid does something *wrong* if she starts to throw darts at her cat. But, again, I fail to see in what sense such an action would be *wrong* in contractualism, if it actually does not break any rule in the contract. *If* the animals have only indirect significance that means they are *not* directly mentioned in the contract. Furthermore, Carruthers does not even think they have to be mentioned when a contractualist considers what sort of person she should become, which is evident from the following passage:

Contracting rational agents should agree to try to develop a ready sympathy for one another's suffering, and sympathy for animal suffering is, on the current proposal, merely a side-effect of this general attitude (1992: 154).

The idea seems to be that the contract deals only with interactions between rational agents (and possibly with interactions between rational agents and marginal cases). One rule in the contract will concern not causing any suffering to rational agents (and possibly also to marginal human cases). If an agent wants to avoid breaking this rule, then she will have to work on her character in such a way as to implant in herself a sensitivity to other rational beings' feelings. However, this feeling of sympathy to rational human beings cannot for various reasons be achieved without also spilling over to non-humans. So sympathy to non-humans is not in any phase of this process something that a rational being strives for. This being so, I cannot see why cruelty to animals would be wrong if "wrong" is defined in terms of breaking a rule in the contract.

This is in a sense a question of how to define your moral terms. Suppose instead we grant Carruthers the conclusion that being cruel to animals is morally unacceptable in the sense that it reveals a lack of sensitivity to rational human beings; it is a manifestation of a character-trait that a rational human being should not have—cruelty. We may then ask why this is so. What is the connection between the attitudes to humans and animals? Why do our attitudes to the animals tell us something about our attitudes to human beings?

10.6 Cruelty and Culture

Carruthers' answer is different from Kant's. Kant, as we have seen, believes that the answer lies in the similarity between humans and animals: "Animal nature has analogies to human nature", Kant says (1976: 122). Carruthers denies this, and claims that the *differences* that exist between animals and humans make it possible to keep the attitudes to these beings psychologically separate:

> That someone can become desensitised to the suffering of an animal need not in any way mean that they have become similarly desensitised to the sufferings of human beings [...]. Because most animals look and behave very differently from humans, it is easy to make and maintain a psychological distinction between one's attitudes to pain in the two cases (1992: 160–1).

The connection is instead, Carruthers believes, culturally conditioned: it is particularly in the Western culture that we can expect a human being who is cruel to animals to be cruel to human beings as well. The first reason is that many of us keep pets and in doing so we "model our relationships with our pets on our relations with other human beings" (1992: 161). The second reason is closely connected with the first one and concerns the fact that this is normally the only direct relation to animals that exists, which also means that we are unable to make any psychological distinctions in the general class of animals. The third reason is that we often use animals as examples in the training of the young, especially in moral training, which means that anthropomorphism is learned at an early age.

Suppose Carruthers is right in his claims. In what ways may we criticize him? I can see at least two problems.

(1) The first problem is, I believe, inescapable for Carruthers and it concerns the fact that he fails to provide the right kind of protection for animals in his theory.

Recall once again the example about Astrid feeding the cat with her grandfather. Why do we object to this kind of behaviour? Well, Carruthers says, because of what it reveals about Astrid's character. And this is in turn explained in the following way:

> I propose that the manner in which we treat our dead is best understood symbolically, the corpse being an embodied image of the person who has died, and perhaps also an image of persons generally. If this is right, then an attack on a corpse would universally be interpreted as a symbolic attack on the dead person. It shows something about one's attitude to the individual person, and perhaps towards humanity generally, that one is prepared to attack their concrete image—that is to say, their corpse (1992: 147–8).

But if the general principle that applies to our treatment of animals is that actions should be condemned in virtue of what they reveal about our character and this in turn is determined by what our actions symbolize, then cruelty towards animals would be morally on a par with cruelty to photos—that is, photos representing real persons—or puppets, and things like that.

To see the problem, we may once again try to modify Carruthers' example. Suppose Astrid has left earth on an irreversible trajectory that will make her lose contact with other humans for ever. As the years pass she becomes bored with her books and so on. Now contrast two cases. In the first case she ties the cat to the wall and uses it as a dart-board. In the second case she places a photo of her grandfather on the wall and uses *it* as a dart-board. Both actions will be performed out of idleness and boredom.

Would not the both these acts be condemned by Carruthers? Throwing darts at the picture of her grandfather would symbolize throwing darts at her real grandfather and this symbolic action would be condemned in view of the fact that it displays cruelty. Throwing darts at the cat can be analysed in a similar manner: in Western culture animals are regarded in an anthropomorphistic manner, according to Carruthers—we make no fundamental difference between animals and humans or at least we regard the animals as in a sense human. This being so, cruelty towards them has to be interpreted as a symbolic cruelty towards real human beings and therefore something that only a person with a morally defective character would display.

And why could not the same kind of reasoning apply also to (one variant of) the original example where Carruthers, as we have seen, asks us to "contrast two cases: in the first case [Astrid] removes the glass cover from the *Mona Lisa* and uses the painting as a dart-board; in the second case she ties the cat to the wall and uses *it* as a dart-board" (1992: 108). If actions should be condemned in virtue of what they reveal and if, in doing so, it is important to take into consideration the symbolic aspect—which, according to Carruthers, will explain why causing suffering to animals is unacceptable— then I fail to see why throwing darts at the *Mona Lisa* out of boredom should not be condemned on the same ground, since I believe that will display a defective character in the same way as would throwing darts at the cat or at a photo of one's grandfather.

If so, then Carruthers fails to show that there is a moral difference between the two cases in his theory, which he definitely wants to do: "I think I would be prepared to grant that Astrid does nothing wrong in throwing darts at the *Mona Lisa* [...] In contrast, it is surely wrong of Astrid to throw darts at the cat out of idle amusement" (1992: 109). If I am right in my interpretation above, then the two cases would be morally on a par in Carruthers' theory, and that would indeed be counter-intuitive.

As a consequence of this, the protection Carruthers can give to animals in his theory is too weak and has the wrong kind of foundation: Carruthers has shown that cruelty to animals ought to be morally condemned precisely because of the fact that it is cruelty, but he is not able to cope with the intuitions saying that there is a fundamental difference between cruelty displayed *vis-à-vis* animals and cruelty displayed *vis-à-vis* non-living matter, such as paintings, photos, and so on. Carruthers is unable, as far as I can see, to make moral sense of the distinction between, on the one hand, actions which have non-rational beings as their objects and that are cruel because of their effects for these beings and, on the other hand, actions that are cruel because of what they reveal about the character of the agent. It is important to take moral notice of both these aspects, according to common sense; it is particularly important to acknowledge the negative value of cruelty towards animals that stems from the fact that *they* are the target of it.

So Carruthers has not yet succeeded in giving a theoretical foundation for the intuition that says that cruelty towards animals is wrong because of what it means for them.

(2) The second problem is closely connected with the first one and concerns the fact that even this weak protection depends on circumstances that may change from one time to another or from one place to another. Carruthers is aware of this, but does not seem to regard it as a problem. Concerning the anthropomorphism in children's literature and the other factors mentioned above, he writes:

These features of our society are highly contingent. There may be (indeed, there are) many other societies in which animals are not accorded these roles. In such a society a dog may be slowly strangled to death because this is believed to make the meat taste better, while it never occurs to the people involved that there is any connection between what they are doing and their attitudes to human beings—indeed, there may in fact be no such connection. While such an action performed by someone in our society would manifest cruelty, when done by them it may not (1992: 162).

This illustrates the weakness in Carruthers' theory. Once again he seems to use a very narrow concept of cruelty. Cruelty, for Carruthers, seems always to refer to human objects—directly or indirectly—whereas *if* animals can suffer—and Carruthers does not in any way base his theory on a denial of this, even if he makes certain attempts towards such a denial at the end of his book—then common sense would call actions that willingly afflicted harm on them (like those described above) manifestations of cruelty. It is unimportant whether or not people would acknowledge a link between their actions and attitudes towards other rational humans; what is important is whether or not they realize that their actions cause suffering to a being that can experience suffering.

And there would be something fundamentally wrong even if Carruthers *were right* in his statement that the behaviour described is no manifestation of cruelty. The problem is once again that he believes that as far as our treatment of animals is concerned, there is no other morally relevant aspect besides whether or not it displays traits of character relevant for our dealings with other rational beings. If the dogs above are capable of suffering, then what these people do is morally unacceptable whether or not it is cruel. A theory which is unable to assign a negative value to suffering as such is unacceptable from the perspective of common sense.

Another question: Carruthers believes that he is able to base the protection of animals in his theory on considerations concerning the symbolic nature of cruel acts towards animals in our culture. But to what extent does he *want* to provide this kind of protection—how desirable does Carruthers find the existence of these features in Western culture?

Carruthers' answer is straightforward:

Concern with animal welfare, while expressive of states of character that are admirable, is an irrelevance to be opposed rather than encouraged. Our response to animal lovers should not be "If it upsets you, don't think about it", but rather "If it upsets you, think about something more important" (1992: 168).

Carruthers believes that there are considerable social and economic costs of placing (further?) restrictions on our treatment of animals, in view of the fact that we are living on a planet where millions of people are starving. It is on them that our moral attention should be focused instead. The problem is that if human beings are the only primary moral targets and if it is possible to regard the animals in a non-anthropomorphistic manner and if, furthermore, placing restrictions on our treatment of animals has certain costs, then it seems that we ought to strive for a society in which there are *no restrictions at all* on our treatment of the animals! Why have such restrictions when they *might* be morally costly? This question is particularly urgent in view of the fact that Carruthers does not, as far as I can see, recognize any moral advantages pertaining to such restrictions.

10.7 Conclusion

I do not find it really meaningful to quantify the degree of counter-intuitiveness of a theory in a precise manner. But at the same time, I believe that I have been able to point out several aspects of Carruthers' theory that are hard to swallow for common-sense morality—particularly the consequence that animal suffering is assigned no negative value for what it is in itself, but only for what it is in relation to the experiences of rational human beings. And the same might with certain modifications be said about the suffering of marginal human cases—it is relevant particularly in so far as it can be related to the experiences of non-marginal human beings. Therefore, Carruthers has failed to give convincing reasons why reflective equilibrium is more easily reached in his theory than in utilitarianism. He might be right when he points out that utilitarianism has serious intuitive drawbacks and he might even be right when he claims that these drawbacks should lead one to abandon utilitarianism, but my point is that he has not succeeded in showing that his own theory is different in this regard. There are serious drawbacks of his theory, and I am not at all sure that they are less fatal than the drawbacks of utilitarianism.

CHAPTER 11

PETER SINGER ON KILLING PERSONS AND NON-PERSONS

It's not the killing of the animals that is the chief issue here, but rather the unspeakable quality of the lives they are forced to live.

John Robbins *Diet For A New America*

One of the main thoughts in Peter Singer's book *Practical Ethics* is that we have to extend the principle of equal consideration of interests—which demands "that we give equal weight in our moral deliberations to the like interests of all those affected by our actions" (1993: 21)—also to the non-human animals. This means that their pain and suffering should be regarded as morally on a par with human suffering. However, Singer is not only eager to stress the moral importance of the animals' interests, but also the moral importance of the distinction between persons and non-persons. These distinctions do not coincide, according to Singer, since some non-human animals are and some humans are not persons. Here I want to consider particularly what relevance Singer wants to assign to the distinction between persons and non-persons.

Singer believes that killing a human being is under normal conditions worse than killing a non-human being, and that this is so not only for indirect reasons, which refers to the effects on other human beings than those killed. At the same time, we cannot, Singer claims, justify this moral difference in terms of intrinsic species differences, since that would be morally arbitrary and would be a violation of the principle of equal consideration of interests: "The biological facts upon which the boundary of our species is drawn do not have moral significance" (1993: 88). Therefore, we have to find a morally significant property that we humans normally have which the animals do not have and which cannot only explain but also justify our placing them in different moral categories. This property is personhood.

But *why* then is personhood morally important?

In the first edition of *Practical Ethics* Singer thought that the distinction between being and not being a person should determine which general utilitarian approach to apply. Singer distinguishes between two approaches (for the sake of simplicity I quote from the second edition). One is called the "total" view,

since on this view we aim to increase the total amount of pleasure (and reduce the total amount of pain) and are indifferent whether this is done by increasing the pleasure of existing beings, or increasing the number of beings who exist (1993: 103).

Despite the fact that Singer speaks exclusively in terms of pleasure and pain here, I believe he regards the approach to be more general than this suggests. The total view is available whatever axiological version of utilitarianism you adhere to, and it is better therefore to use the concept of total amount of utility in the formulation of the total view. (The same reservation is appropriate to make also concerning the second approach.)

Singer continues:

> The second approach is to count only beings who already exist, prior to the decision we are taking, or at least will exist independently of that decision. We can call this the "prior existence" view. It denies that there is value in increasing pleasure by creating additional beings (1993: 103–4).

Now one thought played with by Singer in the first edition was to apply the total view merely to conscious beings whereas the prior existence view would apply only to persons. So he suggested a compromise between the two versions of utilitarianism where the main aim in our dealings "with beings that do not exist as individuals living their own lives" should be to maximize happiness (1979: 103). Switching attention instead to self-conscious beings "we are justified in concerning ourselves first and foremost with the quality of life of people who exist now or, independently of our decisions, will exist at some future time, rather than with the creation of possible extra people" (1979: 103).

This is problematic for various reasons and Singer seems to be aware of this. In the second edition he claims that he has abandoned the mixed strategy:

> I now think that preference utilitarianism draws a sufficiently sharp distinction between these two categories of being [those who are not self-conscious and those who are] to enable us to apply one version of utilitarianism to all sentient beings (1993: xi).

The most natural reading of this passage is that the total view now applies both to persons and to non-persons.[1] However, I hope to show that it is not altogether clear that Singer *has* abandoned the compromise view. In any case, it is not clear to me that his present solution will avoid some of the problems with which the compromise view is afflicted.

What Singer wants to do is show that being a person is something morally special even without the compromise view. Let us see whether or not he succeeds in these attempts.

11.1 The Direct Wrongness of Killing

Singer believes that the status of killing a person is different in his axiological version of utilitarianism compared to the classical one, expounded by Jeremy Bentham and developed by for instance John Stuart Mill and Henry Sidgwick. The main reason is that classical utilitarianism judges actions by their tendency

---

[1] This is also Ingmar Persson's interpretation (1995: 55 f.).

to maximize sensations and emotions like pleasure and happiness and their tendency to minimize feelings like pain and suffering. It is true that these feelings might be analysed in various ways, but it is also fairly uncontroversial that we have to do with something experienced or felt, that is, with states of consciousness:

> According to classical utilitarianism, therefore, there is no direct significance in the fact that desires for the future go unfulfilled when people die. If you die instantaneously, whether you have any desires for the future makes no difference to the amount of pleasure or pain you experience. Thus for the classical utilitarian the status of "person" is not *directly* relevant to the wrongness of killing (1993: 90–1).

This is not to say that being a person has no relevance for this question. On the contrary, being a person means having a conception of oneself. One knows that one has a future and also that this future could be cut short. Therefore, a person who knows that persons like herself are sometimes killed— even if the killing is painless—will naturally fear that she might be killed as well.[2] And, as Singer says, if I know that this might happen at any moment— when I am asleep, for instance—then my present existence will be fraught with anxiety. If instead I know that persons like myself very rarely are killed, then I will worry less.

Therefore classical utilitarianism is able to defend a moral prohibition against killing persons on what Singer calls *indirect* grounds: not having such a prohibition will make people worried and less happy than they will be in the presence of such a prohibition. And Singer says:

> I call this an *indirect* ground because it does not refer to any direct wrong done to the person killed, but rather to a consequence of it for other people (1993: 91).

Unfortunately, classical utilitarianism is unable to provide a strong enough moral prohibition against killing persons, since it does not rule out the *secret* killing of persons. Furthermore, there is also something odd with a theory that will prohibit murder not because of its consequences for the person murdered, but rather for its consequences for other persons. Therefore, the ground for saying that killing persons is prohibited in classical utilitarianism is both insufficient and of the wrong kind, according to Singer.

The solution lies in turning to another version of utilitarianism, which does not judge actions by their tendency to maximize and minimize certain feelings, but instead "by the extent to which they accord with the preferences of any beings affected by the action or its consequences" (1993: 94).

This is known as "preference utilitarianism" and is described in the following way:

> According to preference utilitarianism, an action contrary to the preference of any being is, unless this preference is outweighed by contrary preferences, wrong. Killing a person who prefers to continue living is therefore wrong, other things being equal. That the victims are not

---

[2] Cf. G. E. Moore (1903: 156–7). This idea can have various applications, for instance to the question of euthanasia. See L. W. Sumner (1981: 205).

around after the act to lament the fact that their preferences have been disregarded is irrelevant. The wrong is done when the preference is thwarted (1993: 94).

Singer believes, as I interpret him, that in view of the fact that non-persons are incapable of having any desires concerning their own future existence, the painless killing of that kind of being will not mean thwarting any of its desires and is therefore not *directly* wrong in preference utilitarianism. The status of persons is different precisely because even painless killing means thwarting their desires for the future and such thwarting is, other things beings equal, directly wrong in preference utilitarianism—"preference utilitarianism does provide a direct reason for not killing a person" (1993: 95). This is not so in classical utilitarianism, since the unfulfilment of a desire has no special standing in that theory. So the status of being a person has direct significance in preference utilitarianism but not in classical utilitarianism.

These suggestions can be questioned in many ways. Let me begin with the idea that killing persons is *directly* wrong in preference utilitarianism whereas killing non-persons is only *indirectly* wrong.

I believe that we may have a conflation between two different senses of the term "directly wrong". One may use this concept (1) to distinguish between the kind of wrongness of an action that is to be explained in terms of what is done to the primary object of the action and the wrongness of an action that is to be explained in terms of what the action means to other beings that are not the primary object of the action (1993: 91). (2) Another distinction concerns whether the harm done to the primary victim is positive or negative, that is to say, whether the action will result in a certain amount of positive *dis*utility or merely ensure that a certain amount of positive utility will not be the case. In preference utilitarian terms this distinction concerns the difference between having a preference frustrated and being prevented from having a preference that is satisfied. In colloquial language we make the distinction by contrasting inflictions with deprivations.

Now, for the sake of argument, let us first of all suppose that non-persons cannot be directly wronged in sense (2), that is, these beings have no desires that we can thwart by killing them. This is not to say, however, that killing them does not mean that we do something that is of a negative value primarily to them, since it is still the case that killing them means making it the case that they will not experience the pleasure of having some of their (immediate) desires satisfied. In other words, killing might well mean that we eliminate the pleasure and happiness that the victim would have experienced, had we not killed her.

And it is not at all peculiar to claim that the victim might be *harmed* by an action that will result in such an elimination. The concept of harm is wide enough to accommodate this sense.[3] Therefore, Singer can hardly claim that killing a non-person instantaneously does not mean harming it, and he can

---

[3] See, for instance, Peter Carruthers (1992: 76).

definitely not claim that it does not mean doing something wrong primarily to the victim as long as he accepts that the total view applies to them.[4] So, when Singer claims that classical utilitarianism provides an *indirect* reason against killing persons (see above) and at the same time claims that preference utilitarianism provides a *direct* reason against killing a person (1993: 95), I believe he slides between the direct/indirect distinction in sense (1) and (2).

The only way to argue that persons have a special standing in preference utilitarianism because of the fact that killing them is directly wrong is to understand this in the second sense, i.e. that even the instantaneous killing means the thwarting of a desire for a person who wants to go on living, but not for a non-person. Now I want to question this idea too.

11.2 Positive Frustration

It might be true (by definition) that a non-person is not aware of itself as a distinct entity, with a past and a future, and therefore also true that such a being lacks a plain interest just to continue living (because of a lack of necessary concepts). But this does not mean that such a being necessarily lacks the capacity to have future-oriented wants altogether, since it is one thing to want to go on living and another thing to want certain things to happen in the future. And the point is that the last situation seems to require a less advanced conceptual apparatus than does the former.

Ingmar Persson makes the same point in the following way:

a fish while eating may well be thought to have a desire to go on doing so, i.e. a desire which concerns the most immediate future (1995: 60).

The thought is that many fairly primitive wants can be described as future-oriented, which means that death might have positive frustration as a result also for a being who is capable to accommodate merely these unsophisticated wants, as for instance non-persons are. For instance, if a chicken sees a grain on the ground and desires to eat it, then there will be a space of time—from the moment when the chicken recognizes the grain until it eats it—when sudden death would result in a frustrated desire. And in view of the fact that so much time of an animal's life is devoted to the activity of finding food, one has to admit, I think, that there is a real danger of this kind of frustration in a non-person's life.

Suppose that Singer claims that there is a difference between desiring to continue living and desiring other objects placed in the future and that when he points to the special standing of killing a person, he has in mind that death frustrates the plain desire to go on living. However, this would be problematic for many reasons. First of all, it would appear arbitrary to claim that it is only the positive frustration of desires of a certain kind that

[4] Observe that Singer is well aware of some of these observations (1993: 91).

counts as a direct reason against killing. Secondly, even if a non-person has no concept of itself as a distinct entity existing in the future, the very fact that it has future-oriented desires for certain experiences, means that we can easily *derive* a desire to go on living, a desire that of course will be frustrated the moment a being with this kind of desire is killed. For it seems reasonable to accept a variant of Kant's supposed analytic principle that "Who wills the end, wills also (necessarily, if he accords with reason) the sole means which are in his power" (1964: 85), a variant which says that, other things being equal, given a desire for a certain object, one can be said to desire as well all the necessary means for the obtaining of this object.

Singer is well aware of some of these problems, since what he suggests is not that the instantaneous killing of non-persons fails to be directly wrong (second sense) in all circumstances, but instead that it fails to be wrong in a direct way when the non-self-conscious being is unconscious—"if fish become unconscious, then before the loss of consciousness they would have no expectation or desires for anything that might happen subsequently" (1993: 126)—whereas persons are capable of having preferences that extend beyond short periods of unconsciousness, for instance sleep. Therefore, according to Singer, it is not directly wrong to kill a non-person "while unconscious".[5]

The conclusion to draw from this argument is that the status of being a person has ethical relevance for the question of killing in the sense that it will under normal circumstances be directly wrong to kill a person even when she is temporarily unconscious, directly wrong in the sense that some important future-oriented desires are frustrated in this sense. It will not be directly wrong to kill a non-person while it is unconscious.[6]

The question is what kind of ethical relevance this will have if one adheres to the total view. It seems to me that the difference between what is directly and indirectly wrong should in that case have no fundamental significance, since what counts is merely what is wrong, and one of the thoughts in the total view is precisely this: not only is it wrong to ensure that an existing desire is frustrated, but also that a possible preference does not get satisfied, other things being equal. Therefore, it is not only wrong to kill persons with future-oriented preferences but also non-persons with no such preferences (which will be the case when they are unconscious).

---

[5] But Ingmar Persson notes that Singer "seems to forget this qualification at once for he draws the general conclusion that for conscious beings '[d]eath cannot be contrary to an interest in continued life' (p. 126)" (1995: 60).

[6] It should be noted that this holds merely on condition that we take into consideration only the frustration of *occurrent* preferences and not also the frustration of *dispositional* preferences, which I have claimed is the reasonable attitude.

11.3 Comparing the Quality of Different Lives

Singer also has an argument for the possibility of ordering the value of different lives which employs a distinction which comes very close to Mill's well-known distinction between pleasures of lower and higher qualities. Singer not only accepts this distinction, as it seems, he even uses an argument very similar to Mill's in order to defend and explain the distinction.

Mill thought that some pleasures are more valuable than some others due to their superior quality. Even a smaller amount of these pleasures could out-weigh a much larger quantity of pleasures with an inferior quality, which means among other things that a high-quality pleasure might contain or occasion even discontentment and still be more valuable than pure low-quality pleasure.

Concerning the criteria for high and low quality of a pleasure, Mill says:

Of two pleasures, if there be one to which all or almost all who have experience of both give a decided preference, irrespective of any feeling of moral obligation to prefer it, that is the more desirable pleasure (1972: 8–9).

It goes without saying that Mill claims that mental pleasures are superior to bodily ones. This had been the opinion of many philosophers before Mill, even utilitarian ones. But Mill believes that the superiority of the mental pleasures should be explained in terms of their *intrinsic* nature, whereas the utilitarian writers before Mill wanted to explain it in terms of *extrinsic* advantages—intellectual pleasures are safer, last longer, and so on. What Mill says is that the mental pleasures are *in themselves* such that one cannot ignore their superiority once one has experienced the pleasure in question. Mill writes:

Now it is an unquestionable fact that those who are equally acquainted with, and equally capable of appreciating and enjoying, both, do give a most marked preference to the manner of existence which employs their higher faculties. Few human creatures would consent to be changed into any of the lower animals, for a promise of the fullest allowance of a beast's pleasures; no intelligent human being would consent to be a fool [...] (1972: 9).

Now this idea is problematic in several ways.[7] For one thing, how could a human being possibly know what it would be like to be a pleased lower animal? Furthermore, there is an in-built partiality of perspective in Mill's method. Another problem is that I believe one might question whether Mill's conviction really is correct. Let us consider these problems in turn.

(1) Suppose it is true that a normal human being would refuse to be changed into any of the lower animals, that is to say, she would not want to have its pleasures instead of the human ones, even if they lasted longer and were more intense. However, the question is whether such a test really is neutral, since what Mill says is that human pleasures are more valuable from the human perspective than the pleasures of lower animals, and furthermore that the pleasures of an intelligent human being are more valuable from the

[7] See, for instance, Oswald Hanfling (1987: 142 ff.).

perspective of the intelligent human being than the human fool's pleasures. But how can he be sure that this is not a result of the particular perspective of the one who chooses?

Mill presupposes that one can fully appreciate and enjoy both manners of existence, which in my interpretation means that the one who chooses knows what these lives are like also from the perspective of the one who leads them. But the thing is that the *choice* between these manners of existence nevertheless is made from a particular perspective.

Singer is aware of these problems and searches for a neutral standpoint from which to make the comparison between the value of different lives. The practical problems will always be great, of course, but he does not think that the theoretical problems are insoluble. He writes:

Imagine that I have the peculiar property of being able to turn myself into an animal, so that like Puck in *A Midsummer-Night's Dream*, "Sometimes a horse I'll be, sometimes a hound." And suppose that when I am a horse, I really am a horse, with all and only the mental experiences of a horse, and when I am a human being I have all and only the mental experiences of a human being. Now let us make the additional supposition that I can enter a third state in which I remember exactly what it was like to be a horse and exactly what it was like to be a human being (1993: 106).

Singer believes that in this third state I am able to compare horse-existence with human-existence.

In my view Singer has not succeeded in his attempts to find a neutral standpoint, and this is so in virtue of something that Singer actually points out immediately after the quotation above, when he writes about the third state that in "some respects—the degree of self-awareness and rationality involved, for instance—it might be more like a human existence than an equine one, but it would not be a human existence in every respect" (1993: 106).

Suppose that in this third state I make the decision that the one type of existence is more desirable than the other, for instance that the human life is more valuable than the equine life. How can I make sure that this choice is not a result of the fact the third standpoint is more similar to the human existence than the equine existence? One might reason in the following way. I do not only have certain information when I am in the third state; I will also regard certain things as valuable, for instance that I can make a rational decision as to what kind of existence is most valuable (if I did not regard this as being valuable or preferable, then why would I ever try to reach any decision?). But then I *will* choose from a normative perspective and that might very well affect the decision I make: if in the third state I have a positive attitude to the capacity to make decisions on the basis of certain information, then would I not rather want to be a human being than an equine being, if from the perspective of the third standpoint I had to make a decision as to which of these beings lives the more valuable life? At least, this kind of reasoning does make sense and deserves serious attention.[8]

---

[8] Carruthers has a similar argument against Singer's imaginary device. Concerning the creatures

(2) Suppose that these problems can be solved and that we can make comparisons between the relative value of different lives which are neutral and impartial; that is to say, suppose we can imagine an objective method of judging the comparative value of different lives. Our next task will be to consider what kind of judgements we would reach by such an objective method.

Mill, as we have seen, believes that we would assign a higher value to the pleasures of the intellect than to those of mere sensation, and Singer seems to have a similar idea when he writes:

In general it does seem that the more highly developed the conscious life of the being, the greater the degree of self-awareness and rationality and the broader the range of possible experiences, the more one would prefer that kind of life, if one were choosing between it and a being at a lower level of awareness (1993: 107).

Actually I am not convinced that this is the case.

First of all, what is the criterion used when judging the level of consciousness? As it seems, Singer would say that the level of consciousness is determined by the presence of intellectual capacity. This can be called into question, if by "level" one means something quantitative. Compare the pleasures of reading or writing a book and the pleasures of riding a motorcycle. No doubt, normally the first kind of pleasure requires more intellectual capacity than does the second one. Will this mean that the first kind of pleasure also is associated with a *higher* level of consciousness, that is to say—would we say that we are in general *more* conscious when reading a book with pleasure than we are when riding a motorbike with pleasure? In my view, that would not be the natural way of expressing oneself. The experiences associated with riding a motorbike are to my knowledge in general more *intense* than the experiences associated with writing or reading a book.

Therefore, I am not convinced that the traditional elements in personhood— rationality and self-awareness—are directly connected with *degree* of consciousness, unless by this term we refer to a certain quality of consciousness, or possibly a somewhat greater range of experiences. Emotions which do not require intellectual sophistication might very well be associated with *more* consciousness than emotions which do require intellectual sophistication.[9]

---

in the third state, he says: "[N]ote that the creature in question is supposed to have articulate memories of its previous existences, and is supposed to be able to entertain sophisticated judgements about the relative values of those existences. In these respects the mode of existence of that creature is much closer to ours than to that of the horse. Small wonder, then, that such a creature should prefer the life of a human, since it might be expected to judge the life of the horse to be dull and invaried by comparison" (1992: 89). The difference between this argument and mine is that I am not claiming that the equine existence from the perspective of the third state will appear emotionally less interesting, but only that it will contain less of something that the creatures in the third state shows that he values, given that he wants to reach a judgement concerning the comparative value of different lives. Therefore I consider my argument to be stronger, since it does not build on suppositions concerning emotions.

[9] Also Steve S. Sapontzis has argued that animal feelings might be more intense than ours: "humans are notorious for not getting full enjoyment from present pleasures because they have

Secondly, suppose I am wrong here and that there is a reasonable criterion according to which the degree of intellectual sophistication—rationality and self-consciousness—is directly reflected in the level of consciousness. Then the problem is whether we in general prefer a higher level of consciousness to a lower one.

For instance, take a choice between emotions which do and emotions which do not require a high intellectual capacity: suppose you can choose between experiencing the intense pleasures of having a love affair with a person and experiencing the intense intellectual pleasures of making a psychological analysis of those intense emotions involved in love affairs. Would you automatically choose the latter alternative? I must say that I would not. In general, I would rather have these kinds of non-intellectual emotions themselves than have the intellectual pleasure from analysing them.

This point can be illustrated in many other ways. For instance, I suppose that the degree of intellectual sophistication is proportional to age to a certain extent, so that the level of consciousness of a ten-year-old boy is lower—according to Singer's criterion—than the level of consciousness of a forty-year-old man. Nevertheless, if I had to choose between the experiences of these human beings, I am not at all sure that I would prefer the experiences of the man. On the contrary, I would rather have the experiences of my ten-year-old son than the typical experiences of my colleagues (of approximately the same age as I), which in my view proves that I regard the typical experiences of a child at a lower intellectual level as more valuable—at least in certain respects—than the typical experiences of a grown-up man at a higher intellectual level. This means that I question Singer's thesis.

11.4 Irreplaceability

When in Chapter 6 we discussed the elements in SA, one such element concerned the irreplaceability of human beings. Now Singer wants to show not that human beings are irreplaceable but instead that *persons* are.

In this sense there is a difference between persons and non-persons, and it has to do in part with the fact that killing a person is *directly* wrong in a way that killing a non-person, according to Singer, is not. In order to support this idea, Singer makes what he calls a "test of universalisability". I agree with Ingmar Persson (1995: 57–8) that it is hard to understand what Singer wants to say, since it does not automatically fit in with Hare's well-known

---

fixated on past sorrows and are fretting about future difficulties, while animals, like dogs playing on the beach, do not seem to have their present enjoyment thus diluted. Now, if animal feelings are more intense than ours, then this extra intensity could counterbalance the extra feelings our extensive temporal capacity provides us" (1987: 220). Cf. also David DeGrazia (1996: 239).

test, which roughly amounts to a ban on individual references and which we discussed in a previous chapter (see Chapter 2). Anyway, this is how Singer describes the test:

If I imagine myself in turn as a self-conscious being and a conscious but not self-conscious being, it is only in the former case that I could have forward-looking desires that extend beyond periods of sleep or temporary unconsciousness, for example a desire to complete my studies, a desire to have children, or simply a desire to go on living, in addition to desires for immediate satisfaction or pleasure, or to get out of painful or distressing situations. Hence it is only in the former case that my death involves a greater loss than just a temporary loss of consciousness, and is not adequately compensated for by the creation of a being with similar prospects of pleasurable experiences (1993: 127).

Once again, Singer's idea seems to be the following one. Death for a non-person, provided it takes place when the non-person is not conscious, means only a negative harm done to the victim—a certain amount of positive utility will not occur—whereas death for a person means a positive harm done to the victim—a certain amount of disutility will occur.

This might be thought to have a direct bearing on the question of replaceability. I believe the idea can be illustrated by an example. Compare the lives of two beings: the person Per and the non-person Non-Per. Let us simplify and compare Per's forward-looking desires that extend beyond non-conscious periods only, with Non-Per's desires for immediate pleasures and let the question concern what it would take to compensate for the fact that these two beings are killed while asleep. We assume that the desires of the two beings are equally strong, say 10 units.

Suppose we kill Per. The amount of disutility as a result from this will be 10 units, that is −10, which describes the frustration of the desire to go on living. Suppose furthermore that we create another person Per*, with similar desires for the future as Per and also with similar prospects of having them satisfied as Per would have if we had not killed him. Then we have to add −10 and 10 and the sum will be 0. Thus we seem to *lose* a certain amount of utility when we replace Per with Per*, which amounts to the same as saying that the killing of a self-conscious being is not, other things being equal, adequately compensated for by the creation of another similar being.

Turning to the non-self-conscious beings, things seem to be different. Killing Non-Per, one might say, will only mean that 10 units of utility will *not* occur. If Non-Per had 10 utility units from his pleasurable experiences in life, then killing him means that 10 such units simply should be subtracted. The sum of this operation will be zero. Now suppose that we replace Non-Per with Non-Per*. This means that we may add 10 units to the sum we received from killing the first being, which in turn means that the creation of an another non-self-conscious being will compensate for the fact that a non-self-conscious being was killed—we have 10 units of utility both before and after the killing, which means that this kind of killing would lack moral significance for the one who merely counts changes in the utility level.

This is my interpretation of Singer's idea. My criticism should be judged in the light of that.

(1) Let us first accept this way of putting the question; in other words we ask what it takes to compensate for the fact that a being is killed, and let us furthermore accept, for the sake of argument, the conclusions concerning Per and Non-Per. Our question will then be whether the fact that the utility of Per cannot be compensated for by the creation of Per* really supports the conclusion that Per is not whereas Non-Per *is* replaceable. It seems to me that this is so only in a qualified sense.

Remember that in Chapter 6 we discussed two senses of replaceability which differed only concerning the condition for compensating for the fact that a being is killed. There is a weak and a strong sense of replaceability. A being is replaceable in the weak sense if its death can be compensated for by the creation of additional beings. A being is replaceable in the strong sense if its death can be compensated for by the creation of *one* additional being with similar prospects for the future.

Consider Per's and Non-Per's deaths. We can all see that, according to the way things are described, whereas the creation of Per* will not compensate for the fact that Per is killed, the creation of Per* and Per** actually seems to do so. So, in general and other things being equal, it takes the creation of *two* persons to compensate for the fact that one person is killed.[10]

Singer may indeed point to the fact that this is replaceability in a fairly weak sense and it will preserve a moral difference between the ethics of killing persons and non-persons. However, if we are seriously worried over the possibility that persons are replaceable in some moral theories (particularly classical utilitarianism) in the sense that we may compensate for the fact that one person is killed by the creation of another one, then we will not feel reassured by the conditions of acceptable replacement of a person in preference utilitarianism. If replacing one person with another one is regarded as morally problematic, replacing one person with *two* other persons should be morally problematic as well.

This does not mean that there are no conditions under which one may accept a person as replaceable—there probably are; what it means is just that the difference between the conditions in classical utilitarianism and preference utilitarian is too slight to make up for a solution to the problem of replaceability.

(2) Another problem is that the talk about *compensating* for the fact that a being is killed as well as claiming that killing can be "counter-balanced by bringing into existence similar beings who will lead equally happy lives" (1993: 125) does not easily fit in with the total view, which Singer seems to accept, at least when considering non-self-conscious beings.

---

[10] Bringing in the time factor one may also claim that the killing of a 35-year-old person might be compensated for by bringing into existence another person which will lead an equally happy life until he is 70. The total view is indifferent to how the compensation takes place, as long as the amount of additional utility is doubled in cases like this one.

The problem is that if you accept the total view, then killing one being and replacing it with another cannot be unproblematic, not even when the being in question is non-self-conscious, since the total view claims not only that you are doing something wrong when reducing the total utility but also— and to the same extent—when you knowingly refrain from increasing it.

Rosalind Hursthouse puts the finger on precisely this point when discussing "the replaceability argument":

I am supposed to be maximizing happiness; I kill a chicken and thereby (other things being equal) do wrong by reducing the total happiness. Then, instead of eating a fertilized hen's egg, I arrange for it to be hatched, thereby counter-balancing the earlier reduction. But, given that I am supposed to be maximizing happiness, why do I not arrange for the egg to be hatched *and* refrain from killing the first chicken? I ought to be arranging for eggs to be hatched anyhow— how can my doing so make up for my having wrongly killed the chicken? It is as if my kicking a child were made up for by my giving her a kiss. Why not just give her kisses instead of kicks (1987: 149)?

It seems that we may talk about a moral compensation for the fact that a non-self-conscious being is killed only in very special circumstances, namely when the killing is a prerequisite for the creation of the replacing being. We have this condition when the number of non-self-conscious beings the existence of which depends on our efforts is limited and when the actual number of non-self-conscious beings the existence of which depends on our efforts is optimal in relation to these limits. But are these conditions ever fulfilled?

For instance, Singer seems to believe that the replaceability argument will apply to the farming of chickens, under certain circumstances. The argument would justify raising chickens for their meat on condition that they have pleasant lives, can be killed painlessly and, furthermore, on condition "that for economic reasons we could not rear the birds if we did not eat them" (1993: 133). But even granted the last condition, it is hard to believe that any farmer of chickens is in the position to truly claim that he could not afford to invest the money he gets from killing some of the chickens in order to be able to raise an even larger total amount of chickens in the future.

Singer is aware of some of the limits of the applicability of the replaceability argument. It cannot, for instance, justify factory farming, where the animals live under conditions that are more unpleasant than pleasant, which means that it can probably not justify normal factory farming. It cannot justify killing wild animals either, for instance duck hunting, not even on the condition that the ducks die immediately, since when we shoot ducks there is normally no way to make sure that replacement takes place (1993: 133–4). Add to this the conclusion we reached earlier that the killing of a non-self-conscious being means no positive harm only on the condition that the killing takes place when the being in question is unconscious (since otherwise it may well frustrate future-oriented desires for certain experiences), and we will get a very complicated picture according to which the replacement of a non-self-conscious being can probably never be justified in real life.

(3) Ingmar Persson has questioned Singer's argument that because of a person's aims and plans for the future, the death of a person will inflict a loss which cannot be compensated for by the creation of another person. The following thought experiment explains why Persson has his doubts:

Suppose that when I go to bed tonight, I have certain aims for tomorrow and the further future. Suppose further that during a period of deep sleep, I cease to exist because the elementary particles composing me fly apart. Shortly afterwards in the same place, however, different particles join to constitute a person who in all (macroscopic) physical and psychological respects is indistinguishable from me. In this situation, I think it correct to say that I have been replaced by a numerically distinct, but qualitatively indistinguishable, replica. Consequently, if this happens, my aims for the future will certainly remain unfulfilled. But in the place of my aims the perfectly similar aims of my replica will exist, and these will be satisfied to the same extent as my aims would have been. Thus, replacing me by a replica seems to have no effect on the utilitarian calculus. In other words, persons appear to be replaceable in principle (1995: 57).

This experiment, however, is not free from problems.

One problem concerns whether Singer really would say that my plans for the future remain unfulfilled after this kind of replacement. (Another possibility, which I will not discuss, is that he might as well question whether a replacement really has occurred under these circumstances.) Suppose the replacement takes place within a fraction of a second, so that no one ever notices that it has taken place. Suppose furthermore that I would not really care about this; if I knew that such a replacement was about to take place, I would probably not feel very uneasy about it (since such replacements could have occurred hundreds or thousands of times during the lifetime of the person that I consider to be me, without being noticed by me, for the simple reason that it *makes no noticeable* difference whether or not I am replaced in this way).

But if this is so, if the replacement actually means nothing to me, then why would I embrace wants for which it makes a lot of difference? In other words, if it means nothing to me whether or not I am replaced in this way, then why would it matter to me whether a certain plan of mine is carried out by me or by a perfect replica of me? And if I am indifferent to this, then there seem to be no unfulfilled desires as a result of the replacement. Since I am indifferent as to whether my plans are realized by me or by my replica, the plans I have for the future will just as much be plans for my replica or will be plans for either me or my replica.

This is only a question mark in the margin, and I cannot exclude the possibility that Singer would accept the example more or less as it is described. On the other hand, he might claim that Persson has ignored the point that we tried to make in the example about Per and Non-Per, namely that the positive harm that killing a person with plans for the future means will not be adequately compensated for by the creation of another person, since what we have to compensate for is not merely the absence of the first person's positive utility but also the presence of her negative disutility. Applied to Persson's example this means that the replacement will have as a result not only the negative disvalue stemming from the fact that my plans for the future will remain unfulfilled but also the positive disvalue stemming from the fact that they are frustrated. And, in Persson's words, "[i]t may be urged that this disvalue should be subtracted from the value that falls on the lot of my replica" (1995: 59).

This is exactly the kind of reasoning employed in the example about Per and Non-Per. But Persson is not at a loss for a reply:

> We find an answer to this as soon as we remind ourselves that we are now working on the basis of the total view which admits that we can influence the value level in the world by creating subjects having preferences and affecting these preferences. If, however, creating somebody with a preference which is satisfied is doing something good, just as is satisfying an existing preference, then failing to do this is doing something bad, just as is ensuring the frustration of an existing preference. So, whether or not I am replaced, there is disvalue—of the same magnitude—to subtract from the value accomplished: either the disvalue stemming from the frustration of my future-oriented preferences or from failing to satisfy the same possible preferences of my replica (1995: 59).

Persson's point here seems to be that the reasoning employed for instance in the example about Per and Non-Per will work only on the assumption that the total view does not apply, since if it does, then the death of one person and the creation of another exactly similar one will cancel each other out.

I am not absolutely sure that I follow this reply. But in my view the thesis of irreplaccability can be understood in the following way.

Let us reconstruct the example about Per and Per* in order to make it into an illustration of replacement à la Persson. We imagine that we may decide whether or not Per should be replaced by Per* exactly in the manner described by Persson. We may also add that replacement occurs—if it occurs—as a result of the killing. We have to remind ourselves that the strength of both Per's and Per's* desires to go on living is 10 and also that we can simplify the case by counting merely these desires.

We have two alternatives—either to kill Per and have him replaced or to refrain from killing him. If we choose the first alternative we have to count 10 units of dissatisfaction from Per's case and add to this 10 units of satisfaction from Per's* created desire to go on living. Again, we end up with zero utility units. If, on the other hand, we choose the other alternative, then we can collect 10 units of satisfaction from Per's desire to continuing living. But, on the other hand, since in this alternative we fail to create and satisfy Per's* desire to go on living—by failing to create Per*—Persson's idea seems to be that this is to be counted as a cost if the total view applies, since then frustrating an existing preference, will have, according to Persson, the same status as has the failure to create and satisfy a preference of a possible person. So what we have to count here is 10–10, which again equals zero. If this is the case, then it seems that Per* is replaceable, since we reach the same amount of final utility whether or not we choose the replacement alternative.

I am not here going into a discussion of moral mathematics, but I am somewhat sceptical of this way of describing the relevant calculation operations. I am not, however, capable of defending this scepticism, but I will try instead to point to one consequence that has to be accepted if we choose this way of counting.

One problematic consequence is that the total amount of utility in the world seems to decrease as soon as there exists an alternative way of gaining utility, *even when the total utility would not increase by choosing this alternative*! Once again, let me try to illustrate the point.

Suppose there exist two possible worlds W1 and W2. In W1 I am confronted precisely with the choice between killing Per and letting Per* replace him or doing nothing and thereby refrain from creating Per*. We concluded that whatever choice I make, I will end up with zero units of utility, given this piece of moral mathematics. Now suppose that the only difference between W1 and W2 is that in the second possible world the possibility of having Per replaced by Per* does *not* exist. Using the proposed piece of moral mathematics in this world would mean that we do not have to subtract the failure to create Per*, and thereby make it the case that he develops a desire that can be satisfied, if we refrain from killing Per, for the simple reason that there is no such failure. We have 10 utility units from the fact that Per goes on living and no subtraction from that sum.

Therefore, supposing that other things are equal in W1 and W2, we have to conclude that the total utility level in W2 is higher than that in W2, *even though all other things are equal in W1 and W2 except for the fact that in W1 there is an alternative course of action which, however, would not result in more utility than the one actually chosen*. This is surprising, since here it seems that the existence of the alternative will not make possible an *increase* of the total amount of utility in the world but would instead mean an inevitable *reduction* of the total amount of utility compared to a world in which this possibility was absent.

The upshot of this is that it is in my view still an open question whether or not Persson's objection is fatal for Singer. We need not be concerned about that, however, as long as we are confident that the other two critical points, (1) and (2), retain their full force. And nothing said in (3) suggests anything else. So we can conclude that the irreplaceability argument in my interpretation fails to convince us that persons, in contrast to non-persons, are irreplaceable in preference utilitarianism.

11.5 Singer's Argument for Irreplaceability

The discussion of Singer's irreplaceability argument was built on my interpretation of it, illustrated by Per and Non-Per. Now I intend to discuss instead Singer's *explicit* argument in favour of the idea that self-conscious beings, in contrast to non-self-conscious ones, are irreplaceable and that this is so in virtue of the fact that the "desire to continue living means that death inflicts a loss for which the birth of another [being] is insufficient compensation" (1993: 127).

One of Singer's ideas is that it might be a good thing to satisfy an existing preference. However, "the package deal that involves creating and then satisfying a preference need not be thought of as equivalent to it" (1993: 127–8).

Again, Singer believes that the test of universalizability supports the idea about a non-equivalence here:

If I put myself in the place of another with an unsatisfied preference, and ask myself if I want that preference satisfied, the answer is (tautologically) yes. If, however, I ask myself whether I wish to have a new preference created that can then be satisfied, I will be quite uncertain. If I think of a case in which the satisfaction of the preference will be highly pleasurable, I may say yes. (We are glad that we are hungry if delicious food is on the table before us, and strong sexual desires are fine when we are able to satisfy them.) But if I think of the creation of a preference that is more like a privation, I will say no. (We don't cause ourselves headaches simply in order to be able to take aspirin and thus satisfy our desire to be free of the pain.) This suggests that the creation and satisfaction of a preference is in itself neither good nor bad [...] (1993: 128).

Now Singer does not develop in this passage *why* he thinks that this is the case, i.e., he does not discuss here what philosophical attitude to have to the distinction between satisfying an existing preference and the package-deal of creating and satisfying a preference—he seems merely to express an intuition. Let me comment on the passage anyway.

I agree with the general conclusion that Singer draws—it *is* problematic to regard the creation and satisfaction of a preference as being good in itself. Sometimes it definitely seems not to be. I am not sure, however, that this will block the suspicion that persons are replaceable in preference utilitarianism.

The problem with the argument is that those desires which make the life of a self-conscious being valuable seem to be more like desires the satisfaction of which are highly pleasurable than desires merely to avoid what is unpleasant. Recall what Singer in an earlier quotation said about the killing of a self-conscious being with desires that extend beyond periods of temporary unconsciousness. Remember also his examples: "for example a desire to complete my studies, a desire to have children, or simply a desire to go on living, in addition to desires for immediate satisfaction or pleasure, or to get out of painful or distressing situations" (1993: 127). These are the desires that make a self-conscious being irreplaceable, according to Singer.

But if we look at them, we see that with the exception of the last mentioned desire to get out of painful or distressing situations, there are no examples of preferences that are like privations. On the contrary, many of these desires seem to be desires the satisfaction of which is highly pleasurable and therefore we might well see a value not only in satisfying them when they exist but also in the package-deal of creating and satisfying them, according to Singer.

It is true that this is not the case concerning the desire to get out of painful or distressing situations, but, on the other hand, this desire seems to be out of place on Singer's list, since this is *not* a desire that will be frustrated by killing a being. We do not have to compensate for the frustration of these desires by creating a new being, for the simple reason that we have no frustration here—on the contrary, death *is* an effective means of getting out of painful or distressing situations.

Therefore, it might well be true that satisfying an existing desire and creating and satisfying a new one is in some cases non-equivalent. But in view of the examples given by Singer this contention seems to be irrelevant to the question of whether or not persons are replaceable, since those desires which must be compensated for if one self-conscious being is killed do not seem to be associated with this non-equivalence.

11.6 Life as a Journey

Let me comment on one of Singer's metaphors designed to give an *explanation* why non-self-conscious beings, in contrast to self-conscious beings, might be replaceable.[11] Singer's idea is that the lives of self-conscious beings might be seen as "arduous and uncertain journeys, at different stages, in which various amounts of hope and desire, as well as time and effort have been invested in order to reach particular goals or destinations" (1993: 130).

The analogy seems to be the following one. Compare two situations. In the first you are about to plan to make a journey. You are thinking of going from Lund to Princeton to meet someone who might help you with a mathematical problem. You write a letter to the person and ask if he is prepared to meet you. Unfortunately he is not, and therefore the journey never takes place. This is no serious cause of concern in view of the fact that your plans were cancelled at a very early stage. You have time to search for other mathematicians who might help you to solve the problem you are racking your brains over.

The other situation is quite different. Here you have written to the mathematician at Princeton and he has declared himself to be prepared to discuss the problem with you. Now you start to prepare for the journey— you contact your travel agency, you spend some months formulating your thoughts in writing, you even buy the tickets. But just before the planned day of departure you receive a letter in which the mathematician wants to cancel the meeting with reference to the fact that he might not be the right person for you to meet. In this situation you are naturally much more disappointed than you are in the first situation, in virtue of your mental preparations and the time and effort invested.

[11] I will not consider all the alternative ways of looking at the irreplaceability of persons, not, for instance, the so called "moral ledger" model, which has been the target of what I think is fatal criticism elsewhere. See for instance Persson (1995).

Now Singer's thought seems to be that the first situation is an analogy to the killing of a non-self-conscious being—for instance a foetus—or alternatively to a decision not to bring an infant into the world whereas the second situation is an analogy to the killing of a self-conscious being who has not yet been able to fulfil all his plans in life. Singer describes the difference in the following way:

one can regard not to bring an infant into the world as akin to preventing a journey from getting underway, but this is not in itself seriously wrong, for the voyager has made no plans and set no goals. Gradually, as goals are set, even if tentatively, and a lot is done in order to increase the probability of the goals being reached, the wrongness of bringing the journey to a premature end increases (1993: 130).[12]

Observe that there is a difference between this irreplaceability argument and the argument which was illustrated by Per and Non-Per. The difference is that the present argument seems to focus on the fact that the preparations from a utilitarian perspective are made unnecessarily—there will be no one to enjoy the fruits of one's effort if one is prematurely killed—whereas the former argument instead was concentrating on the frustration of one's plans.

This difference is fatal, since here it is no doubt that Singer's argument will be hit by Persson's thought experiment. It is true that the argument can explain why under normal conditions it is worse to kill a person than a non-person. Lacking plans for the future, the non-person will not make any preparations for fulfilling such plans either. But it does not, Persson claims, underpin the irreplaceability of persons:

If [...] a person is not just killed, but replaced by a replica [in the manner described in Persson's thought experiment above], the benefit saved up for will not be lost: it will be enjoyed by the replica instead of the original person (1995: 66).

The reason is simple—enjoying the fruits of the original person's efforts does not require being identical with her. If you save money for many years in order to retire at the age of 60 and dedicate the rest of your life to beekeeping, but suddenly at the age of 59 are replaced in the manner described by Persson, then your replica will enjoy your retirement as much as you would.

11.7 Does the Total View Apply to Persons?

Before reaching a conclusion I want to address a question touched upon early in this chapter, namely whether or not Singer believes that the total view applies to persons. He does indeed claim that one version of utilitarianism should apply to all sentient beings, but he is also willing to confess that he is

---

[12] At the end of life it decreases again, which explains why, as Nagel says, the "death of Keats at 24 is generally regarded as tragic; that of Tolstoy at 82 is not" (1979: 9). However, Nagel wants to explain this reaction in terms of years of life of which a person is deprived.

"not entirely satisfied with [his] treatment of this whole question of how we should deal with ethical choices that involve bringing a being or beings into existence" (1993: xi). And this kind of uncertainty has, I think, made an impression on Singer's book.

For instance, certain passages seem to suggest that he does not at all want to apply the total view to self-conscious beings. One idea is problematic, according to Singer, since it "commits us to the total view, and implies that, other things being equal, it is good to bring into existence children without disabilities" (1993: 124).

This looks like a rejection of the total view (applied to persons). And he definitely seems to repudiate the conclusion drawn from the total view, when he claims that the journey model of a person's life "does not require us to hold that there is an obligation to bring more children into existence, let alone to regard people as replaceable once life's journey has properly begun" (1993: 131).

This is enough to get into the following problem: if there *is* a value in bringing non-self-conscious beings into existence—which there must be since the total view applies to them, which is evident from, among other things, the fact that they are replaceable—but no such value in bringing self-conscious beings into existence, then it seems that we should devote as much as possible of our time to bringing as many non-self-conscious beings as possible into existence. This will of course take very much of our time and effort, but the more important point is that it will inevitably reduce the living-space of the self-conscious beings in the future; it seems that they will by some kind of mathematical and moral necessity be superseded by the non-self-conscious beings, unless we can point to some biological niche which is exclusive for the self-conscious beings.

This follows from the fact that if bringing self-conscious beings into the world reduces, even slightly, the living-space for non-self-conscious beings, actual and possible ones—and everything points to this being the case—then we have to abstain from bringing this kind of being into the world, since there is an obligation to bring into existence as many as possible of the non-self-conscious beings but no such obligation as far as the self-conscious beings are concerned. And this is of course an unwelcome conclusion.

11.8 Conclusion

My conclusion is that Singer has not been able to show that the distinction between being and not being a person has the kind of moral relevance he believes it has, for instance as regards the ethics of killing.

I have tried to show, first, that the distinction is of no vital importance for the directness of killing—even the painless killing of a non-person might result in positive preference frustration for the non-person. Only under the presupposition that the beings are unconscious will it, typically, be directly wrong to kill the person but not the non-person.

Secondly, I have also questioned an idea that concentrates not on the *kind* of wrongness of killing a person compared to a non-person, but instead on the *degree* of it. The idea is that it is more wrong to kill a person than a non-person in virtue of the superior quality of the normal person's experiences. I questioned whether it is possible to decide such questions in an impartial manner and furthermore I questioned whether an impartial test—provided that it exists—of the desirability of different kinds of experiences really would favour the experiences of rational beings at the expense of non-rational ones.

I also tried to show that Singer's replaceability argument was unable to do the job it is designed to do, namely to give an account of our intuitions concerning the value of a person's life. It turned out that at best persons are irreplaceable in a very qualified sense given preference utilitarianism. Furthermore, it turned out that at least some of Singer's suggested models of thinking about when a being might be considered as replaceable and when not, were defective in certain respects.

Finally, I questioned whether Singer really has abandoned the idea of a mixed utilitarian strategy or not. It seems that he has not and I pointed out the fatal consequences following from this.

Summary and Conclusions

Let me sum up chapter by chapter.

Part 1: Problem and Method
Chapter 1. Traditionally in the West we regard the property of being human as something morally significant. In what does this significance consist? Is membership of our species important in itself, or does the importance lie in having the properties that a normal grown-up human being has? I believe that this distinction is commonly neglected in discussions about a special human value or a human dignity. In this study Chapters 3–9 deal with the importance of being a human being *per se* whereas Chapters 10 and 11 deal with two kinds of theories in which being human is important on indirect grounds. What I want to claim is that there is a way of arguing for the existence of a value which proceeds from the assumption that most of us believe that being human is something important *per se*. The advantage of founding the idea of a human dignity on this kind of reasoning is of course that it allows *all* human beings to have a share in this value, which would not be the case if the argument had instead proceeded from the assumption that being human is valuable only in an indirect sense.

In the traditional view, however, it is not only important to regard *all* human beings as having a share in a special human value; it is normally important as well to regard all human beings as having this share *to the same extent*. Not only is it the case that human beings are more valuable than non-humans, all human beings are *equally* valuable. This second aspect of the importance of being human is only given a brief treatment in this study.

Chapter 2. I discuss three theoretical demands on an ethical theory or principle, namely simplicity, consistency and intuitive plausibility and their relevance for the question of human dignity. As far as simplicity is concerned, I believe that there is a pedagogical value in this feature. This is something that has to be kept in mind when assessing the theoretical foundation of a special value of being human.

When it comes to consistency I let the requirement of universalizability exemplify this demand. I claim that partiality to the human species will not violate this principle, for instance if this partiality is expressed in judgements to the effect that a certain being should be treated in a certain way merely because it does not belong to the human species. Given a genetic species concept, it will make sense to apply a universalizability test to such a judgement and ask whether the speaker would be prepared to accept that she ought to be treated in the same way if it turned out that she did not belong to the human species.

Singer has claimed that the universal aspect of ethics provides a reason for taking a broadly utilitarian position. I do not think so, although I believe that it will perhaps give us reason, though not conclusive, for sorting out certain kinds of partiality to oneself, even universal kinds. I believe that there are certain difficulties associated with applying the universalizability test to universal egoism. The alternatives to this position, however, is not only universal altruism or utilitarianism.

My attitude to intuitions is somewhat ambiguous. In spite of the problems of intuitionism, I believe that intuitions should have a place in this study, particularly because of the fact that our intuitions are so hard to ignore and that there is no obvious alternative. I claim that intuitions are important both as evidential value and as indications of actually existing attitudes, which I believe are important to take into account whatever their intrinsic value as evidence. In this study, however, it is the second kind of importance that plays the leading role.

Part II: Direct Importance
Chapter 3. The intuition upon which this study is built is the one which says that it is morally important to be a living human. This is roughly what Roger Wertheimer has called the Standard Belief, which says that being human has moral cachet. I modify Wertheimer's term and call this the Standard Attitude (for the obvious reason that I do not think it is exclusively a belief), SA, and just like him I believe that the attitude in question really deserves its name—it is a *standard* attitude in the sense that in one way or another it is important for most of us.

I penetrate both Wertheimer's and William E. May's account of SA. Once again I conclude that it is notoriously hard to say whether SA is about an intrinsic importance of the property of being human or something else. Furthermore, I discuss May's idea that our humanity is a gift either from God or from our fellow men. The problem with the last alternative is that it seems to be too inclusive if you want to say that human beings differ radically *in kind* from other beings, since it seems that some humans are prepared to ascribe moral worth to other beings than humans. The problem with a religious foundation of human dignity, on the other hand, is related to the idea that humans have their moral significance in virtue of having a soul. Why is it more wrong to kill a being with a soul than one without a soul? And when does a human being get a soul? The last question turns out to be logically problematic.

The chapter ends with a decision to understand SA as an attitude towards the direct importance of being a member of the biological species *Homo sapiens.*

Chapter 4. To claim that a property is directly important can mean both (a) that the property is valuable in itself and not because of typically being found together with some other property and (b) that the property is valuable in itself and not because of what it leads to or is a necessary condition for. I think that SA is about direct importance in both these senses, whereas when we talk of an *indirect* importance of being human we normally have in mind distinction (a).

I consider two positions. According to one position, subjectivism, things have value only in relation to valuing subjects. In objectivism, on the other hand, things can be valuable independently of any attitudes. Given subjectivism we can place a special value on being human in so far as this property is intrinsically valuable *for humans*. This is the theoretical foundation of human dignity upon which this study rests. The reason why I choose to proceed from subjectivism is partly that I personally find this position more attractive than objectivism, but also that it is interesting to defend the idea of human dignity from a subjectivistic position when such an idea normally is rejected by the subjectivists.

I also discuss the conditions on which subjective value is conferred on a property. This includes considering two assumptions which I partly defend. First that so-called now-for-then preferences and secondly that so-called external preferences—that is, altruistic preferences as well as preferences for other objects than experiences—have moral importance. I am fairly convinced that things, personal or impersonal, the existence of which I am not aware of, may have value for me. I am less sure that past wants of still existing beings should have a voice in the moral matter, and even less sure that past preferences of past people ought to have such a voice. These questions have to do with the scope of SA.

Chapter 5. Some investigations carried out in Sweden in the eighties seem to contradict the thesis about a universal SA—two Swedes out of three seemed to believe that humans and non-humans are equally valuable. I question the seriousness of the attitude expressed in the investigation. I believe that in what-ever sense we understand a moral attitude—as a belief, preference or emotion —its practical consequences will be included in a criterion for seriousness.

From the perspective of subjectivism, a moral attitude or intuition will have a moral relevance in virtue of being connected with our preferences, and more exactly with our *intrinsic* preferences. The same is true of preference utilitarianism. I claim that it makes sense to reason in a preference utilitarian manner about SA whether you accept or reject preference utilitarianism as the ultimate moral theory. In other words, if we humans have a special value in virtue of having this value in the eyes of other humans beings, then it seems reasonable to assume that the magnitude of this value is a function of the strength and scope of people's attitudes.

Chapter 6. In previous chapters we have discussed the scope and seriousness of SA, but not its exact content. SA seems to be about a moral privilege of humans. In this chapter I discuss what this privilege consists in, i.e. in what sense we believe that humans are special.

I discern the following elements in the phenomenology of SA. First *objectivity*, which means that we believe that the value to be attached to every human being in virtue of her species membership is independent of the value she has for others. Second *inviolability*, which means that we believe that it is more valuable to protect the human beings that exist than to bring new human beings into existence. Third *irreplaceability*, which is mentioned as a separate element but which, I believe, is a consequence of the second element and says roughly that the killing of one human being cannot be compensated for by the creation of another one. Fourth *dignity*, which is the famous Kantian thought that people ought to be treated always as ends in themselves and never simply as means. Fifth *equality*, which says that all human beings are equally valuable, or rather that they have the kind of value that SA is about to the same extent. I believe that the fifth element is included in the phenomenology of SA, but I am not sure that this is a serious belief.

Chapter 7. I have decided to understand SA as an attitude concerning an intrinsic importance of belonging to the human species. Now I have to test this claim.

In order to show that it is not intrinsically important to be a biological human, Tooley constructs three thought experiments. The third one is considered in some detail. In this example Tooley asks us to imagine what it would be like if there existed non-human inhabitants of some other planet who were mentally, intellectually and culturally on a level with mankind. Would we really regard the killing of such a being as less morally serious than the killing of a human one? Tooley believes not.

I have my doubts. For instance, it would make biological sense if we nevertheless discriminated between these Martians and human beings, since the genetic difference, by hypothesis, between them and us is greater than the genetic difference between another human being and us. So from an evolutionary angle, discriminating between the Martians and other human beings could be explained. However, it is one thing to be able to explain a certain reaction and quite another to prove its existence.

Suppose then that we do not discriminate between these Martians and human beings. My other strategy is to explain this in a way that will not affect the truth of SA. I say that maybe we, as it were, *half-believe* that these Martians are human beings after all, in virtue of their similarity to humans. This would refute Tooley's argument. However, I conclude that the evidence for the existence of the phenomenon of half-believing in this particular case is too weak. So we seem to have an argument against SA.

Chapter 8. In this chapter I try to find an argument *for* SA instead. I consider Warnock's argument concerning a prohibition against using plainly human embryos *in vitro* for experimental purposes. She makes two claims. First that these embryos should have a very strong protection compared to if they had been non-humans. Second that plainly human beings should be more strongly protected than merely human organisms, for instance early human embryos.

I believe that it is difficult to argue for Warnock's first claim in the way she has formulated it. I also question the way she has designed her example. However, with the inspiration of her example I try to construct a new one, which in my view could support a weak version of Warnock's first claim, and which therefore would also support SA. Furthermore, I try to construct an example which supports Warnock's second claim.

So we have examples against SA and examples for SA. The thesis I want to defend is that SA is applicable only to cases where we deal with non-persons.

Is it possible that SA can be applied to some cases but not to others? In the second part of the chapter I try to argue for this. The structure of this part is somewhat complicated since I argue against both Rachels' argument *against* a similar thesis and Kagan's argument *for* a similar thesis.

I end up with the following description of the differences between Rachels, Kagan and the view defended here: Rachels believes that a distinction might be important in some cases but not in some others, but in that case there is some other factor present that will account for this importance. Kagan too explains the fact that a distinction might be important sometimes by pointing to the presence of some other factor or factors. The difference between Rachels and Kagan seems to be that in Rachels' eyes it is these other factors that explain the importance of the distinction, whereas Kagan believes that it is the distinction together with these other factors that explain it. I claim that some cases provide the necessary background for the distinction to have moral importance in itself, or that they make it possible for us to *detect* its intrinsic importance.

Chapter 9. What I have tried to do in this study is argue for the thesis that given subjectivism and the existence of an intuition or preference to the effect that a human being has a special moral standing precisely in virtue of being human, then we have a foundation of the idea of human dignity. This is true whether or not we may find any further theoretical foundation of the moral belief that is part of the intuition the existence of which our defence of dignity is built upon. So an intuition might be relevant from a subjectivistic perspective whether or not we are able to place it in a larger theoretical context. Quite the contrary, we run into difficulties as soon as we try to give a rational defence of intuitions like SA, which is what I try to show in this chapter.

I discuss three attempts to defend the idea that being human is something morally special. According to Willard Gaylin the explanation can be found in a list of human attributes, for instance conceptual thought, capacity for technology, etc. Gaylin assigns weight to the fact that many of the attributes on his list are evolutionarily significant. One problem with accounting for human dignity in terms of attributes that have proved themselves to be evolutionarily useful is that the human species is not the only species that can exhibit properties which have played an important role in evolution.

Actually this is one aspect, or as Regan prefers to state it, one *phase* of the "argument from marginal cases". The argument has two phases and Gaylin's list will be hit by both of them, as far as I can see.

Jean Beer Blumenfeld tries to avoid this problem by rejecting moral individualism, which claims that it is only the individual's properties that should decide how the individual is to be morally treated, and she argues instead that group membership has moral significance. I claim, among other things, that this principle is counter-intuitive.

Nozick too claims that he has an answer to the argument from marginal cases. He makes two suggestions. First, that any species may legitimately give their fellows moral privileges. Second, that human beings have their value in virtue of being parts of a rich human tapestry. This is problematic for various reasons, and I claim that Nozick has *not* escaped the argument from marginal cases.

Part III: Indirect Importance
Chapter 10. The two philosophers discussed in this part are prepared to acknowledge the *indirect* importance of being a biological human in so far as this is accompanied by the property of being a person. They are not, however, prepared to assign *direct* significance to the property in question. My position is in a sense the very opposite one: I acknowledge the direct value of being a human, and naturally, I am also willing to acknowledge its indirect importance. But I am not ready to make so much of the property of being a person as these philosophers are. I think they underestimate the moral importance of being a biological human whereas they overestimate the moral implications of being a person.

In this chapter I criticize Peter Carruthers' contractualism. Carruthers' strategy is to show that his theory is a more reasonable basis for our treatment than is particularly Peter Singer's version of utilitarianism. I believe Carruthers fails in his attempts to show this. I believe, just like Carruthers, that utilitarianism has results that will strongly offend moral common sense, and I also think that this is a big problem. But I suspect that Carruthers' contractualism in the end is at least as counter-intuitive as is utilitarianism.

Chapter 11. In this final chapter I discuss Peter Singer's thesis according to which there is a morally important distinction to draw between being and not being a person. This will explain why, under normal circumstances, it is morally worse to kill a human being than to kill a non-human being. Since non-persons are incapable of having any desires concerning their own future existence (they lack the conceptual resources) the painless killing of an unconscious being of this kind will not mean thwarting any of its desires and is therefore not directly wrong in utilitarianism. This means that non-persons are replaceable in a way that persons are not. I assert that the difference is merely a question of degree and that it will not reassure those people who believe that people should not be replaceable. This part of my criticism is built on an interpretation of Singer. I also criticize two of his explicit irreplaceability arguments.

References

Anderson, Elizabeth (1993). *Value in Ethics and Economics*, Cambridge, Mass.: Harvard University Press.

Aristotle (1943). *Politics*, New York: Walter J. Black.

Beauchamp, T. L. & J. F. Childress (1994). *Principles of Biomedical Ethics*, fourth edition, New York & Oxford: Oxford University Press.

Bermúdez, José Luis (1996). "The Moral Significance of Birth", *Ethics*, Vol. 106, No. 2, pp. 378–403.

Bennett, Jonathan (1993). "Negation and Abstention: Two Theories of Allowing", *Ethics*, Vol. 104, No. 1, pp. 75–96.

Benson, Thomas L. (1983): "The Clouded Mirror: Animal Stereotypes and Human Cruelty", in H. B. Miller & W. H. Williams (eds.): *Ethics and Animals*, Clifton, New Jersey: Humana Press, pp. 79–90.

Berglund, Stefan (1995). *Human and Personal Identity*, Lund: Lund University Press.

Blumenfeld, Jean Beer (1977). "Abortion and the Human Brain", *Philosophical Studies*, Vol. 32, pp. 251–68.

Boesch, C. (1991). "Teaching among wild chimpanzees", *Animal Behaviour*, Vol. 41, pp. 530–1.

Braithwaite, R. B. (1964). "Half-Belief", *The Aristotelian Society*, Suppl. Vol. 38, pp. 163–74.

Brandt, R. B. (1979). *A Theory of the Good and the Right*, Oxford: Clarendon Press.

Brink, D. O. (1994). "A Reasonable Morality", *Ethics*, Vol. 104, No. 3, pp. 593–619.

Carruthers, Peter (1992). *The Animals Issue*, Cambridge: Cambridge University Press.

Carter, Ian (1995). "The Independent Value of Freedom", *Ethics*, Vol. 105, No. 4, pp. 819–45.

Clark, Stephen R. L. (1983). "Humans, Animals, and 'Animal Behavior'", in H. B. Miller & W. H. Williams (eds.): *Ethics and Animals*, Clifton, New Jersey: Humana Press, pp. 169–82.

Dancy, Jonathan (1981). "On Moral Properties", *Mind*, Vol 40, pp. 367–85.

Dancy, Jonathan (1993). "Intuitionism", in Peter Singer (ed.): *A Companion to Ethics*, Oxford UK & Cambridge USA: Blackwell, pp. 411–9.

Dancy, Jonathan (1993a). *Moral Reasons*, Oxford UK & Cambridge USA: Blackwell.

DeGrazia, David (1996). *Taking animals seriously*, Cambridge: Cambridge University Press.

Deigh, John (1994). "Cognitivism in the Theory of Emotions", *Ethics*, Vol. 104, No. 4, pp. 824–54.

Deigh, John (1995). "Empathy and Universalizability", *Ethics*, Vol. 105, No. 4, pp. 743–63.

Diamond, Jared (1993). "The Third Chimpanzee", in P. Cavalieri & P. Singer (eds.): *The Great Ape Project*, London: Fourth Estate, pp. 88–101.

Donceel, Joseph (1984). "A Liberal Catholic's View", in Joel Feinberg (ed.): *The Problem of Abortion*, Belmont: Wadsworth.

Dworkin, Ronald (1977). *Taking Rights Seriously*, Cambridge & Massachusetts: Harvard University Press.

Dworkin, Ronald (1986). "We Do Not Have a Right to Liberty", in R. M. Stewart (ed.): *Readings in Social and Political Philosophy*, New York & Oxford: Oxford University Press, pp. 297–305.

Dworkin, Ronald (1993). *Life's Dominion*, London: Harper Collins.

Egonsson, Dan (1990). *Interests, Utilitarianism and Moral Standing*, Lund: Lund University Press.

Egonsson, Dan (1997). "Kant's Vegetarianism", *The Journal of Value Inquiry*, Vol. 31, pp. 473–83.

Ellis, Anthony (1995). "Thomson on Distress", *Ethics*, Vol. 106. No. 1, pp. 112–19.

Feldman, Fred (1992). *Confrontations with the Reaper*, New York & Oxford: Oxford University Press.

Foot, Philippa (1967). "The Problem of Abortion and the Doctrine of the Double Effect", *The Oxford Review*, No. 5, pp. 5–15.

Forsman, Birgitta (1996). "En vetenskaplig oreda: Om fusk, slarv och annan oredlighet inom forskningen", VEST Tidskrift för vetenskapsstudier, Vol 9, No. 1, pp. 53–71.

Francione, Gary L. (1993). "Personhood, Property and Legal Competence", in P. Cavalieri & P. Singer (eds.): *The Great Ape Project*, London: Fourth Estate, pp. 248–68.

Frey, R. G. (1980). *Interests and Rights*, Oxford: Clarendon Press.

Frey, R. G. (1983). *Rights, Killing, and Suffering*, Oxford: Basil Blackwell.

Gaylin, Willard (1984). "What's So Special about Being Human", in Robert Esbjornson (ed.): *The Manipulation of Life* (Nobel Conference), San Francisco: Harper & Row.

Gibbard, Allan (1990). *Wise Choices, Apt Feelings*, Oxford: Clarendon Press.

Glover, Jonathan (1977). *Causing Death and Saving Lives*, Harmondsworth, Middlesex: Penguin Books.

Goldman, Alvin (1976). *A Theory of Human Action*, Princeton, New Jersey: Princeton University Press.

Green, O. H. (1979). "The Expression of Emotion", *Mind*, Vol. 79.

Griffin, James (1996). *Value Judgment*, Oxford: Clarendon Press.

Haksar, Vinit (1979). *Equality, Liberty, and Perfectionism*, Oxford: Oxford University Press.

Hanfling, Oswald (1983). "Real Life, Art and the Grammar of Feelings", *Philosophy*, Vol 58, pp. 237–43.

Hanfling, Oswald (1987). *The Quest for Meaning*, Oxford UK & Cambridge USA: Blackwell.

Hansson, M. G. (1991). *Human Dignity and Animal Well-being*, Stockholm: Almqvist & Wiksell International.

Hare, R. M. (1963). *Freedom and Reason*, Oxford: Clarendon Press.

Hare, R. M. (1981). *Moral Thinking*, Oxford: Clarendon Press.

Hare, R. M. (1985). "Ontology in Ethics", in Ted Honderich (ed.): *Morality and Objectivity*, London, Boston, Melbourne & Henley: Routledge and Kegan Paul, pp. 39–53.

Hare, R. M. (1987). "An Ambiguity in Warnock", *Bioethics*, Vol. 1, No. 2, pp. 175–8.

Hare, R. M. (1988). "Comments on Vendler", in D. Seanor & N. Fotion (eds.): *Hare and Critics*, Oxford: Clarendon Press, pp. 280–7.

Hare, R. M. (1989). *Essays in Ethical Theory*, Oxford: Clarendon Press.

Hare, R. M. (1989a). "Prudence and past preferences: Reply to Wlodzimierz Rabinowicz", *Theoria*, Vol. LV, Part 3, pp. 152–8.

Hare, R. M. (1989b). "Universalizability and the summing of desires: Reply to Ingmar Persson", *Theoria*, Vol. LV, Part 3, pp. 171–7.

Harman, Gilbert (1977). *The Nature of Morality*, New York: Oxford University Press.

Harris, John (1983). "*In Vitro* Fertilization: The Ethical Issues", *The Philosophical Quarterly*, Vol. 33, No. 132, pp. 217–37.

Harris, John (1985). *The Value of Life*, London: Routledge & Kegan Paul.

Harris, John (1993). *Wonderwoman and Superman*, Oxford & New York: Oxford University Press.

Hart, H. L. A. (1986). "Between Utility and Rights" in R. M. Stewart (ed.): *Readings in Social and Political Philosophy*, New York & Oxford: Oxford University Press, pp. 306–19.

Hermerén, Göran (1969). *Representation and the Meaning in the Visual Arts*, Lund: Läromedelsförlagen (Scandinavian University Books).

Herrnstein, Richard J. & Murray, Charles (1994). *The Bell Curve*, New York, London, etc.: The Free Press.

Hill, Thomas E. Jr. (1992). *Dignity and Practical Reason*, Ithaca & London: Cornell University Press.

Hogarth, Robin M. (1987). *Judgment and Choice*, New York: John Wiley.

Honderich, Ted (1982). "'On Liberty' and Morality-Dependent Harms", *Political Studies*, Vol. 30, No. 4, pp. 504–14.

Hull, D. L. (1976). "Are Species Really Individuals?", *Systematic Zoology*, Vol. 25.

Hume, David (1896). *A Treatise of Human Nature*, Oxford: Clarendon Press.

Hurka, Thomas (1996). "Monism, Pluralism, and Rational Regret", *Ethics*, Vol. 106, No. 3, pp. 552–75.

Hursthouse, Rosalind (1987). *Beginning Lives*, Oxford UK & Cambridge USA: Blackwell.

Huxley, Julian (1944). *Man in the Modern World*, New York: Mentor Books.

Jeffner, Anders (1988). *Människovärde och människovärdering*, Uppsala Universitet, Tros- och livsåskådningsvetenskap, Rapport.

Kagan, Shelly (1988). "The Additive Fallacy", *Ethics*, Vol. 99, No. 1, pp. 5–31.

Kamm, F. M. (1992). *Creation and Abortion*, New York & Oxford: Oxford University Press.

Kamm, F. M. (1992a). "Non-consequentialism, the Person as an End-in-Itself, and the Significance of Status", *Philosophy & Public Affairs*, Vol. 21, No. 4, pp. 354–89.

Kamm, F. M. (1993). *Morality, Mortality*, New York & Oxford: Oxford University Press.

Kant, Immanuel (1964). *Groundwork of the Metaphysic of Morals*, trans. and analysed by H. J. Paton, New York, Grand Rapids, Philadelphia, etc.: Harper Torchbooks.

Kant, Immanuel (1976). "Duties to Animals", in Tom Regan & Peter Singer (eds.): *Animal Rights and Human Obligations*, Englewood Cliffs, New Jersey: Prentice-Hall INC.

Kleinig, John (1991). *Valuing Life*, Princeton & New Jersey: Princeton University Press.

Korsgaard, Christine M. (1983). "Two Distinctions in Goodness", *Philosophical Review*, Vol. 92, pp. 169–95.

Kripke, S. A. (1980). *Naming and Necessity*, Oxford: Blackwell.

Kuhse, Helga (1987). *Sanctity-of-Life Doctrine in Medicine*, Oxford: Clarendon Press.

Kuhse, Helga & Peter Singer (1985). *Should the Baby Live?*, Oxford, New York & Melbourne: Oxford University Press.

Kymlicka, Will (1990). *Contemporary Political Philosophy*, Oxford: Clarendon Press.

Kymlicka, Will (1993). "The social contract tradition", in P. Singer (ed.): *A Companion to Ethics*, Oxford: Blackwell, pp. 186–96.

Leahy, Michael P. T. (1994). *Against Liberation*, London & New York: Routledge.

Leeton, John F., Alan O. Trounson & Carl Wood (1982). "IVF and ET: What it is and how it works" in W. A. W. Walters & P. Singer: *Test-Tube Babies*, Oxford, Auckland, New York: Oxford U. P, pp. 2–10.

Lemos, Noah M. (1994). *Intrinsic Value*, Cambridge: Cambridge University Press.

Lippert-Rasmussen, Kasper (1994). "Moral Status and the Impermissibility of Minimizing Violations" (unpublished).

Locke, John (1964). *An Essay Concerning Human Understanding*, Glasgow: Collins Fount Paperbacks.

Lyons, William (1980). *Emotion*, Cambridge, London & New York: Cambridge University Press.

Mackie, J. L. (1977). *Ethics. Inventing Right and Wrong*, Harmondsworth, Middlesex: Penguin.

Maclean, Anne (1993). *The Elimination of Morality*, London & New York: Routledge.

Masserman, Jules H., Stanley Wechkin & William Terris (1964). "'Altruistic' Behavior in Rhesus Monkeys", *American Journal of Psychiatry*, Vol. 121, pp. 584–5.

May, W. E. (1974). "Abortion and Man's Moral Being", in R. L. Perkins (ed.): *Abortion: Pro and Con*, Cambridge & Massachusetts: Schenkman, pp. 13–35.

Mayr, Ernst (1963). *Animal Species and Evolution*, Cambridge, Massachusetts: Harvard University Press.

Mayr, Ernst (1976). "The Biological Meaning of Species", in C. N. Slobodchikoff (ed.): *Concepts of Species*, Stroudsberg, Pennsylvania: Dowden, Hutchinson & Ross, pp. 267–76.

McDowell, John (1985). "Values and Secondary Qualities" in Ted Honderich (ed.): *Morality And Objectivity*, London: Routledge and Kegan Paul, pp. 110–29.

McMahan, Jeff (1988). "Death and the Value of Life", *Ethics*, Vol. 99, No. 1, pp. 32–61.

250 REFERENCES

Mele, Alfred R. (1996). "Internalist Moral Cognitivism and Listlessness", *Ethics*, Vol. 106, No. 4, pp. 724–53.
Meyer, Michael J. (1989). "Dignity, Rights, and Self-Control", *Ethics*, Vol. 99, No. 3, pp. 520–34.
Midgley, Mary (1984). *Animals and Why They Matter*, Athens: The University of Georgia Press.
Mill, J. S. (1972). *Utilitarianism*, London & Melbourne: Dent.
Mill, J. S. (1978). *On Liberty*, Indianapolis & Cambridge: Hackett.
Miller, Harlan B. & William H. Williams (eds.) (1983): *Ethics and Animals*, Clifton, New Jersey: Humana Press.
Morris, Bertram (1946). "The Dignity of Man", *Ethics*, Vol. 57, No. 1, pp. 57–64.
Moore, G. E. (1903). *Principia Ethica*, Cambridge, London, New York, etc.: Cambridge University Press.
Moore, G. E. (1922). *Philosophical Studies*, London: Kegan Paul, Trench, Trubner & CO.
Moore, G. E. (1966). *Ethics*, Oxford: Oxford University Press.
Munthe, Christian (1992). *Livets slut i livets början*, Stockholm: Thales.
Nagel, Thomas (1979). *Mortal Questions*, Cambridge, London, New York, etc.: Cambridge University Press.
Nagel, Thomas (1986). *The View from Nowhere*, New York & Oxford: Oxford University Press.
Nordenfelt, Lennart (1993). *Quality of Life, Health and Happiness*, Aldershot, Brookfield USA, Hong Kong, etc.: Avebury.
Norman, Richard (1983). *The Moral Philosophers*, Oxford: Clarendon Press.
Noske, Barbara (1993). "Great Apes as Anthropological Subjects — Deconstructing Anthropocentrism", in P. Cavalieri & P. Singer (eds.): *The Great Ape Project*, London: Fourth Estate, pp. 258–68.
Nozick, Robert (1983). "About Mammals and People", *The New York Book Review*, pp. 11–30.
Oksenberg Rorty, Amélie (1990). "Persons and *Personae*" in C. Gill (ed.): *The Person and the Human Mind*, Oxford: Clarendon Press, pp. 21–39.
O'Neill, Onora (1993). "Kantian ethics", in P. Singer (ed.): *A Companion to Ethics*, Oxford: Blackwell, pp. 175–85.
Parfit, Derek (1984). *Reasons and Persons*, Oxford: Clarendon Press.
Parfit, Derek (1986). "Overpopulation and the Quality of Life", in P. Singer (ed.): *Applied Ethics*, Oxford University Press.
Perry, R. B. (1954). *General Theory of Value*, Cambridge, Mass.: Harvard University Press.
Persson, Ingmar (1981). *Reasons and Reason-governed Actions*, Lund: Studentlitteratur.
Persson, Ingmar (1995). "Peter Singer on Why Persons are Irreplaceable", *Utilitas*, Vol. 7, No. 1, pp. 55–66.
Piper, Adrian M. S. (1996). "Making Sense of Value", *Ethics*, Vol. 106, No. 3, pp. 525–37.
Popper, K. R. (1966). *The Open Society and Its Enemies*, fifth edition, London & Henley: Routledge & Kegan Paul.
Price, H. H. (1964). "Half-Belief", *The Aristotelian Society*, Suppl. Vol. 38, pp. 149–62.
Price, H. H. (1969). *Belief*, London: George Allen & Unwin.
Pritchard, Michael S. (1971–2). "Human Dignity and Justice", *Ethics*, Vol. 82, pp. 299–313.
Rabinowicz, Wlodzimierz (1979). *Universalizability*, Dordrecht, Boston & London: D. Reidel Publishing Company.
Rabinowicz, Wlodzimierz (1989). "Hare on Prudence", *Theoria*, Vol. LV, Part 3, pp. 145–51.
Rabinowicz, Wlodek & Jan Österberg (1996). "Value Based on Preferences", *Economics and Philosophy*, Vol 12, pp. 1–27.
Rachels, James (1987). "Do Animals Have a Right to Liberty", in T. Regan & P. Singer (eds.): *Animal Rights and Human Obligations*, Englewood Cliffs, N. J.: Prentice-Hall, pp. 205–223.
Rachels, James (1986). *The End of Life*, Oxford, New York & Melbourne: Oxford University Press.
Rachels, James (1991). *Created from Animals*, Oxford & New York: Oxford University Press.

Rachels, James (1993). "Moral Philosophy as a Subversive Activity", in E. R. Winkler and J. R. Coombs (eds.): *Applied Ethics: A Reader*, Oxford UK & Cambridge USA: Blackwell.

Rachels, James (1993a). "Why Darwinians Should Support Equal Treatment for Other Great Apes", in P. Cavalieri & P. Singer (eds.): *The Great Ape Project*, London: Fourth Estate, pp. 152–7.

Railton, Peter (1986). "Facts and Values", *Philosophical Topics*, Vol. 14, pp. 5–31.

Ramsey, Paul (1970). *The Patient as Person*, New Haven: Yale University Press.

Raphael, D. D. (1994). *Moral Philosophy*, second edition, Oxford & New York: Oxford University Press.

Rawls, John (1972). *A Theory of Justice*, Oxford, Melbourne, Cape Town: Oxford University Press.

Regan, Tom (1976). "McCloskey on Why Animals Cannot have Rights", *The Philosophical Quarterly*, Vol. 26, No. 104, pp. 251–7.

Regan, Tom (1979). "An Examination and Defence of One Argument Concerning Animal Rights", *Inquiry*, Vol. 22, Nos. 1–2, pp. 189–219.

Regan, Tom (1984). *The Case for Animal Rights*, London, Melbourne & Henley: Routledge & Kegan Paul.

Robbins, John (1987). *Diet For A New America*, Walpole: Stillpoint Publishing.

Rodd, Rosemary (1990). *Biology, Ethics, and Animals*, Oxford: Clarendon Press.

Rollin, Bernard E. (1983). "The Legal and Moral Bases of Animal Rights", in H. B. Miller & W. H. Williams (eds.). *Ethics and Animals*, Clifton, New Jersey: Humana Press, pp. 103–18.

Rosati, Connie S. (1996). "Internalism and the Good for a Person", *Ethics*, Vol. 106, No. 2, pp. 297–326.

Ross, W. D. (1930). *The Right and the Good*, Oxford: Clarendon Press.

Ryder, Richard D. (1979). "The Struggle Against Speciesism", in D. Paterson & R. D. Ryder (eds.): *Animals' Rights — a Symposium*, London, Sussex: Centaur Press.

Ryder, Richard D. (1989). *Animal Revolution*, Oxford, Cambridge, MA: Blackwell.

Rønnow-Rasmussen, Toni (1993). *Logic, Facts and Representation*, Lund: Lund University Press.

Sapontzis, Steve F. (1980). "Are Animals Moral Beings?", *American Philosophical Quarterly*, Vol. 17, No. 1, pp. 45–52.

Sapontzis, Steve F. (1987). *Morals, Reasons, and Animals*, Philadelphia: Temple University Press.

Sapontzis, Steve F. (1993). "Aping Persons — Pro and Con", in P. Cavalieri & P. Singer (eds.): *The Great Ape Project*, London: Fourth Estate, pp. 269–77.

Scanlon, T. M. (1982). "Contractualism and utilitarianism", in A. Sen & B. Williams (eds.): *Utilitarianism and beyond*, Cambridge, London, New York, etc.: Cambridge University Press., pp. 103–28.

Scheffler, Samuel (1992). *Human Morality*, New York, Oxford: Oxford University Press.

Shaw, William (1980). "Intuition and Moral Philosophy", *American Philosophical Quarterly*, Vol. 17, No. 2, pp. 127–34.

Sidgwick, Henry (1907). *The Methods of Ethics*, London: MacMillan.

Singer, Peter (1979). *Practical Ethics*, Cambridge, London, New York, etc.: Cambridge University Press.

Singer, Peter (1993), *Practical Ethics*, Second edition, Cambridge, London, New York, etc.: Cambridge University Press.

Singer, Peter (1995). *Rethinking Life & Death* Oxford: Oxford University Press.

Sinnott-Armstrong, Walter (1992). "Intuitionism" in Becker & Becker (eds.): *Encyclopedia of Ethics*, New York & London: Garland Publishing, pp. 628–30.

Slobodchikoff, C. N. (ed.) (1976). *Concepts of Species*, Pennsylvania, Stroudsberg: Dowden, Hutchinson & Ross.

Smart, Ninian (1984). *The Religious Experiences of Mankind*, third edition, New York: Charles Scribner's sons.

Smith, Michael (1994). *The Moral Problem*, Oxford UK & Cambridge USA: Blackwell.

Smith, Michael (1995). "Internal Reasons", *Philosophy and Phenomenological Research*, Vol. 55, No. 1, pp. 109–31.

Smith, Peter (1990). "Human Persons", in C. Gill (ed.): *The Person and the Human Mind*, Oxford: Clarendon Press, pp. 61–81.

Snowdon, P. F. (1990). "Persons, Animals, and Ourselves", in Christopher Gill (ed.): *The Person and the Human Mind*, Oxford: Clarendon Press, pp. 83–107.

Sober, Elliot (1993). *Philosophy of Biology*, Oxford: Oxford University Press.

Sorensen, Roy A. (1992). *Thought Experiments*, New York & Oxford: Oxford University Press.

Sturgeon, Nicholas L. (1996). "Anderson on Reason and Value", *Ethics*, Vol. 106, No. 3, pp. 509–24.

Sumner, L. W. (1981). *Abortion and Moral Theory*, Princeton, New Jersey: Princeton University Press.

Sumner, L. W. (1995). "The Subjectivity of Welfare", *Ethics*, Vol. 105, No. 4, pp. 764–90.

Sverdlik, Steven (1996). "Motive and Rightness", *Ethics*, Vol. 106, No. 2, pp. 327–49.

Taurek, John (1977). "Should the Numbers Count?", *Philosophy and Public Affairs*, Vol. 6, No. 4, pp. 293–316.

Taylor, Paul W. (1986). *Respect for Nature*, Princeton, New Jersey: Princeton University Press.

Thomson, J. J. (1975). "Killing, Letting Die, and the Trolley Problem", *The Monist*, Vol. 59, No. 2, pp. 204–17.

Thomson, J. J. (1990). *The Realm of Rights*, Cambridge, Mass.: Cambridge University Press.

Tooley, Michael (1983). *Abortion and Infanticide*, Oxford: Clarendon Press.

Tribe, L. H. (1990). *Abortion: The Clash of Absolutes*, New York: Norton.

Trigg, Roger (1882). *The Shaping of Man*, Oxford: Blackwell.

Tännsjö, Torbjörn (1976). *The Relevance of Metaethics to Ethics*, Stockholm Studies in Philosophy: Almquist & Wiksell International.

Unger, Peter (1996). *Living High and Letting Die*, New York & Oxford: Oxford University Press.

Vendler, Zeno (1988). "Changing Places?", in D. Seanor & N. Fotion (eds.): *Hare and Critics*, Oxford: Clarendon Press, pp. 171–83.

Walker, Stephen (1983). *Animal Thought*, London, Boston, Melbourne & Henley: Routledge & Kegan Paul.

Warnock, Mary (1983). "*In Vitro* Fertilization: The Ethical Issues", *The Philosophical Quarterly*, Vol. 33, No. 132, pp. 238–49.

Warnock, Mary (1985). *A Question of Life*, Oxford: Blackwell.

Warnock, Mary (1987). "Do Human Cells Have Rights?", *Bioethics*, Vol. 1, No. 1, pp. 1–14.

Wertheimer, Roger (1974). "Philosophy on Humanity", in R. L. Perkins (ed.): *Abortion: Pro and Con*, Cambridge & Massachusetts: Schenkman, pp. 107–28.

White, M. (1981). *What Is and What Ought to be Done*, New York: Oxford University Press.

Williams, Bernard (1990). "Who might I have been?", in *Human Genetic Information: Science, Law and Ethics* (Ciba Foundation Symposium 149), Chichester, New York, etc.: John Wiley, pp. 167–79.

Index